SIDE DISHES

LATINA AMERICAN WOMEN, SEX, AND CULTURAL PRODUCTION

MELISSA A. FITCH

RUTGERS UNIVERSITY PRESS

New Brunswick, New Jersey, and London

LIBRARY OF CONGRESS CATALOGING-IN-PUBLICATION DATA

Fitch, Melissa A., 1964–
Side dishes : Latina American women, sex, and cultural production/Melissa A. Fitch.
    p.   cm. — (New directions in international studies)
    Includes bibliographical references and index.
    ISBN 978–0–8135–4524–0 (hardcover : alk. paper)
    ISBN 978–0–8135–4525–7 (pbk. : alk. paper)
    1. Women—Latin America. 2. Sex—Latin America. 3. Pornography—Latin America.
    4. Feminism—Latin America. 5. Postmodernism (Literature)—Latin America. I. Title.

    HQ1460.5.F58 2009
    305.48'9631098—dc22

                                                                          2008043712

A British Cataloging-in-Publication record for this book is available from the British Library.

Visit our Web site: http://rutgerspress.rutgers.edu

Manufactured in the United States of America

This book is dedicated to David William Foster, mentor and scholar extraordinaire, esteemed colleague, and beloved friend. I could never have imagined where life would take me when I knocked on his office door in August 1987, and he briefly glanced away from his computer, lost in thought, and distractedly waved me in, "Yes, yes, come in . . . I'll be right with you."

CONTENTS

ACKNOWLEDGMENTS

The organizational structure for this book came from the Food Network, or, more precisely, from my aspiring chef and partner's addiction to the Food Network, in particular the show "Iron Chef." His irrepressible glee at learning each show's secret ingredient was something that for me, as a non-cook, was difficult to understand. The book's title is also connected to a feminist road trip film, *Boys on the Side*, from 1995, starring Whoopi Goldberg, Drew Barrymore, and Mary-Louise Parker. At the time I saw the movie, I was living in Winston-Salem, North Carolina, far from my beloved border, a newly minted Ph.D. teaching Spanish and Latin American literature in one of the state's many universities. When I saw the blue skies and adobe structures of Tucson, where the film's three characters unexpectedly end up on their way from New York to San Diego, I was entranced. The film was forgettable; the sky was not. It was under that cloudless turquoise sky that my grandmother crossed the border from Ciudad Juárez into El Paso at the beginning of the last century; it was under that deep blue dome that my mother, as a young woman, would take a bus from her hometown of El Paso to Los Angeles, the city where I would be born. As I watched the film, I was certain that it was there in Tucson, roughly the mid-point on my mother's journey, where I was destined to live.

There are many people who have patiently helped me work through many of the ideas contained within *Side Dishes*, in particular my two research assistants, Araceli Masterson and Jennifer Phillips. Araceli's work related to the chapter on women's studies programs in Latin America was invaluable. She was the ideal sounding board for many of the thoughts found within the pages, teasing out relations I had not considered, enthusiastically pushing me in new directions. Jennifer's complete dedication to the project over this last year, her superlative work on the Appendix that lists Latin American women filmmakers who have won international awards, and her willingness to drop everything in her own life to provide me with a careful reading was a great comfort. Liz Rangel also offered invaluable support. Antonio Otero provided a humorous, yet supportive push during a moment when I found it difficult to find the right words. My colleague Kamran Talattoff cheered me on by regularly bringing me delicious Persian food while I worked on the final stages of the manuscript. My sisters, as always, provided their own considerable gifts; Allison Fitch gave freely of her offbeat humor and creativity while Pam Handley afforded a wellspring of common sense and patience.

My colleague Eliana Rivero was a great source of inspiration for her own work in cultural studies and her fearless inclusion of her own voice in her intellectual work. I am profoundly indebted to Leslie Mitchner from Rutgers University Press. Leslie's quick and detailed response to the manuscript proposal, one that came literally within days of the submission, made me an instant fan. The editor of the series "New Directions in International Studies," Patrice Petro, similarly, was able to provide a reader's report in record time, a feat that was deeply appreciated. Mitchner and Petro make an unbeatable team, and I look forward to reading the other books that emerge from this series.

My undying loyalty goes to University of Arizona College of Humanities Dean Charles Tatum, himself an expert on Chicano popular culture. He will never regret having had such faith in me.

While it is customary to thank a foundation for providing the financial support necessary to write a book, I have none to thank. That said, I *have* had a foundation during this time, my partner, Fabio Lanza. An immense debt of gratitude goes to him for his unwavering belief in the project and willingness to do everything possible to provide me with the conditions that would enable me to finish it. This amounted to the single greatest gift of selflessness I have ever received. Thanks to Fabio, I had a cozy room in Cambridge, Massachusetts, where I could write uninterrupted daily during the winter; I ate fabulous, healthy, creative meals every day; and I benefited from his careful reading of each chapter. He injected large doses of silliness, love, and patience into the entire experience.

SIDE DISHES

INTRODUCTION

APPETIZER

I admit it. I was hungry. After sitting at the dinner table, staring at the familiar meal set before me, a steady diet of canonical texts by Latin American and Latina women, I craved something different. I needed something beyond the same female novelists, playwrights, poets, and testimonial voices routinely found in courses on Women's Writing in Latin/o America. But what are the dietary restrictions of the discipline that keep us from conceptualizing other possibilities for understanding women's cultural production and consumption in the region, for bringing other voices, as it were, to the table?

In *Side Dishes*, I argue that there is a need to broaden our understanding of Latin American and Latina women's cultural narratives and notions of authorship and activism to move beyond the "main dish" that is the traditional corpus of works. It must be clarified that efforts to offer a more varied intellectual fare are constrained by the political economy of cultural commodities: the canon of Latin American women's writing will necessarily be limited and restricted by the circulation of texts. We end up using in our courses only those cultural artifacts that are already easily available in their ready-to-buy form, be it a book or DVD. A large part of this commodification takes place outside of Latin America and oftentimes in the United States and, as such, it is subject to the ever-changing U.S. cultural market.

This book includes myriad cultural artifacts and heretofore-understudied themes, almost all of which show a greater focus on the cultural narratives of everyday life. A "dish" was a slang term common in the first half of the twentieth century used to describe an attractive woman, so the book's title plays with this double meaning. The individuals included in *Side Dishes* are, quite literally, the women on the side of traditional academic fare.

The first answer to my what-is-missing question was smut. Where are the Latin American or Latina women who are producing texts, films or Web sites that, instead of showing women as sexual victims of male aggression, show women with hearty, or even voracious, sexual appetites? What about these Latina American women who talk, write, and draw about sex graphically? How can we analyze cultural artifacts both in print and online that, for lack of a better term, could be classified as pornography? But smut wasn't the only answer. What about that which traditionally has been conceptualized as pop culture, such as science fiction, for example, or even the work of cartoonists or stand-up comedians; where are these voices on traditional academic menus? Another chapter was born.

Then a new thought occurred to me, instead of looking for textual clues in fictional works that provide a glimpse of women's lives and activism, why don't we go directly to the feminist activists and critics themselves, to the women who are writing about culture in feminist journals, in print or on the Web, or establishing gender studies programs in their respective countries? How can these elements round out our notions of women's intellectual contributions in Latin America? Historically, all roads and highways in South America led from the interior to the ports, where raw goods would be shipped to Europe or the United States. Has this been mirrored by intellectual trends as well? Has feminist theory in Latin America developed more through its association with the Northern Hemisphere than with neighboring nations? Has feminist theory made its way into academic institutions? If so, when, and with what degree of obstacles or level of success?

But there was one final dish that needed to be prepared: now more than ever a large number of films are being written and directed by women in Mexico, Argentina, and Brazil and these women are meeting with great success in their own countries and internationally. But where were these directors in recent books or courses on Latin American women or for that matter in courses on Latin American film?

In the wildly popular international television show "Iron Chef," the duel between the two top chefs always hinges on their talents at creating a full meal, from appetizers to dessert, with one key ingredient. The moment of revelation ("Frozen Peas!!") is always presented at the start of the show with great fanfare, music, and lighting. Audible gasps rise from the audience. In *Side Dishes* the secret ingredient—one that flavors each chapter—is sex.

Chapter One, "Lust," discusses areas of sexuality often deemed "tasteless" by critics, including the explicit sexuality prevalent in most of the artifacts studied—many of them classified as "pornographic" and dealing with bisexuality, lesbianism, sadomasochism, or masturbation. "Lust" also provides the theoretical key to understanding the four chapters or side dishes that follow: "Pop," "Issues," "Flicks," and "Class." Chapter Two, "Pop," concerns science fiction writers, cartoonists, and stand-up comedians: the equivalent of a side of fries or a one-night stand. Chapter Three, "Issues," is the first academic study to deal with the critical issues, both literal and figurative, of three leading Latin American feminist journals published during the span of time from 1990 to 2007: *debate feminista* from Mexico, *Feminaria* from Argentina, and Brazil's *Cadernos Pagu* as well as a number of contemporary online feminist journals from these regions. Chapter Four, "Flicks," discusses the representation of women's sexuality in the work of feminist filmmakers in Brazil, Argentina, and Mexico over the last twenty years. Finally, Chapter Five, "Class," traces the rise and development of women's studies and gender studies programs in this region. The Epilogue, "Leftovers," discusses future areas of inquiry that are either not fully explored or are not addressed in this text that would serve to further extend the boundaries of what is considered Latin American or Latina women's cultural production.

Side Dishes combines Latina, Brazilian, and Spanish American ingredients, in an attempt to provide a more comprehensive view of Latina America. A jambalaya of critical approaches is used in order to illuminate the topics addressed taken from feminist and post-colonial studies, queer theory, reception theory, cultural studies, and postmodernism. In cultural studies, most artifacts are deemed worthy of analysis for what they reveal about the webs of signification, or the grids of intelligibility of a given group. In this case, *Side Dishes* presents Latin American and Latina women not merely or exclusively as writers, but also as editors, directors, academics, cartoonists, pornographers, and comedians.

Adding these side dishes to the plate of traditional academic fare is still not enough to convey the range of women's production and contributions. It is no easy fix. But *Side Dishes* opens the door towards moving in the direction of inclusiveness, of thinking in ways that extend beyond the literary text, and moving into new areas of inquiry, thus providing a broader and more comprehensive understanding of the wealth of Latin American and Latina women's creative and intellectual work. It is precisely for this reason that these "side dishes" make the meal. Admit it. You were hungry, too.

1

✤

LUST

It has been called sperm, semen, ejaculate, seed, man fluid, baby gravy, jizz, cum, pearl necklace, gentleman's relish, wad, pimp juice, number 3, load, spew, donut glaze, spunk, gizzum, cream, hot man mustard, squirt, goo, spunk, splooge, love juice, man cream, and la leche.

—Lisa Jean Moore, *Sperm Counts:*
Overcome by Man's Most Precious Fluid

The year 2007 was a watershed for semen. It marked the publication in academia of three tomes to systematically treat the topic: Lisa Jean Moore's *Sperm Counts: Overcome by Man's Most Precious Fluid*, Murat Aydemir's *Images of Bliss: Ejaculation, Masculinity, Meaning*, and Angus McLaren's *Impotence: A Cultural History*. Moore's unusual first line, cited above, was an eye-opener, not only because of the unusually imaginative terms, but also because ten of the twenty-eight terms are food-related. Curious, I immediately searched for slang terms related to women's orgasmic fluid. I was unable to find any at all.

The three texts mentioned above all discuss the cultural meaning of sperm, and how the privileging of male sexuality has served to limit everyone, not just women. Each book fits neatly into the category of gender studies. Moore draws on historical and medical documents, pornography, children's sex-education books, and sex-worker narratives to examine the meaning of sperm. She shows that while the significance has shifted somewhat according to place and time, the depiction of sperm as active, heroic protagonists has been fairly constant. And the egg? The egg doesn't do much. It has no personality. It just hangs around, waiting for the big moment.

This first Side Dish is not about bored eggs. It is not about the representation of women as victims of rape, incest, or other forms of sexual violence, either. It is about lust. Specifically, it is about the production and consumption of representations of women with insatiable sexual appetites. When the pornography wars raged in the 1990s, Catherine McKinnon versus Andrea Dworkin, what the anti-porn feminists refused to acknowledge was that there could be a porn-viewing population of women. Women who were not dupes, nor forced by their male partners to watch, but who did so of their own free will. In retrospect, it now seems naive to assume that women were exclusively victims of the porn trade.

Porno por/para Mujeres

Both in the United States and in Latin America, women who twenty or thirty years ago might have been reluctant to buy a girlie magazine at a newsstand or enter a porn movie house—activities conducted in a public space—are now partaking more than ever before of nonpublic viewing of pornography on DVDs, cable TV programs, and on the Internet. Web sites have been created around the world for these new consumers. Some recent Internet surveys have found that as many as 25 percent of the users are women (Internet Filter Review).

Female lust has also started to appear prominently outside the privacy of the Internet, on the big screen. In 2004, one of the most successful films released in Chile was *Mujeres infieles*, [Unfaithful Women], dir. Rodrigo Ortúzar Lynch, a film that humorously showed, among other things, the value of sex toys and masturbation. One hundred and fifty thousand spectators saw the film in Chile and it became the most popular Chilean film ever released in Spain. It was also the most popular foreign film (not American) released in Peru that year. There have been other recent important milestones in feminist pornography. Erika Lust, a Swede, won the prize for short film of the year at the Festival Internacional de Cine Erótico [International Festival of Erotic Cinema] in Barcelona for her movie *The Good Girl* (2004). Canada's Good For Her, a store that sells sex toys exclusively to women, had its very first Feminist Porn Awards ceremony in June 2007. Their promotional information included the following:

"Good For Her came up with the idea for the Feminist Porn Awards because people don't know they have a choice when it comes to porn," said Chanelle Gallant, manager of Good For Her and the event's organizer. "Yes, there's a lot of bad porn out there. But there is also some great porn being made by and for women. We wanted to recognize and celebrate the good porn makers as well as direct people to their work."[1]

The event brought 350 guests and included a roundtable discussion about how these feminist filmmakers and performers have changed the ways women and people of color are shown in adult films.

There are any number of porn sites in English for women, including www.sssh.com, www.forthegirls.com, and www.hotmoviesforher.com. Frustrated by the lack of feminist porn in Latin America, the Web site www.feministasanónimas.com, created by women in Mexico City, put out a public call for action on November 18, 2006, "Queremos una pornografía para mujeres" [We want pornography for women"]. Still another Web site, "El sentido de la vida," from Spain, proudly proclaims that their Web site will be number one on the list for anyone who googles "niña ninfomaniaca." The site includes an ongoing survey. "¿Alguna vez te han metido un dedo en el culo?" [Have they ever stuck a finger in your anus?]. It discusses how the Internet has revolutionized porn consumption and provides links to graphic discussions of masturbation in pages entitled Las pajas I and II. It is important to note that Web sites from Spain are read throughout the Spanish-speaking world (www.elsentidodelavida.net).

Returning to Latin America, however, the Web site for the Gender Studies program at the Universidad Nacional Mayor de San Marcos in Lima, Peru, www.des-ubicadas.com, has a number of sections devoted to pornography. The des-ubicadas cite the www.girlswholikeporno.com Web site in Spain as proof that feminist porn is possible and that it is "desestabilizando dicotomías, yendo más allá de categorías, siempre gozando" [destabilizing dichotomies, going beyond categories and always enjoying] (17 Feb. 2007). Links to previous online issues include the "Encuentro feminista lésbico" [Feminist Lesbian Encounter] and one entitled "My pussy is magic!!" Spaniards are seen as leading the way for Latin Americans: "Hay muchas más páginas sobre post-pornolinkeadas en girlswholikeporno. Seguiremos navegando para ver qué propuestas encontramos en Latinoamérica!" [There are many more pages like the pornolinkadas and girlswholikeporno, we will keep looking to see what we find in Latin America] (ibid.).

In Argentina, one porn director, Martín Lucas, decided that, in an effort to accommodate the many women who are working in the production of his films, he would focus less on the gratuitous violence and humiliation scenes so common to porn from earlier decades (*La nación* Chile 9/9/2005 www.lanacion.cl). Mariano Martínez Lacarre, the marketing genius behind the most important adult cable channels in Argentina, affirmed in an article in that country's *Clarín* newspaper in 2005 that 61 percent of females watch porn with their partners, 15 percent with their male or female friends, and 19 percent alone (Bassani). He also mentioned that 30 percent of customers in adult stores in Buenos Aires now are women, a marked change from the past when the clientele was almost exclusively male. It is because of this interest on the part of female consumers that he attributes the surge in cable subscriptions to porn channels in Argentina. That not withstanding, we cannot generalize for all of Latin America. Chilean sexologist Ellen Sepúlveda has said "La mujer argentina es distinta a la chilena. Ellas tienen una concepción cultural de lo erótico y la sensualidad absolutamente distinta a la nuestra, tienen menos pudor y más asumida su corporalidad. En resumen, son dueñas de vivencias respecto de la corporalidad y el placer diferentes a las chilenas" [The Argentine woman is distinct from Chilean woman. They have a cultural concept of the erotic and of sensuality that is completely different from ours, they have less shame and they assume their physicality more. In short, they are the owners of experiences of the body and of pleasure that are different from Chilean women].[2]

The site www.blog.innerpendejo.net discussed the topic of women as consumers of porn in August 2007, pointing out that according to Internet Filter Review Source fully one-third of all porn users are women, and 9.4 million women access it monthly ("Pornografía para mujeres" 8 Aug. 2007). But do women enjoy porn as much as men? In a study at the McGill University Health Care Centre in 2006, it was found that both sexes reach peak arousal within ten minutes, on average, upon viewing pornography, something that dispels two myths: (1) that women are not aroused by porn; and (2) that they take longer to become sexually aroused (Khamsi).

This volume starts precisely from the assumption that women not only are aroused, but that they have sexual appetites, they have lust, and that this can be and has been represented in various creative forms by Latin American and Latina women. This chapter is about the textual representation of women with voracious sexual appetites. It is about the representation of women as sexual aggressors or pleasuring themselves. For the latter, male presence or participation is not required. But for now, let's return to *la leche* [the milk].

On the Difficulty of Transcending Taboos

In *Images of Bliss*, Murat Aydemir undertakes an original and extensive analysis of images of male orgasm and semen in literature, art, and hardcore pornography. It offers a critical exploration of ejaculation in Western culture. Angus McLaren, meanwhile, in *Impotence*, draws on medical texts, marriage manuals, pornography, and other sources to explore cultural preoccupations with male potency or lack thereof. He discusses how Viagra became the "fastest selling pharmaceutical in history," pointing out that most insurance companies paid for Viagra prescriptions, whereas women for 40 years had been denied coverage for oral contraceptives. Moore, McLaren, and Aydemir all to varying degrees highlight the importance attached to semen, something also addressed a few years back in a different academic tome.

In 2003, *Solitary Sex* (Laqueur), the first scholarly book to deal with masturbation, hit the bookshelves. I immediately rushed to the university bookstore to grab my copy, finding it on a display table near the entrance. When I reached the front of the line to make my purchase, the woman at the counter glanced at me, slightly distracted, "I think there is some sort of promotion going on." She grabbed the thick volume and thrust it high into the air over her head, shouting across the store to another sales clerk; "How much is *Solitary Sex*?" I resisted the urge to respond, "Hasn't it always been free?" Instead, I cast a glance behind me to see if any of my colleagues or students happened to be standing in line. They weren't. Still, I wanted to shout at those who were waiting, staring at me disapprovingly (was it my imagination?): "This is a serious area of intellectual inquiry!! It is not gratuitous smut!!" I didn't have the chance. The sales clerk had gotten the price check, completed the transaction, and handed me my book. I greedily took it back to my office and immediately checked, as I always do, the bibliography and index. But wait, what's this? In the index there is a subcategory for women? I checked to see if men had their own subcategory. Nope. In other words, in a tome of 501 pages the assumption, of course, was that we only need to read about men. Women are almost a postscript. Or, to be fair, we were covered on 74–77; 200–204, mentioned on 257, 339–55, 93–95, 100, 104, 372–76, 392–94, 398–404, a total of 31 pages. Best yet, following the page listings I found the helpful cross-reference "see also Feminism: Nymphomania" (501). So women masturbators might be feminist nymphomaniacs? Tsk Tsk.

How could there be a total of 31 pages devoted to women and masturbation, out of 420 pages of text, when women account for more than half of the population? After all, masturbation is one of the most democratic activities around. It knows few boundaries; all economic classes, ages, and races can participate. Why the focus on men? Of course, one never reads in the newspaper police blotters of women sitting in their cars or in the bushes leering at young men or women and caught in the middle of a masturbatory frenzy. Beyond that, the ol' hand to the crotch move, even in public, is considered a gesture of hypermasculinity, albeit a somewhat vulgar one.

And yes . . . of course . . . there are all of those historical notions of the "wasted seed" and what not. I have always been a staunch believer that a little wasted seed never hurt any man, indeed, the over preoccupation to preserve the precious semen has led to some pretty grim consequences in many parts of the world. A button on the bulletin board in my office proclaims: "Not every ejaculation deserves a name." Still, I had so hoped that this, the first official academic book on masturbation, written by a scholar from Berkeley, no less, would at least provide equal coverage of all masturbators. Sigh.

Here's the rub (pun fully intended): in spite of the lack of coverage of women in the text itself, 75 percent of the illustrations used for the book, including the cover, are of women in masturbatory poses, not men. Of course! If the implied reader is the heterosexual male, why would he possibly want to see a bunch of men touching themselves—not much enchantment to be found there. The dominant male gaze is alive and well.

What is unusual is that, in spite of this, in an interview with Peter Monaghan, entitled "Knowing Thyself: A historian explains how the stigma of 'solitary sex' rose . . . and fell" (a wink-wink nudge-nudge for male readers), Monaghan points out that in Laqueur's book, "it affected women as much as men. In fact, argued the experts, girls and women were particularly prone to myriad ailments. Full-blown nervous collapse might land them in asylums—if they didn't die of consumption first." He then quotes the author directly, "Solitary sex broke the gender barrier." Well, if solitary sex did, then why didn't he? To be fair, Laqueur does credit the women's movement, the sexual revolution, and the gay-and-lesbian movement for making masturbation more socially acceptable: "The first, easiest, and most convenient way to experiment with your body" proclaimed the Boston Women's Health Book Collective in *Our Bodies, Ourselves* from 1971. So we have feminists to thank for the widespread acceptance of masturbation? Maybe not.

As Monaghan points out, printing of *Solitary Sex* was delayed because Zone Books' usual American printer declined the job. The publisher's staff members found a Canadian press capable of handling the book's high-quality graphics, but they worried that it would be denied entry at customs. Five bookstores invited Mr. Laqueur to talk about his work, but three others refused, describing themselves as "family bookstores." Beyond that, the prominent scholar found that he was not invited to radio and television talk shows to discuss his latest research (Internet Filter Review A14).

A similar puritanical bent greeted Rachel Shteir when her book, *Striptease: The Untold History of the Girlie Show*, was published by Oxford University Press in 2005. "I had begun thinking about writing *Striptease* during the years, back in the mid-90s, when Catherine McKinnon and Andrea Dworkin were going at it, declaiming the evils of pornography and its exploitation of women—an era whose heat I thought had disappeared by the time my book was published." It hadn't, as she describes:

> The bookstore at the University of California at Los Angeles, for example, "banned" me. I say "banned" because UCLA had invited me to give a talk on the LA leg of my tour and then disinvited me. From what I could surmise, an administrator had caught wind of the book's subject and, along with some donors, deemed it, if not downright pornographic, at least inappropriate for a college campus. They seemed to believe that my talk would send the message that the university condoned stripping, or pornography, or something generally inappropriate for young minds. (B15)

But let's return to masturbation. I've come to think that this male reluctance to acknowledge (or analyze) women and masturbation has to do with the following: nothing quite elicits as much discomfort on the part of the self-identified straight male as the idea of being found sexually disposable by women. This has come to my attention repeatedly over the years. The first time was while reading the amusing reaction of Latin American writer Albert Fuguet to what he termed was the "recent breakthrough bestseller" in Chile, *Los siete días de la señora K* (1993) [The Seven Days of Señora K] by Ana María del Río. The book chronicles a week in the life of a woman masturbating. "A mí me hubiera gustado más si se hubiera acostado con alguien" [I would have liked it more if she had slept with someone.] (21). Why? It is interesting that in Spanish "alguien" [someone] is a gender-neutral pronoun, so I assume that either sex would have worked for Fuguet. The idea of serving as a voyeur to lesbian sex has long been known to be a fantasy of many men. Yet Del Río demonstrates complete sexual independence for her protagonist. And it is precisely that independence that is seen as such a threat to some men, as is illustrated below.

Rachel Maines, author of *The Technology of Orgasm: "Hysteria" the Vibrator, and Women's Sexual Satisfaction*, thought she had stumbled onto a fascinating topic, turn-of-the-century vibrators, and yet she found resistance when she attempted to discuss her findings at conferences. "[. . . M]any men, she realized, seemed to take her findings as a personal criticism." One went so far as to argue that the "sexual experience of women using vibrators was 'not the real thing'" (8). Clarkson University, where Maines was teaching, decided to fire her for fear, in part, that donations to the university would dry up if they knew someone on their faculty was researching vibrators (9). It was not until her findings were published in the journal *Technology and Society*, however, that the perceived "legitimacy" of her work was established. It is also of note that the journal's subscription rates rose considerably after the publication of her article (9). What both of these reactions suggest is that a woman's manual or machine-aided orgasm is an anxiety-producing topic for men, bringing some to the point—dare I say it—of hysteria.

If women no longer need men economically, nor sexually, then one can reach the uncomfortable conclusion that men are at least to some degree disposable. In an infamous recorded statement, Prince Charles told Camila Parker that he wanted to live inside her "like a tampon." Of course, His Royal Highness was forgetting that women dispose of tampons shortly after they have been used. What academic critic Maines had felt so interesting in researching her topic was the way in which "androcentric medical tradition had pathologized clitoris-centered female sexuality" turning it into a taboo topic (8).

This notion that women cannot have sexual appetites (or if they do, they better not talk or write about it) is not something of the past, as Shteir also found when she tried to publicize or discuss her book. And the taboo against women openly discussing lust and sexual gratification remains.

In "The New Sex Scribes: Female columnists spark interest and controversy at student newspapers," Eric Hoover discussed the uproar over female columnists of college newspapers who are writing weekly sex columns, such as Meghan Bainum who has written about sex outdoors, sodomy laws, and masturbation. Over the last few years, sexually explicit columns caused a controversy at several institutions, including Yale University. Sex columns vary: columnists may provide graphic personal accounts or they may offer clinical advice. They generally agree that undergraduate men are poor lovers. When the *Yale Daily News* published a column written by sophomore Natalie Krinsky called "Spit or swallow? It's all about the sauce," in which she "recalled childhood sexual experiments with produce, reported on the fat content of semen, tweaked Hamlet's most famous soliloquy to reframe the question posed in her title, and revealed her personal preference," the campus was in an uproar. Hundreds of messages poured in to the newspaper, many sharply criticizing the undergraduate. The response showed how deeply divided society remains on the topic of women's lust (A33). The idea that "nice girls" don't write or talk about sex is still prevalent.

The Masturbatory Woman in Argentina and Brazil

This topic of a woman's sexual gratification has been an important theme in literature written by Latin American women over the last forty years. This is all the more interesting when one takes into account the historical regulation of women's sexuality and the climate of machismo that permeates much of the region. One of the more comical events that I have witnessed involved the lecture of demure, sweet elderly Argentine author Alicia Steimberg when she came to Arizona to discuss her work. Steimberg had recently won the Sonrisa Vertical award in Spain for her novel, *Amatista* (1989), a masturbation-focused text (although it must be noted that it is not one focused on a woman's private sexual gratification, thus not generating much anxiety on the part of male readers). There was something mildly unsettling about the incongruity of the real life image of the woman to her passionate, funny, and erotic prose. Like Dr. Ruth, Steimberg hardly embodied one's image of exactly the sort of writer who would create such a lusty text. She herself seemed somewhat shy when the topic was broached, preferring to dwell on her well-known novel that deals with her Jewish immigrant family, *Músicos y relojeros* (1971) [Musicians and Watchmakers].

    Amatista may be the first Hispanic novel, up until the time of *Los siete días de la Señora K,* that has focused explicitly on masturbation as a central theme. In it, the protagonist is the instructor of a man on the techniques of gratifying a woman sexually. She initiates, discusses, and controls the sexual act, and her student is exceptionally interested in the subject matter. Her pupil willingly obliges her every instruction.

The woman speaks; the man is mute. She controls language and occasionally supplies him with answers or attributes. She is the voice of sexual experience, recounting the sexual exploits of Amatista, a personage that may be assumed to be either directly the narrator or to be a projection of her fantasies. The incidences that the teacher recounts all have the classic formula of pornography in the "glorious beauty, the superb proportions, and the unfettered lugubricity of the performers the narrator evokes" (Foster, "The Case" 267). While the *Amatista* stories privilege genital contact, the instructor's lessons to her student focus on the entire body. The tease, the thrill of the delayed orgasm, as opposed to immediate gratification, is considered of primary importance and contrasts with the stereotypical image of male sexuality. This is what makes Steimberg's text significantly more than just a reworking of typical male porn formulas. The arousal, according to the teacher, must be sustained, increased, and orgasm delayed so that the final incident of the insertion of penis into vagina becomes of secondary importance.

The teacher demonstrates for her pupil that masturbation is of great importance. It is presented as a gratifying act unto itself and it is shown as an option to be engaged in either alone or with another, as a suitable outlet and variation on the erotic theme. The narrator encourages masturbation, shows the student how to engage in it, and requires him to do so at times. It is seen as a complement to genital penetration as well as the eroticism of the entire body.

Like Steimberg, Brazilian writer Helena Parente Cunha emphasizes the importance of masturbation and lust in her *Mulher no espelho* [Woman Between Mirrors] (1985).

In the current literature written by Brazilian women there is a trend to discuss sexuality openly, if not militantly. As David William Foster has stated, "[t]he fact that this production has come from a large-market society like Brazil has undoubtedly to do with the greater incorporation in that country of a project of modernity that incorporates explicit space for cultural products that in a loose way can be called pornographic" ("The Case" 4). *Mulher no espelho* is just one of the many notable literary works dealing openly with women's eroticism and life circumstances in a changing Brazilian society following the demise of the dictatorship.

Parente Cunha's novel won the country's Cruz and Sousa Award in part for its capacity to portray the enigma of a woman's experience, but also for the profound psychological delineation of the protagonist. The text forms part of an innovative trend in women's writing in Brazil in which there is an attempt to extend the parameters of literary creation beyond those traditionally accepted by the canon. As Darlene Sadlier points out,

> Narrative realism has given way almost entirely to surrealistic and self-reflexive writing, and in some cases to "magical" and "postmodern" techniques [. . .] Internal monologue becomes completely decentered, or is framed by various forms of metanarrative; a concern with women's problems and women's subjectivity remains the dominant feature, but the contemporary stories are more radical in their attitude towards language. (II)

Mulher no espelho may be seen as a response to the growing movement of feminist consciousness in Brazil, which while stunted somewhat by the authoritarian regime, was never undermined. The novel is an exploration of the effects of patriarchal authoritarianism on feminine—if not feminist—consciousness. The novel focuses on the family life of an upper-middle class Bahian woman on three levels: the memory of her childhood, her lived present, and her imagination and subconscious. The protagonist, who remains nameless, finds herself, at the age of forty-five, meditating on her life in front of a multipaneled mirror. She narrates her story using the first-person while her image in the mirror uses the second-person to provide an alternative understanding of the past and present.

The transgression of sexual taboos is the most salient dimension explored in the process of identity formation in *Mulher no espelho*. Physical pleasure, historically denied, regulated and repressed in women, is a necessary component in self-discovery. Initially, the protagonist allows herself only to feel the sensual pleasures of dance, later to be humiliated by her sons who find her in the living room, moving about to the pulsating sounds of their disco records. Later, she discovers the joy of exploring her own body in a clearly masturbatory fashion:

> As minhas mãos percorrem o meu corpo, de alto a baixo. Detêm-se na nuca e se misturam aos cabelos pra soltá-los, livres, sobre os ombros. As minhas mãos descem, contornando os seios, levemente sobre as

pontas endurecidas, que somente conhecem as mãos balofas e suadas de um homem. Sinto que haverá um prazer à espera dos meus seios solitários. As minhas mãos descem pela cintura, pelas nádegas, se afundam no sexo [. . .]

[My hands moved along my body, from top to bottom. They are detained at the nape of the neck and mix in with my hair, which is freed to fall over the shoulders. My hands descend, rounding the breasts, lightly over the hardened points that only know the clumsy and sweaty hands of a man. I feel that pleasure awaits my solitary breasts. My hands descend to the waist, to the buttocks, they become lost in my genitals.]. (109)

She is able to look at her body in the multipaneled mirror unabashedly, to take pleasure in her aging body: "Não é um corpo jovem, mas vejo um corpo bonito, suaves curvas, carnes rijas, petulantes" (108). [It isn't a young body, but I see a pretty body, soft curves, rigid, petulant flesh]. The excitement and pleasure she feels herald her long repressed but awakening sexuality: "A minha nudez me atrai, me exita, me assusta" (39). [My nakedness attracts me, excites me, frightens me.]

Beyond *Mulher no espelho*, Márcia Denser's *Muito prazer* (1982), a series of erotic short stories by contemporary Brazilian writers, also appeared in the 1980s. The title, "Much Pleasure" is a play on the traditional greeting used when first meeting someone. When the original text was greeted with overwhelming enthusiasm, Denser edited the second anthology a mere two years later with the traditional response to the first greeting, again imbued with sexual meaning: *O prazer é tudo meu* (1984) or "The pleasure is all mine."

While repeated references to lesbian sex in the stories of *Muito prazer* are probably the first of their kind in the country, the subject of gay love was first dealt with in Brazil during the last half of the nineteenth century in *Bom Crioulo* [Good Criollo] (1895) by Adolfo Caminha (Foster, *Gay and Lesbian Themes* 1). In 1984, Olga Savary published an anthology of women's erotic poetry entitled *Carne viva* [Live Flesh]. As Foster points out, Brazil has always had a tradition of erotic culture. While the country is fraught with heterosexism, racism, and sexism, it does, nonetheless, provide a much more inviting, if not accepting, climate in which an author may produce erotic works, certainly to a greater extent than in Spanish-speaking societies (Foster, *Gay and Lesbian Themes* 32). *Muito prazer*, *O prazer e tudo meu*, and

Carne viva, all form part the "nova ficção feminina" [new feminine fiction] in which the depiction of eroticism plays an increasingly significant role (Novães Coelho 22).

It helps at this juncture to discuss the term erotic versus pornographic, as Linda Williams attempts to do:

> The very notion that erotica as "good," clean, non-explicit representations of sexual pleasure in opposition to dirty, explicit pornographic ones is false. The one emphasizes desire, the other one satisfaction. Depending on who is looking, both can appear dirty, perverse or too explicit . . . We need to see pornography in all its naked explicitness if we are to speak frankly about sexual power and pleasure and if we are to demystify sex. (227)

While, traditionally, "erotic" has been privileged over "pornographic," this is still a highly charged issue in feminism, as Jill Dolan explains "hegemonic anti-porn feminism has so successfully infiltrated lesbian discourse in the 1980s that even erotica has been flattened out and carefully monitored for any evidence of politically incorrect sex practice" (270).

In terms of the compilation edited by Denser in 1982 and its sequel in 1984, whether the stories exemplify eroticism or pornography is open to interpretation. What is certain, however, is that the stories were published upon the demise of an authoritarian period in the country that lasted for more than 20 years, ending in 1984 with the election of Tancredo Neves. Eroticism in Brazilian women's writing at this time emerged as part of the "nova imagem" [new image] of women writers in Brazil who attempted to go beyond a subversion of the hegemonic order seeking a new way of connecting with themselves after the period of "bloqueio absoluto ao sexo" [absolute block of sexuality] during the dictatorship (Novães Coelho 17).

It is important to clarify that when referring to "women," "woman," or "woman's identity" I enter another polemical area. While Julia Kristeva argues against the use of the category "women," she is unable to make the distinction between "women" the historical actors and "woman" the abstract noun, both of which presuppose some form of gender identity. Kristeva's argument is that the stability of the subject is called into question and the sign "woman" has been shown to signify lack, and thus we cannot posit anything like gender identity particularly for women. However, since the make-up of the body is a fixed determinant of forming gender identity, then gender identity ought to be thought of as one of the more stable determinants of the individual. Thinking of it in this way allows us to talk about "women" and "men" and the unfixed power differences between the two. How can feminism form an agenda for action if there is no sort of central tenant that may be said to bring women together, in spite of class, race, or sexual determinations? The answer for some is strategic essentialism. The one constant that has been noted, and is virtually universal, is that women have served as the primary victims of sexual oppression. As Amy Kaminsky states,

> For though self-critical feminist theory has in recent years incorporated into its analysis the specificities of race, class, and nationality that inform and shape the oppression of women, in most feminists accounts, sexuality remains a constant of women's subordination. (xiii)

What is specific to women's oppression is the impulse to regulate female sexuality, which in turn depends on the enforcement of heterosexuality. It is in this way that *Mulher no espelho*, *Muito prazer*, and *O prazer é tudo meu* are such radical texts. Eroticism, for many of these women authors, is a form of existential interrogation.

Censorship and the Lesbian Body

Reina Roffé belongs to the generation of authors who came of age during the neofascist Process of National Reorganization. In 1969, at the age of 17, Roffé wrote her first novel, *Llamado al puf* [Called to the Ottoman], which met with immediate critical acclaim and won the Pondal Ríos Prize in Buenos Aires in 1975 for the best novel by a young writer. *Llamado al puf* chronicles many of the events in the author's life. She has termed it an "análisis casero de mi infancia" [homegrown analysis of my childhood] and it documents the suffocating and repressive atmosphere of life within a middle-class Buenos Aires family. The novel is upbeat and optimistic, finishing with the departure of the protagonist from her dismal home life and her entrance into the world (142). In spite of the success of the novel, Roffé was greeted by much criticism from literary specialists. She was told that her writing had too many feminine registers and that it was necessary that she try to present greater social conscience (*La rompiente* 9). Roffé took the comments into consideration, and in the process she betrayed "el mensaje individual, subjetivo, femenino" (*La rompiente* 10) [the individual, subjective and feminine message] as reflected in her next novel, *Monte de Venus* [Venus' Mount], completed at an inauspicious time, the beginning of 1976.

On March 24, 1976, the new military government was installed and Roffé's text was immediately censured. Because her narrative posed a fundamental challenge to patriarchy (as represented in the form of authoritarianism) and was a deconstruction of gender representation and female sexuality, she was silenced and eventually forced to go into exile. The experience was devastating for Roffé. She moved to Madrid and wrote little in the way of fiction in the years that followed, conserving her attachment with the literary field by working as a journalist, editor, and book reviewer in such newspapers as *Clarín*, *Convicción*, and *La Opinión*.

The book was censored due to its representations of women's political activism and sexual lust. Sexual and political transgressions are obviously not easily separated: since Foucault's groundbreaking work on the "technology of sex," we know that proper sexualization is a crucial concern of the modern state, and even when surveillance is entrusted to the family or internalized by the individual, sex remains a central issue for the survival of the social body as a whole (Foucault; De Lauretis). The borderline between political criticism and sexual transgression is accordingly very thin in Roffé's novel.

When asked about the censorship of the novel, the author said, "Creo que la prohibieron porque era cosa molesta. También había una crítica al sistema educativo y la situación de la mujer" (Domínguez 6). [I think they banned it because it was bothersome. Also, there was a criticism of the educational system and women's situation.]

What Roffé does not mention is the theme of homosexuality, which may have accounted in large part for its banning by the censors. The inadhesion to the ideology of compulsory heterosexuality for the good of the Fatherland was only one of Roffé's transgressions. Others had to do with the representation of a system that worked against individuals who attempted to initiate social change.

In the novel, the women attempt to better their lives through the system. Two stories emerge. The first, narrated in third person, is that of Barú, one of the returning students who finds her "voice" through political activism; the second is that of a lesbian, Julia Grande, who asserts her identity through recounting her life story into a tape recorder for Victoria Sáenz Ballesteros, one of the instructors who takes a personal interest in Julia's life as the possible subject of a novel. Both attempts at self-articulation are thwarted. Barú comes to realize that the minor changes she had managed to achieve in order to be treated with greater dignity by the school officials were inconsequential. Julia's instructor blackmails her by threatening to expose her taped intimate confessions (which include having killed a man in self-defense while working as a prostitute) if Julia does not give in to her demands for her child.

One of the most interesting elements in the *Monte de Venus* that undoubtedly was scandalous to the censors is the description of Julia's voracious sexual appetite and her adhesion to the "butch" stereotype of lesbian behavior. The issue of appropriate behavior for lesbian feminists remains hotly contested. The idealistic and sanitized view posited by many mainstream feminists is that somehow lesbian sexual relations are more noble than gay male sex because they prioritize loving relationships and sexual relationships over the rough impersonal sex thought to be primarily the domain of men. This view of women and sex ironically rests on the very same Victorian ideology that so many mainstream feminists have derided in the past, one which presents women as asexual, or at least mildly erotic, and pure. It also fosters the regulation of sexual conduct, setting itself up as yet another authoritarian discourse that denies the possibility that there be such a thing as lesbian lust (De Lauretis).

The fact that Roffé's graphic portrayal of lesbian passion follows along the butch/femme model has caused it to be somewhat derided by critics such as Elena Martínez, who writes:

In the presentation of the lesbian character in this novel, the reader finds all the cultural clichés and myths created around lesbians and their social behavior: such as the strong attachment of the lesbian with the father, who is the main source of affection and nurturance, and the rejecting mother. The view the author presents of lesbianism follows the Freudian perspective of identification with the father and a desire to be male and to be seen as a man, which makes the lesbian character dress like a boy and perform activities that society and culture have long associated with males. Julia feels her true identity to be masculine while her feminine identity is viewed by her as something fake that she assumes while betraying herself [. . .] *Monte de Venus does not present a lesbian perspective* and is rather a mosaic of stereotypical constructions that reiterate prejudices of society. (38, my emphasis added)

Martínez does not allow for the possibility that some women may, in fact, adhere to the stereotype and that this may be a legitimate lesbian "perspective." Some women may, like Roffé's Julia Grande, enjoy sex outside of the context of a romantic relationship, have casual sex, or enjoy pornography. The key to understanding this particular model of sexual activity, according to Pat Califia, is fantasy. The participants are engaging in behavior that enhances their sexual pleasure and the activity may be connected to drama or ritual (168).

Should lesbians that do adhere to the heterosexual paradigm for the purposes of their own heightened sexual pleasure be, in the words of Califia, "tarred and feathered and ridden out of the lesbian ghetto on a rail"? (11) The butch/femme model may be an authentic language of lesbian desire instead of what some mainstream feminists, authors, and academics consider an anachronism to be rejected by all enlightened, modern feminists including Latin American feminist literary critics.

Califia has argued for the rights of women to express any dimension of their sexuality, and has nothing but scorn and derision for those authors during the 1980s who, "in bids for literary legitimacy, chose to remain closeted and write about things other than their own lives. Even novelists, journalists, and academics who were ostensibly out of the closet could only bear to write about lesbian reality in sanitized, strained and compartmentalized ways" (15).

In contrast to the above, Roffé's treatment of lesbian sexuality in 1970s Argentina is explicit. Julia Grande is a "butch" dyke. She is in many ways a parody of a man, where each lover for her is another notch on the belt. Adopting a masculine stance for Julia is an attempt to enter into the realm of phallocentric power. Furthermore, this transvestism calls attention to the constructed nature of gender. Julia breaks with the erotic and social role assigned to her, proving in the process that the model is flawed, incapable of fixing any identity, be it hetero- or homosexual. Roffé, in presenting Julia Grande, is also breaking with the erotic and social role assigned to her, as a "respectable" author.

In many ways, *Monte de Venus*'s sanction of censorship should not come as any surprise given that the book deals with the position of working class, lesbian, activist women. By providing a text sympathetic to the working class and to women's sexual liberation while at the same time presenting an open and sharp condemnation of the patriarchal and authoritarian system, Roffé was truly engaging in radical activism. She risked speaking openly about the sexual and political frustrations of women in a society in which they are exploited and oppressed. Barú with her politics and Julia Grande with her sexuality dared to enter into the masculine sphere of power and failed.

In the exploration of the limits of discourse and the marginalization of identity, it would help to discuss the consequences of the book's publication in Argentina in 1976. As mentioned earlier, in 1976, a few months after its publication, a court order proscribed the book in Buenos Aires for reasons of "immorality." Later it was banned in the entire country. I refer to Roffé:

> Durante el tiempo que el libro estuvo en las librerías, los críticos sacaron algunas notas; los reporteros me entrevistaron; el editor invertía, dentro de la precariedad económica del momento, algún dinero en publicidad. Pero inmediatamente después de la prohibición, o mejor dicho, un poco antes—cuando se corrió el rumor que *Monte de Venus* era "provocativa" y, por tanto, destinada a caer bajo la picota de la censura—, el periodismo me silenció; el editor no sólo hizo desaparecer del depósito los ejemplares que quedaban, sino que al libro y a mí nos eliminó del catálogo; los libreros apuraron las devoluciones, y hasta los amigos escogieron no mencionar la novela. [During the time that the book was in bookstores, the critics wrote up a few things on it, the reporters interviewed me, the editor invested, within the precarious economy of the moment, some money in publicity. But immediately following the prohibition, or better yet, a bit before, when the rumor began to circulate that it was "provocative " and therefore, destined to be censored, journalism silenced me, the publisher not only made the remainder of the texts disappear, but both the book and I were eliminated from the catalogs; the booksellers hurriedly returned it and even my friends chose not to mention it.] ("Omnipresencia" 915)

In *Monte de Venus*, Roffé was able to mark the struggle to find one's voice and the subsequent euphoria that accompanied the belief that one could participate openly in debate only to find frustration at the realization of the impossibility of the project.

Roffé stopped writing for many years. For her, writing was much like politics for her fictional character Barú, and what the tape had meant for her character Julia Grande. It was a way to "salir de la oscuridad" [come out of darkness], and to find her voice. With the prohibition of the text, Roffé turned into a character worthy of her own novel and felt the same sensation of having been raped, that is, violated and denigrated.

Although *Monte de Venus* was silenced for deconstructing in different ways
the mechanisms and myths of the dominant system, which offers so few alter-
natives for self-realization, it is not a text void of hope. Promise may be found
in Julia Grande's "Última grabación pasada en limpio" [Final recording]
which she recorded for her instructor: "Pero antes que nada que quede claro
que soy una persona con más bronca que tristeza. Mi bronca es lo único noble
que tengo" [Before anything else let me make it clear that I am a person with
more anger than sadness. My anger is the only noble thing I have.] (267). In
my perspective, it is precisely this acknowledgement of anger, instead of res-
ignation, that marks a concrete step towards liberation.

Audré Lorde, in her book, *Use of the Erotic: The Erotic as Power*, (1978)
defines eroticism as a source of power for women in connection with other
spheres of life. According to Lorde, the erotic is connected to a sense of self
and to an internal sense of satisfaction, and it is an integral aspect of emo-
tional bonding among women. Thus the fact that Roffé is incapable of providing a literary representation, which could reclaim women's bodies from
cultural and social constrictions and liberate them from taboos, may allow
the reader another optic with which to understand her protagonist's psychological dislocation.

Other Pleasures: Sexual Sadism and Bisexuality

Argentine Alejandra Pizarnik (1936–1972) is now considered one of the most
acclaimed poets of her country, and yet she achieved her greatest notoriety
after her death by her own hand in 1972. While Pizarnik lived in France, she
had become obsessed with the figure of Erzébet Báthory, a Hungarian countess from the fifteenth century who was the subject of a book by Valentine Pen-
rose. Pizarnik decided to write a book concerning the enigmatic countess, *La
condesa sangrienta* [The Bloody Countess]. The text was first published in the
Mexican journal *Diálogos* [Dialogues] in 1965 and finally in book form in 1971.

Pizarnik's fascination with the countess has left many critics perplexed.
Bárthory was infamous for torturing more than 600 young women in sexual rit-
uals that were associated with her desire for eternal youth. The gruesome ceremonies form the foundation of Pizarnik's text, vignettes concerning the various
torture techniques of the countess. Pizarnik does not condemn the noble-
woman's actions, but rather simply recognizes that society's concept of "civi-
lized" versus "uncivilized" behavior is arbitrary and that the countess's actions
may be understood as the result of her simply wielding too much power.

In the first three sections of *La condesa sangrienta*, Pizarnik writes about the particular torture instruments used, such as "La virgen del hierro" [The Iron Virgin], "Muerte por agua" [Death by Water], and "La jaula mortal" [The Lethal Cage]. All three of the tools allow the countess to fulfill her sexual and sadistic fantasies. The descriptions are provided in the present tense and in much detail. For example, the countess's habit of wearing white (suggesting innocence and virginity) is mentioned as well as the clothing's transformation to red as the blood begins to soak the fabric during the torture session. The descriptions are lyrical, almost poetic. In the fourth vignette, Pizarnik begins to deviate from mere description to provide commentary on the motivations of the countess. In "El espejo de la melancolía" [The Mirror of Melancholy], Pizarnik makes reference to the countess's possible lesbian persona. Throughout the text an odd conjugation of positive and negative elements provide jolting contrasts. The text also provides a voyeuristic dimension. The countess is portrayed as the ultimate voyeur: she observes and contemplates the scene, seemingly inviting the reader to do the same. The final passage of the text is a meditation on the ramifications of the possession of unlimited power. *La condesa sangrienta* emerges as a disturbingly beautiful depiction of sexuality and death.

Pizarnik continues to be one of the most commented upon Argentine poets of the last fifty years and her death, if in fact it did not initiate her rise in popularity, at least contributed to making her an almost mythical figure in the Argentine literary realm in large part due precisely to her unusual take on women's eroticism.

Pizarnik's compatriot Griselda Gambaro wrote a novel that similarly left readers perplexed, a parody of pornography called *Lo impenetrable* [The Impenetrable Madame X] (1984), which has as its protagonist a bisexual woman.

Marjorie Garber has discussed the anxiety connected to bisexuality in her text, *Vice Versa* (1995). Bisexuals are seen as sexual outcasts, unable to assume a place in gay circles and suspect in straight ones. As Garber states, "[m]any bisexuals feel alienated from the queer community as well as the heterosexual community suggests that the opposition of bisexuality is a mode of sexual prejudice" (21). There seems to be, according to Garber, this idea that bisexuality means "having your cake and eating it, too" and that no one should be able to engage in the pursuit of total satisfaction before announcing one's "full-fledged" membership in the gay community (71).

Bisexuality was and is seen as an ambiguous position because it is often perceived as "between" identities. There is an idea that bisexuals simply are incapable of making a decision or that this is merely an "intermediate" step before announcing one's full-fledged membership in the gay community by coming to terms with his or her "real" sexuality. According to Garber:

> To the disapproving or the disinclined it connotes promiscuity, imma-
> turity, or wishy-washyness. To some lesbians and gay men it says
> "passing," "false consciousness," and a desire for "heterosexual privi-
> lege." To psychologists it may suggest adjustment problems; to psy-
> choanalysts an unresolved Oedipus complex; to anthropologists, the
> narrowness of Western (Judeo-Christian) world view. (40)

The rallying cry for feminism in the 1970s was "Feminism is the theory, lesbianism is the practice." In other words, "real" feminists were expected to
walk the talk and this meant in some cases forsaking relationships with patriarchal oppressors. Somehow it was thought that politics could be aligned
with lust in a systematic fashion. I would like to examine just this notion in
the critical response to Gambaro's *Lo impenetrable*.

Gambaro is known as one of Argentina's preeminent dramatists. Her novels have received considerably less critical attention. It has been *Lo impenetrable* that has garnered the most critical attention. Although the theme of
same sex sexuality appears in *Ganarse la muerte* and in *Dios no nos quiere contentos* the idea of lesbianism or bisexuality is also flirted with, it isn't until *Lo
impenetrable* that Gambaro develops an openly bisexual character in the form
of her protagonist Madame X.

The novel is a parody of male pornography. Although she maintains a sexually active life with her maid, Marie, Madame X believes that she must be
penetrated by a man in order to be fully sexually satisfied. Madame X does not
feel that her liaisons with Marie are, in fact "real" sex. The novel details her
pursuit of the penis to literally fill the void in her sexual life. Jonathan is the
man she pursues and his letters promising sexual fulfillment leave Madame X
anxious with desire. The novel recounts her frustrations at ever actually
reaching the point of copulating with Jonathan because he is incapable of
controlling his premature ejaculations. When he leaves Madame X sexually
frustrated, she turns to the comfort and sexual attentions provided by Marie.

What is interesting about this depiction of bisexuality is that the relationship of Madame X with Marie, while clearly being the more sexually gratifying

of the two, is never presented as completely gratifying because of the maid's lack of a penis. Madame X is enthralled by the possibility of the commanding power that she is certain the penis will exert over and into her. In the meantime a woman will suffice. However, Jonathan's member cannot make good on the promise and renders itself useless. This exposes, as Duncan points out, the myth of the phallus (168). Her insatiable desire emasculates him. At the end of the novel Madame X has turned her attentions to yet another potential suitor and yet the possibilities are as bleak as ever.

Duncan points out that "*Lo impenetrable* reconfigures the penis as a source for feminine displeasure" (168), citing the Hite Report that shows how women are in fact less likely to achieve orgasm through penal penetration than by direct clitoral stimulation. This, in Duncan's eyes would seem to demonstrate that Marie is the only "real" option that Madame X has for sexual gratification. I disagree, however, with what appears to be Duncan's conclusion that Gambaro is making some sort of case for lesbianism by suggesting that Madame X really should confine her attentions to Marie. Desire resists control, and orgasms aside, the desire for a sexually fulfilling relationship with a man is clearly of great importance to the protagonist, whether it "should" be or not.

What is probably most interesting about the way *Lo impenetrable* has been interpreted is the extent to which the "real" identity of Madame X is assumed by critics to be that of a lesbian instead of a bisexual woman. If it is the belief of fundamentalist church organizations that homosexuality can be "cured" with reindoctrination that includes a steady diet of heterosexual pornography, it must also be cautioned that bisexuality cannot be wished away by critics anxious to chalk up another text for the gay canon.

The fact is, for whatever reason, Madame X does desire men. If desire were based on intellect and not on some other source of attraction there are plenty of individuals who would prefer to recast their own sexual histories to be more compatible with their politics. So although the Hite report, as Duncan notes, demonstrates how penal penetration is not, ultimately, a great source of orgasmic gratification for women during intercourse, one cannot ignore that desire to be penetrated exists among many women (and men). Duncan believes that Madame X is merely a woman who "buys into the system and denies her sexual needs on the basis of socially constructed ideals" (168). Furthermore, Duncan states that Marie is "the one character in the text most in touch with her sexual nature" (169), as though being "in touch" can only mean the possibility of lesbianism and that there is, in fact, one true nature that we can all aspire to know. Chicana and lesbian author Cherríe Moraga has said:

> What the white women's movement tried to convince me of is that lesbian sexuality was *naturally* different than heterosexuality. That the desire to penetrate and be penetrated, to fill and be filled, would vanish. That retaining such desires was "reactionary," not "politically correct," "male identified." And somehow reaching sexual ecstasy with a woman lover would never involve any kind of power struggle. Women were different. We could simply magically "transcend" these "old notions," just by seeking spiritual transcendence in bed." (*Loving in the War Years* 126)

The problem with this, as she goes on the say, is that "lesbianism has become an 'idea'—a political response to male sexual aggression, rather than a sexual response to a woman's desire for another woman" (129). Moraga is the last writer to be discussed as part of this first side dish.

Her Lips, Her Tongue

Moraga, as a biracial writer, linguistically moves in and out of the spheres she inhabits. Although she was not raised speaking Spanish, she refuses, like many hybrid authors, to circumscribe her writing to one language. Instead, she embraces both (and in the process potentially alienates readers familiar with only one language). Moraga's first text was co-edited with Glória Anzaldúa, *This Bridge Called My Back: Writings by Radical Women of Color* (1981). The text took on a life of its own during the 1980s and became required reading for most Women's Studies majors around the country because it was seen to be a groundbreaking and definitive voice reflecting the experiences of U.S. women of color.

Loving in the War Years: Lo que nunca pasó por sus labios [What Never Passed Her Lips] (1983) was Moraga's first single-authored book. It is a combination of genres: essay, poetry, and short stories. The combination of Spanish and English in the title demonstrates the primary concern of Moraga as an author with her hybrid identity; language is literally "tongue," imbued with all of its sexual connotations. Thus, her writing is about language and body, culture and sexual desire, in short, what it means to be a Chicana lesbian. It is the mouth, seen also as the vagina, which is both a source of empowerment at the same time a site of conflict. What is passing through the lips of the author, from the mouth, as in the book's title, is tantamount to the birth of the baby through the vagina.

Loving in the War Years is a book about birth on many levels, not only the birth of language and of a separate voice. Desire is also seen as a coalition-building mechanism. Moraga does not restrict herself to lesbian desire, making a public stance against lesbian separatism as a viable option. Nor does she restrict herself to lesbian readers, voicing an interest in what her heterosexual sisters can share about their own experience of desire (139). As a lesbian living openly she is a potential victim, and she shows that women loving women under patriarchy is the same as loving in the war years. Moraga traces her Hispanic identity and her love of women through her mother, and her grandmother before her:

> *Sueño: 7 de enero, 1983. En el sueño trataba de tomar yo una foto de mi abuela y de mi mamá. Mientras una mujer me esperaba en la cama. The pull and tug present themselves en mis sueños. Deseo para las mujeres/la familia. I want to take a photo of my grandmother because I know she is dying. I want one last picture. The woman keeps calling me to her bed. She wants me. I keep postponing her.*
>
> [Dream: January 7, 1983. In the dream I was trying to take a photo of my grandmother and of my mother. Meanwhile a woman waited for me in bed. The pull and tug present themselves in my dreams. Desire for women, for family.] (iv original emphasis)

Her connection to women is further reinforced with "There is something I knew at that eight-year-old moment that I vowed never to forget—the smell of a woman who is life and home to me all at once. The woman in whose arms I am uplifted, sustained. Since then, it is as if I spent the rest of my years driven by this scent toward la mujer" (94).

For Moraga, sex and freedom are intertwined (v). Although she identifies culturally with her mother she acknowledges that her father was the "queer" one. She voices much ambivalence about this relationship and clearly marks him as a failure for his inability to satisfy her mother sexually. *"This is the queer I run from. This white man in me"* (8). It is, in fact, her construction of his perceived lack of masculinity that is among the most interesting aspects of the text. By perceiving him to be weak, she feels the need to fill the void that her mother feels.

> She asks me, have I noticed how he's "so soft, not very manly?" she goes on "I think he's different like you entiendes? Pero no lo digas a tu hermana." (10–11) "I bite my tongue down hard, holding it. I must not say too much. I must not know too much. But I am so excited, thinking

of the possibility of my father awakened to touch. Imagining my father
feeling *something* deep and profound and alive.

Alive. (II, original emphasis)

[I think he is different like you, you understand? But don't tell your
sister.]

Moraga is pleased at the thought that her father could be a passionate man—
that he could truly feel anything at all and at the same time she is saddened
and feels protective of her mother and of the years that she has spent. Grabbing my hand across the table, "Honey I know what it's like to be touched by
a man who wants a woman. I don't feel this with your father," squeezing me,
"Entiendes?" (II) [Understand?]

In one essay Moraga is watching as the woman that she desires, Elena,
dances with another. She identifies with both roles, the butch and the femme,
the seducer and the seduced, while at the same time remembering her father
and mother dancing and how her mother was always in control. Knowing how
to dance, watching Elena learn, renders the narrator capable of finally fulfilling that need from her mother. The need to be led. She wants both roles, as
Negrón-Muntaner point out (258). Moraga's development of a lesbian identity is seen as a response in some way to her desire to please her mother and
her rejection of the father. She is dismayed, even repulsed by his effeminacy.
She is disgusted by his lack of passion. She identifies completely with her
mother, although it is her mother that, in fact, conveys a racist attitude
toward Chicano culture. Nonetheless, it is the narrative voice that seeks to fill
the space of the father and fulfill the mother, as Negrón-Muntaner points out
(257). There is anger at her father's inability to be a "real" man, even as Moraga herself is unable to fulfill the societal script of a "real" woman.

Moraga identifies with her mother, against her Anglo father. She becomes
a Chicana in the process of identifying with these women in her life, but
acknowledges that, in fact, in many ways the lack of a Chicano father provided
her with a greater freedom with which she could question women's sub-
servience. She notes, significantly, that her other activist Chicana friends had
fathers that died or left when they were young:

[. . .]it is important to say that fearing recriminations from my father
never functioned for me as an obstacle in my political work. Had
I been born of a Chicano father, I sometimes think I never would have
been able to write a line or participate in a demonstration, having to

repress all questioning in order that the ultimate question of my sexuality would never emerge. Possibly, even some of my compañeras [women friends] whose fathers died or left in their early years would never have had the courage to speak out as Third World lesbians the way they do now, had their fathers been a living part of their daily lives. The Chicana lesbians I know whose fathers are very much apart of their lives are seldom "out" to their families. (113)

Moraga's attachment to her mother and her adoption of her mother's name was a way to reclaim her culture, in spite of her *güera* appearance and having to learn Spanish by Berlitz, and yet it is her public adoption of a lesbian identity that serves as the greatest obstacle: "What I am saying is that the joys of looking like a white girl ain't so great since I realized on the street I could be beaten for being a dyke" (52).

Lesbians can be disarming (or maybe arm is the wrong appendage) to a straight-identified man. There is a fear, among some of the more macho straight-identified men that they could not be needed economically or sexually. That is why the topic of masturbation and of vibrators can elicit such a jolt of discomfort. Most of the straight Latino men I have known have had a common line about lesbian sexuality, and that is that those were only the women "who couldn't get a man." The agency is completely removed from the equation, as is desire. It could not possibly be that a woman would have such desires for other women; the only thing that could make her a lesbian was that she was not deemed sufficiently attractive enough to have a man. Her responses are merely a reaction to his lack of interest. The idea that she might not hunger sexually *for him* never enters the equation.

Hunger, again. A woman is supposed then to hunger for a man, and it can't be by chance that his precious bodily fluid is often referred to in food-related terms. So let's keep thinking about our meal. Although I was unable to find any terms for women's orgasmic fluid, in the interest of symmetry I close this first chapter with food-related slang for the vagina. And so, moving on, in Chapter Two, our next side dish is an analysis of the *bearded clam*, *the honey pot*, *the cherry pop*, *the Furburger*, or, my favorite, the *Pink Taco* in popular culture. In other words, pink tacos in pulp fiction.

2

POP

I am gay. Um, queer. In action, deed, shoes, hair, and diet . . . I eat a lot of tofu.

—Marga Gomez

One momentous evening in Detroit, food, pop culture, and sex all converged, when Gael Greene, who, a decade later, would become the food critic for the *New Yorker* magazine, had sex with Elvis. The sex was forgettable, but not the fact that afterwards, he asked her to call room service and order him a fried egg sandwich. Her destiny was marked in that moment. This chapter traces that same greasy combination of pop culture, food, and sex, through stand up comedy, cartoons, and science fiction, all created by Latina or Latin American women. Pop culture may be seen as the cultural equivalent of fast food. It is McSex. And yet, pop culture serves an important function in society. For better or for worse, it is a mirror of a given community. Its success is predicated on the identification of those who read, watch or listen to it. If high culture aims at the head, pop culture aims at the gut, or, in the cases of what we will be discussing in this chapter, even lower. In "Pop," I continue to discuss how food and sex converge, bearing in mind that gluttony and lust constitute two of the seven deadly sins (and, it is said, they both contributed to the fall of the Roman empire).

Throughout this chapter, in addition to the focus on lust, I will underscore politics of reception tied to the cultural production examined. But before doing so, a few definitions are in order. The adjective "pop" is used to show that something is "reflecting or aimed at the tastes of general masses of people" (*The Random House Dictionary of the English Language* 1504). What is perhaps most exciting is that now, with the advent of YouTube and MySpace, forums that allow people to post their thoughts online, it is possible to gauge the reactions of these "general masses" like never before. For the first time, we can actually have a sense of who these previously nameless and faceless consumers are. They are . . . bad spellers.

Popular culture encompasses any cultural artifact that impinges on a daily basis on the lives of individuals. Newspapers, radio, television, music, sports matches, movies, public ceremonies, and advertisements all contribute to pop culture. These particular elements tend to tap into collective concerns of any imagined community that is, in fact, a nation, or region, reflecting the common interests related to quotidian issues of life, love, death, family, and employment. Popular culture deserves attention precisely because of its mass diffusion, its ability for large groups of individuals to "get" it. It reflects the uncertainties of each day, it informs and is informed by the collective consciousness in a symbiotic relationship, and yet, probably because of the negative connotations of kitsch culture and most forms of mass media, popular culture has been a topic often ignored by serious academic professionals. That said, the case may be made that such canned cultural artifacts, mass produced and consumed, are, in fact, often much more representative, at least with regard to Latin/o America, of that region than the canonized texts of "magical realism," for example, that are devoured worldwide and viewed as "authentic" representations of Latin/o American cultural production.

For a long time it was thought that popular culture sinisterly manipulated consumers into accepting the status quo. We were all dupes, the theory went, mindlessly watching TV, eyes glazed over, too busy to think about politics, revolution, the poor, or foreign wars because we were too busy planning how to get enough money to buy the products advertised. This was the legacy of the Frankfurt school. Then academic scholarship went the opposite direction, and all of a sudden, popular culture was seen as a way to undermine the status quo. Scholars began to read all cultural narratives as "subversive" (Modleski 8). In this new line of thinking, everything from soap operas to Harlequin Romances was biting social commentary. As Modleski points out, "No doubt there are many reasons why scholars increasingly are abdicating their responsibility to criticize popular culture and instead are celebrating it as subversive and emancipatory. Many of us fear being called elitist; we don't like to appear to be in the business of policing other people's fantasies" (8). And yet, she continues, "Cultural Studies scholars are in a unique position to see through popular culture's biggest alibi—that it is mere escapism—and to understand how it influences and is affected by people's fantasies, desires and anxieties, as well as how society might respond to those desires and anxieties in meaningful ways. If we abdicate our scholarly responsibilities and choose to become, essentially, publicists for the popular-culture industry, we lose our very reason for being. And society loses one of the last places in which critical analysis of contemporary culture is possible" (8).

This chapter will discuss the theme of lust as seen (and heard) in the routines of Latina stand-up comediennes, Marga Gomez, Sandra Valls, Marilyn Martinez (U.S.) and Cecilia Rosseto (Argentina). In the case of all four, my focus is on the public response, or reception, to their comedy as much as to the comedy itself. In the case of Marga Gomez, this is examined via the responses to her vlog, begun in February 2007, and perhaps less convincingly (only because the final product was subject to editing) on her 1997 CD, *Hung Like a Fly*. For Valls and Martinez, it comes from the responses to their MySpace and YouTube pages as well as the audience reactions to their routines as part of the *Original Latin Divas of Comedy* special taped for *Showtime* in November 2006 and released on DVD on December 11, 2007. In the case of Rossetto, the audience response to her comedy show "Cecilia Rossetto en Madrid," is measured in one particular instance, a show seen in Madrid on March 14, 2004, just days after the train bombings in that city and a few short blocks from the Atocha station where 89 of the 191 victims had been killed. The chapter then goes on to explore the mass popularity of Rossetto's compatriot, cartoonist Maitena Burundarena, and her internationally famous comic strip *Maitena*. The final flavor of this Pop side dish is devoted to science fiction, where we look at the short stories by Daína Chaviano (Cuba), Adriana Simon (Brazil), Angélica Gorodischer and Ana María Shua (both from Argentina) and attempt to answer the question that has baffled great minds through the ages: if a married woman has earth-shattering sex with a well-endowed alien, can it really be considered infidelity?

The Stand-up Comediennes: Marga Gomez, Sandra Valls, Marilyn Martinez, and Cecilia Rossetto

Marga Gomez, as the epigraph states, likes to eat tofu. And other things, perhaps less wholesome. The comic, according to Robin Williams, is a lesbian Lennie Bruce. Marga is the writer/performer of six one-woman shows that have been produced coast to coast. She tours nationally as a comedian and has been featured in short films and documentaries, including the documentary *De Colores*, directed by Peter Barbosa, that premiered at the San Francisco Lesbian and Gay Film Festival in 2001, *Desi's Looking for a New Girl*, directed by Mary Guzman, the short *Miss Clairol*, directed by Melissa Howden, the short *Traveling Companion*, directed by Paula Goldberg, and the docu-comedy *Laughing Matters*, directed by Andrea Meyerson. She has appeared on *Showtime*, *Comedy Central*, *PBS*, and *HBO*. As the artist states, she aims her comedy at everyone regardless of ethnicity, sexual orientation, or hairstyle (www. margagomez.com). Her work has been published in several anthologies including *Extreme Exposure*, *Out, Loud & Laughing*, *Contemporary Plays by American Women of Color*, and *Out of Character*. On February 7, 2007, Marga began a vlog on YouTube, regularly adding excerpts from her video journal for all subscribers. Her subscribers write to give her their opinion of her posts, and she, in turn, will often write back. The conversation with her audience has radical implications for the study of reception theory, long seen as one of the foundational pillars of performance studies.

Reception theory underscores the importance of evaluating the specific moment of a performance, as opposed to merely the text, because the original meaning of the text may be rendered insignificant or radically transformed in the moment it is performed. This transformation in meaning will take place in part because of the effect the spectators will have on the performers. "Aun cuando el espectador no exteriorice ruidosamente sus reacciones, éstas son percibidas por el emisor: un silencio absoluto, súbito, una inmovilidad acrecentada (el espectador "retiene su aliento"), indican al actor el momento en el que él emociona" [Even when the spectator doesn't make evident loudly her or his reactions, these are still perceived by the emissor. An absolute silence, all of a sudden (the spectator holds his or her breath) indicates to the actor the moment in which they are moved] (Ubersfeld 54).

The primary dimension of reception takes places within the performance itself because, as Mario Rojas explains, a representation is pluridimensional. The spectator receives simultaneously words, space, color, movement, music, sound effects, in short, all of the signs that the director, the technicians, and actors bring to life in a show. These are all semiotic cues that require a synthesis, interpretation, and understanding. It is up to the audience to decode, or decipher, what they are seeing. But it is also known that spectators will necessarily see and hear different things. Their own reading of a show will depend upon where they elect to place their attention, their capacity to concentrate throughout the performance and any number of other factors (Rojas 187).

In addition to the specific moment of the production, reception will always be conditioned by the horizons of expectations on the part of the spectator, to use Hans Robert Jauss's term. In other words, what is the audience expecting to see? What are the particular frames of reference that he or she is working with? In this case, these may be the result of any number of factors, including age, social class, gender, or in the case of some of the comediennes discussed here, sexual preference. If a spectator is expecting to see something, whether or not that expectation is met will also color his or her positive or negative reception of a given performance (Jauss qtd. in Ubersfeld 54).

This sort of reaction is very difficult to gauge in a performance that has been edited for television or for a CD. But what is most exciting about the widespread use by comedians of Web sites is that their fans are not merely reacting in a theater or nightclub, but now they are responding on Web sites directly to postings of comedy skits by the artists. And the artists, at least in the case of Gomez, respond.

Marga's routines often play with both the audiences' horizon of expectations and her own. She pokes fun at how her expectations infrequently match the reality of a given situation, most often seen in her frustrated attempts to score with women. An example of this may be found on one of her postings to her Web site, www.margagomez.com, in which she talks of how she was going to perform at New Jersey Pride "because I couldn't get laid in New York." Why? She explains,

I didn't have a graduate degree. It's always something with women. I thought in New Jersey it would be easier. I would be enough, maybe more than enough. I wouldn't have to try hard or keep up on current events. I wouldn't have to read at all. I could impress a date just by watching television. I was beginning to feel a tingly sensation like I was about to meet my perfect partner and my opposite. A woman who dresses like Melanie Griffith in that movie *Working Girl*: short skirts, high heels and tight low-cut tops. A woman who would never want to borrow my clothes. We could live happily ever after, never sharing. My big haired NJ soulmate was out there. I just had to wrap her up and take her home. But when I scoped out the crowd at New Jersey Pride, I couldn't see any big hair, all the women were wearing baseball caps. None possessed the slutty secretary vibe I craved. These ladies looked more like retired softball players. ("Intimate Details")

Marga released her first and only CD in 1997, *Hung Like a Fly*. On it, she categorizes herself as "Half Latina, half lesbian and not into labels." She gleefully shares her tales of wanton lust, "Let me see if this turns you on like this turns me on. I was on a flight and the pilot was a woman. Does that turn you on? I didn't know until I heard her voice, 'This is your captain.' I was wet for the entire flight, all the way to New York. My seat cushion became a flotation device. I couldn't wait to land so that I could meet her and try. Right in front of the cockpit." [There is a pause, scattered laughter in the audience before she continues.] "I guess it is the pussy pouch for her." Her attempt to seduce the pilot is thwarted when Marga tells her "you're the bomb!" and security is called to escort her off the plane.

Marga likes to eat, and practice safe sex, so she appreciates how these two interests have converged in the form of the strawberry and chocolate flavored dental dams, used for oral sex. "Who wouldn't want to take a bite?" she asks, and deadpans, "Men have salami, nachos and beer flavors."

Marga's horizons of expectation are again thwarted in her attempts at Internet sex. Paranoia sets in when, after weeks, not one woman has hit on her: "Is it my typing? My punctuation? Why don't they like me?" She tells us that "Juicy" is a popular handle with lesbian chat rooms and recounts an experience trying to have online sex with a lesbian by that name. Her attempt fails this time because she tried to have a little conversational foreplay before going right to the deed. Juicy accuses Marga of being a man masquerading as a woman. She pleads, "No, Juicy, I'm a woman, really, ask me about Tampax!!" but Juicy leaves the chat room. Frustrated, she tries to satisfy her lusty intentions through lesbian porn, only to find that the lesbians are unconvincing: "I've rented lesbian porn. I wasted money. I've seen these videos and every single time I question the sexuality of the women. I believe in safe sex, so it is alarming when you look at the fingernails on these women. And then they are so rough! I'm like, 'It's a pussy not a piñata!'"

This conflict between frustrated expectations based on women not adhering to the semiotic cues that constitute lesbian identity are seen yet again in Marga's most popular YouTube video, a clip from a routine about *The L word* television show that she did in a show called "Laugh Baby Laugh" at Berkeley's La peña in April 2007. More than 13,831 viewers have seen the routine. In it, she laments that the character meant to be a Latina butch, Papi, is a fraud. "That's the Latina butch? Papi? That . . . that . . . girl, girl, GIRL?" She realizes that she is being unforgiving, and pokes fun at herself and her own inability to adhere to the "butch" stereotype, "I'm not rigid, I mean, I think its okay for a butch to wear a little pink lip gloss [she pauses, looks down, audience laughter]. And a shirt like this one [she points to her patterned shirt], but I've never seen a butch with an updo." In fact, in most of her postings, Marga does not look very butch, but rather more like a mischievous elf, a Sandy-Duncan-as-Peter-Pan look. She is usually dressed in jeans and tee shirts, though for dress-up occasions, she is seen clad in men's shirts, wide tie and glasses.

Marga's attempts to master the new landscape for her comedy via the Internet have been somewhat problematic. She registered for her YouTube site, incorrectly listing her name as Gomez Marga. The mistake immediately became part of her routine, "Hi! I'm Gomez Marga!" The videos she has posted are uneven and many are not very funny. There is a decidedly not-ready-for-prime-time quality that characterizes the short clips, mostly amateurish in nature. Will such a site help or hinder her fame? The truth is that while they may not be expertly edited, or polished, there is a raw quality, an endearing element, to the clips. In examining the audience responses to her vlog, we find the following (all kept in their original form):

> Bjshowz said, "Wow—I just stumbled into the world of Marga Gomez and I ain't leavin'! Pick any topic it won't matter to me I AM HOOKED ON MARGA!!!!!" Marga responds, "How much coffee have you had today BJ? Thanks!"
>
> KekoaT tells her, "lmao [laughing my ass off]—that bit in the middle about the denial blew my mind. i almost choked! i think u are slowly becoming one of my favorite comedians!" Marga responds, "KekoaT, Say it 3 times and click your heels—Marga Gomez is my favorite comedian."
>
> Mpcardenas23 tells her "I was having a horrible day, but a friend forwarded one of your clips to me. I feel so much better now after laughing. Gracias!" Marga answers, "Hi MP I was having a bad day too but you made me feel better so we're even."

What is clear in tracking her responses is that she is gracious, genuine, self-deprecating and yes, funny. She explains on her YouTube site, "I'm a comedy and theater performer with terrible computer skills. I first went on YouTube to send samples of my performances to the Internet community. Then I started watching the vlogs and getting to know some of the vloggers and it's endlessly interesting to me. So now my channel is half performance videos but more and more I'm posting day in the life/vloggy stuff."

Returning to Jauss and reception theory, it must be understood that the Internet audience for Marga is self-selecting. One would not happen upon the site, as one might happen upon a book in a bookstore. The tag words that someone would have to enter in a search engine to be brought to Marga's site include "comedy" "stand up" "lesbian" "gay" and "latina" for anyone who did not directly put in her name based on one of her shows or word of mouth. In other words, it isn't as though the sampling of accolades is representative of say, the woman on the street. That said, the number of hits to her site have been impressive. After the L-word video, Marga's most viewed clips of the 33 posted on her site are "Mojitos and Labels" from February 22, 2007, with 4,269 hits; "Dinah, Lesbians, Golf and Cookies" from April 2, 2007, with 3,835 hits; and "Anna Nicole Smith" from February 26, 2007, with 3,496.

What is most worthy of note about Marga's discussion of her sexual frustrations is how she codes gender and sexuality semiotically, something that inevitably leads to frustration as she, and others, are simply not butch or lesbian enough. Her less-than-successful attempt to fill the role as Casanova dyke are humorous, showing the spectrum of possibilities for self-representation remains constrained even among the intentionally more fluid phrasing as "queer" that she pokes fun of in my opening epigraph. As David William Foster points out, "Queer theory is a critical deconstruction of the assumptions of heteronormativity and compulsory heterosexuality and an inquiry into the foundations of any and all sexual ideologies. As such queer does not equal gay, to the extent that the latter represents a new form of normativity (the legitimacy of same-sex desire), and queer theory is all about questioning normativities, even gay ones." What Marga would seem to be pointing out, playfully, is that the dissolution of the label of gay, to then use the word "queer," does not dissolve the acceptable paradigms and assumptions for behavior *within* that community, in other words, the homonormativity (as contrasted to the "heternormativity" that is often discussed in queer theory). In other words, you can call it whatever you want, but it doesn't change the fact that prevailing assumptions or ingrained notions of identity remain, forming our horizon of expectations. There are "acceptable" forms of homosexuality, and unacceptable, a right way to be queer, and a wrong way, a true way and a false way. In other words, gay, straight, bi, transgender, queer, we must still only color within the lines. Papi isn't butch enough on *The L-word*, Marga isn't butch enough for Juicy, lesbian porn stars aren't lesbian enough to be credible. Everyone falls short. Everyone is, in some way, a fraud. Except, perhaps, that pilot.

Filmed November 25 and 26, 2006 at the San Bernardino Theater of Performing Arts, *The Original Latin Divas of Comedy* brought together some of the most prominent Latina comediennes in America. It starred Colorado-born Mexicana Marilyn Martinez, New Yorican Sara Contreras, San Diego's Cubana Monique Marvez, and Laredo Texas's Tejana Sandra Valls. In a somewhat token fashion, each of the major Latino populations in the United States was represented, with one gay comedienne thrown in for good measure. The show was seen during the first two weeks of May 2007 on *Showtime* and released on DVD on December 11, 2007. I will discuss two of the divas here, Sandra Valls and Marilyn Martinez.

In the case of *The Original Latin Divas of Comedy*, the fact that there were two shows spliced together to form one show that was distributed makes it difficult to gauge audience reactions. The camera shots throughout the hour and a half move from the comediennes on stage to the audience, but it was impossible to know if the "reaction" shots on the part of the public were directly connected to what was happening on stage or edited in afterwards. Furthermore, it is probable that the audience was being cued (as television audiences often are, with big signs that say "Laughter"). They are expected to laugh hard, and doing so might even get their face on television, so not surprisingly they do. This is not to say that the material of the four comediennes did not warrant sustained laughter. In many cases, it did. But in others, it did not. For this reason, in the case of both comediennes, the Web sites also become of paramount importance for understanding the impact of their work.

Sandra Valls describes herself on her MySpace page as: "A FUNNY MOFO . . . IN YOUR FACE STAND UP COMIC. . . . My comedy career began just after this girl broke up with me then signed me up for comedy classes as a consolation prize. Who feels funny after being dumped? BUT I turned lemons into lemon sorbet and now I'm a successful comic. . . . thanks bi-tch!" She tells the audience for Latin Divas that she is a lesbian, but then says that she understands the confusion they must be feeling given that she is wearing spiked heels with her baggy men's suit and tie. "Straight girls wear fuck-me shoes, gay girls wear the fuck-you shoes." She is wearing the former, playing with the semiotic cues for sexual preference and audience expectations. As Judith Butler reminds us,

> . . . gender is in no way a stable identity of locus of agency from which various acts proceed; rather, it is an identity tenuously constituted in

time—an identity instituted through a *stylized repetition of acts*. Further, gender is instituted through the stylization of the body and, hence, must be understood as the mundane way in which bodily gestures, movements, and enactments of various kinds constitute the illusion of an abiding gendered self. (Butler 1997: 402)

Valls describes her realization from early childhood of her attraction to females, wondering why her mother didn't catch on when she only wanted to eat Wilma from the Flintstones vitamins. A child raised on pop culture, with all of the associated referents, she admits desiring MaryAnn over Ginger from *Gilligan's Island*, making the association between food and sex, "I would have traded all of my GI Joes just for a taste of that coconut cream pie." The link is highlighted again when she talks about her difficulty coming out to her parents. "How was I supposed to come out?" she asks the audience, imagining the dinner conversation, "Mami, Pappi, I eat pussy. Pass the salt." She then goes on to discuss the reaction she imagined her mother would have, assuming that it was an implied complaint about the meal, "My mom probably wouldn't understand—'Mija, esta noche preparé tacos, si tú quieres comer pussy, pues, vete a buscar take-out!'" [Honey, tonight I prepared tacos, if you want to eat pussy, well, go and get take out!]

Sandra Valls' routine posted on May 7, 2007, "Coming out Mexican, Calling in Gay," filmed at the Outlaugh Festival on Wisecrack, had 2,625 hits and garnered five laudatory responses from viewers. The second half of the routine dealt with announcements by religious groups that there is a "cure" for being gay, "If there is a cure, then it is a sickness, qué no?" she asks the audience, and waits a beat before continuing, "Then I deserve a sick day!" She picks up an imaginary phone, coughing, "I can't come in today, I'm calling in gay. I don't know what happened last night, I went to bed straight, but then I just woke up this morning feeling gay." While Sandra Valls has not answered any of the people who posted a response to her comedy, she has posted to Marga Gomez's MySpace as well as to the MySpace of her fellow Latin Diva, Marilyn Martinez.

Martinez was considered the "anchor" of the Latin Divas group. "She used to tell me she was a triple minority. She was fat, she was a woman, she was Hispanic," David Crowder, her husband, has said. Martinez connected with her Mexican roots and in the mid-1990s joined Latina troupe the Hot and Spicy Mamitas. She later toured solo with comic Paul Rodriguez from 1996 to

2003. Her comedy sketches often revolved around her weight and her unapologetic love of food. Perhaps most interestingly, they are about her unbridled lust. "I never get to sit on anybody's face—I never do. I never get that call. And it pisses me off cuz you fuckers brag all the time, 'Oh, I'm benching 200, I'm benching 250,' well, bench me mother fucker." In her Latin Divas sketch, she talks about attending Weight Watchers meetings and raising her hand to ask the chirpy thin leader just how many points swallowing semen counted for in the food plan. Martinez's routine seemed to garner the greatest laughs from the audience at the theater in San Bernardino, her red sequined gown working in competition with her in-your-face humor. There was nothing understated about her performance.

Only four months after filming the Latin Divas special, Martinez collapsed on stage on March 28, 2007, and was rushed to the emergency hospital. It was found that she was in the advanced stages of colon cancer. As a comedian, she had no health insurance, and was unable to pay her hospital bills. An appeal went out on her MySpace:

> Marilyn, having no insurance, was informed by doctors that she needed to make a payment of $20,000 the day after her surgery for her hospital stay and surgery. She will then have to follow up with chemotherapy for the next couple of months. This news has forever changed her life and the lives of her family and friends. Marilyn has stage 4 colon cancer. She also has no health insurance; so many of her comedy family have been doing a series of benefits for her to help her with her finances. Her hospital stay alone is over $100,000. If you'd like to make a donation, please go to marilynmartinez.com or click the Make a Memory for Marilyn Banner. Any amount helps. Thank you for your support.

When Martinez's peers found out about her condition and predicament, they began to host benefit shows. Cheech Marin hosted a show at the Comedy Store. The Ice House in Pasadena held a show in April 2006 in which Carlos Mencia, Paul Rodriguez, George Lopez, Alex Reymundo, and Joey Medina, collectively known as the Latin Kings of Comedy, all appeared.

Martinez died on November 3, 2007. The comedians gathered at the Comedy Store for the eulogy, something that, given the ribald humor for which she was famous, probably wouldn't have worked in a church. Dominican comedian Ludo Vika spoke of the happy moments she had shared with

Martinez, fairly unremarkable and standard eulogy fare. At the end of her speech, however, Vika pointed to the picture of Martinez on the stage and said, "make a memory" (in honor of one of the comedian's best known routines). She removed the belt in her trench coat, flashing her naked body. It was a eulogy few will forget. "As dysfunctional as our family is, we really know that our job is to be the ones who heal people with laughter," said Sandra Valls, who had orchestrated many of the appeals for medical funding from the time of Martinez's illness. "When it's one of our own who is down, it's just natural for us to come together and heal each other" (Sandoval).

Coming together to heal was a task that fell to another comic in the last few years, Argentine Cecilia Rossetto. While earlier sections of this chapter have dealt with audience reception as seen on DVDs, measured from postings on the Internet, or heard on CDs, the evaluation of the reception to this comedienne is radically different because it was one experienced firsthand based on a show seen in Madrid in 2004. Rossetto's show, like those of her three peers discussed earlier, speaks to the importance of comedy in everyday life. It is comedy as a reflection of community but also as release valve.

On March 13, two days after the bombings that killed 191 people and injured 1,600 in Spain, I bought tickets to see Argentine cabaret singer and comedian Cecilia Rossetto in the Nuevo Teatro Alcalá the following night. Theaters had been closed Thursday, the day of the bombings, and Friday was declared a national day of mourning. Saturday night was the first night everything would reopen. Rossetto had premiered her show "Cecilia Rossetto in Madrid" only one week before, on March 5. In it she sang and danced, teased the audience and joked both with them and with her pianist Freddy Vacarezza. It was her first extended engagement in the Spanish capital after nearly thirteen years living abroad, with the last three spent in Barcelona where she had earned accolades for her versatility as a performer. In an interview with the Spanish press before her show had opened she had said "me han comentado, a lo largo de las décadas que llevo trabajando, que de mis espectáculos se sale con ganas de vivir. Una vez una señora en la Argentina me dijo que venía a verme una vez por mes y con eso se ahorraba el psicoanalista" [I've been told, throughout the decades that I have been working, that people leave my shows with the desire to live. Once a woman in Argentina told me that she came to see me once a month and that this saved her from having to see a psychoanalyst] (57). In the case of the audience members that night, her importance was magnified.

Rossetto pushes the stereotype of spicy sexpot so far that she denaturalizes it and reveals its ludicrousness. Cecilia Rossetto, the character, is all about voracious sexual appetite. Her performance plays at devouring the men in the audience, flirting with them, toying with them (and their wives or partners in the audience). What she is doing is feminist camp cabaret, a performance form "related to masquerade and rooted in burlesque, which articulates and subverts the 'image and culture making processes' to which women have traditionally been given access" (Robertson 10). But Rossetto's feminist camp cabaret is predicated on the audience's understanding of her wink-wink nudge-nudge humor.

To camp something up is to occupy it temporarily. "If camp 'is' something, it is the crisis of identity, of depth and of gravity. Not a stable code but a discourse produced by the friction with and among other discourses" (Cleto 34). As Caryl Flinn clarifies, "Camp adores cliché, surface image. With its emphasis on textures, appearances, materials, and bodies, camp poses a challenge to depth models of textuality (going against, for example, structuralism's insistence on meaning being embedded within the deep structures of a text) and models of identity (repudiating the belief that external signs of one's appearance 'express' inner truths a stable, 'real' self)" (440). Cecilia Rossetto in her double role as writer and director has simply created a show around an Argentine character that happens to share her name.

For feminists, camp's appeal resides in its potential to function as a form of gender parody (Robertson 10). Mary Ann Doane believes that the credibility of images of the feminine can be undermined by a "double mimesis" or parodic mimicry. Parodic mimicry, she says, allows one to disconnect from a seemingly naturalized femininity: "Mimicry as a political textual strategy makes it possible for the female spectator to understand that recognition is buttressed by misrecognition" (182). In Rossetto's outrageousness and flamboyance, in her exaggeration of the feminine gender code, her excessive artifice, theatricality, and self-sexual objectification she knowingly produces herself as feminist camp.

The over-the-top feminist camp cabaret can be viewed as problematic by some feminist scholars because it is simultaneously critical of, while at the same time being complicit with, the dominant patriarchal ideology, a problem that Roselyn Constantino has cited with respect to Astrid Hadad ("Politics" 205). This is one potential area of conflict for the spectator. Beyond that, as mentioned, the show requires complicity and interaction with audience members to be effective. Thus, the viewer's sense of humor (and shared grid of cultural understanding) and his or her own particular frame of mind during the performance will be of paramount importance for its interpretation and reception.

Anyone who saw the advertisements for Rossetto's show would have been aware to some degree of what they were going to see. Wearing an off-the-shoulder black blouse that fades into the background of the ad itself, displaying her shoulders and neck, the actor's bright red hair appears to stand on end. It matches her bright red lips as well as the color of the child-like writing on the page announcing her show. Her bottom lip juts out comically to the right. A clothespin is attached to her nose. Her eyes bulge out and her eyebrows are in two all-too-perfect painted arches. She looks exactly like the "cantante, sex symbol clown" (singer, sex symbol, clown) she bills herself to be. In other words, unless someone was given a ticket and had absolutely no idea what to expect, the audience members who are present at "Cecilia Rossetto in Madrid" have already self-selected. But then we must ask: did audience members make the choice to see her before or after the bombing? Was this something planned weeks in advance or was it similar to my own case, an attempt to find an escape hatch in the midst of a few days of collective grief? All of these factors will have an effect on the spectator's degree of participation.

What must be underscored by way of this discussion is that Roman Jakobson's standard communication model, that is, addresser > message (including code, contact and context) > addressee, extends much further in theater. It starts before a performance has begun, in the moment one contemplates buying the ticket and it even encompasses whatever mitigating circumstances were involved in buying the ticket (for example, is such an expenditure a rare luxury or commonplace? Will it require a special trip to the city?). As Pierre Voltz explains "la actividad teatral se sitúa, por un lado, en el nivel de la representación del espectáculo, pero por el otro, *comienza antes*, continúa durante, y se prolonga después, cuando se leen los artículos, cuando se habla del espectáculo, cuando se ve a los actores, etc. Es un circuito de intercambios que concierne al conjunto de nuestra vida." [the theatrical activity situates itself, on one hand, at the actual moment of the show, but on the other, it *begins before* the show, continues during, and is prolonged after, when one reads articles, talks of the show, when the actors are seen, etc. It is a circuit of exchanges that have to do with the totality of our life.] (Voltz qtd. in Ubersfeld 96 "Recepción," my emphasis). Beyond that, what is unique to theater is that the communicative code also works in reverse.

Theatrical signs in a given performance adhere to the linguistic code of signifier> signified> referent and will always have a *double* referent, the first directly on stage that corresponds to the theatrical logic and the second in the world just outside the theater doors. As such, grids of intelligibility and interpretation are always woven into the performative moment. Meaning is constantly negotiated and will also be constrained by the audience's specific cultural determinants.[1] All of this is to say that meaning in theater cannot be conveyed or contained solely by the written text. Connections with the "real" world are made before, during, and after a given representation.

Reception will always be, first and foremost, about how an audience is able to read and interpret theatrical signs. Phenomenologist Maurice Natanson has elaborated on Jauss' horizons of expectation, explaining how our consciousness posits horizons of *probabilities*, which then constitute the expectations. In performance, these are created in four interdependent ways:

> 1) the daily experiences and cultural assumptions that inform the experience each spectator brings to the performance; 2) performance experiences similar to or different from the one that each is having now; 3) expectations created by publicity, word of mouth, etc.; and 4) what happens within the frame of the performance that one is attending. (Natanson qtd. in Zarrilli 24)

For purposes of the discussion of Rossetto we will be concentrating on the first and fourth of these postulates, although it must be cautioned that this is predicated on a fundamental assumption, namely that the daily experiences of the audience members at "Cecilia Rossetto in Madrid" were in some way similar during the forty-eight hours prior to the show's representation, something impossible to ascertain. What can be guaranteed is that at least a *minimal* level of similarity was there—the shock and sadness. But the levels of engagement with the tragedy are unknown, that same shock and sadness could quite possibly have been greater or lesser depending on each spectator's connection to the event—as victim, witness, co-worker, medical personal responding to the emergency, or Madrileño/a [a resident of Madrid]. What is clear is that the audience is sharing, in general, a particular frame of mind, and that this will be crucial to the show's reception.

Rossetto is part of the Argentine diaspora. Official estimates say that there are 80,000 to 120,000 Argentines now living in Spain illegally, though other sources say the numbers are actually much higher, closer to 200,000 or even

250,000 (Pisani "Beneficiará"). The majority arrived after the economic crisis in 2001 that left almost one-half of the country's population living below the poverty line ("Argentina" *CIA Factbook*). Between that year and 2003 the number of Argentines in Spain actually doubled, making Argentina one of the greatest sources of illegal immigration from South America. It is a dubious distinction. Argentines have always taken pride in coming from one of Latin America's richest and most advanced countries, a European country that by some fluke of history ended up in the Southern Hemisphere. It was a nation that had welcomed immigration at the turn of the last century, primarily from Italy, Spain, and Eastern Europe. The population is considered highly educated, intellectual, and for many years, it had been one of the most developed manufacturing sectors of Latin America.

So it is with no small measure of irony that the same descendents of those who came to "hacer la América" [make it in America] at the end of the end of the last century are now forced to return back across that same ocean to the countries of their grandparents and great grandparents, Spain and Italy.

The terrorist attacks on March 11 claimed the lives of people from many different countries, among the Latin Americans were five Ecuadorians, four Peruvians, three Dominicans, two Hondurans, two Columbians, a Brazilian, a Chilean, and a Cuban. They were part of an estimated 200,000 or more illegal aliens living in the outlying regions of Madrid, the less expensive areas that are connected via local trains to the city center. It is clear that Madrid is feeling the strain of adapting to this new wave of visitors from other countries and it is reflected in the attitudes of the native-born inhabitants, 46 percent of whom view the newcomers with suspicion.[2]

PERFORMATIVE CONTEXT. MARCH 13, 2004, MADRID

It has been raining for two days now. I have spent the moments since Thursday morning bombarded by the grotesque images that arrive via television, newspapers, and magazines. As the magnitude of the tragedy becomes clear, 191 dead, 1500 injured, stillness descends upon the city like one I had rarely experienced before.

Thirteen bombs, on four trains all departing between 7:00 and 7:15 from Alcalá de Henares, the city where I was living. Three trains had a capacity of 1,500 people and the fourth, 1,800, for a total of over 6,000. That meant that 27 percent of the riders on those four trains were either killed or injured. Eleven nationalities were represented beyond Spain, 47 of the total number killed. The people who died were workers and students, not wealthy individuals, and many were immigrants living illegally in the country. They were going to work at menial jobs in the city.

The rainy evening before Rossetto's performance, on March 12, one-fourth of Spain's population took to the streets in silent protest, 11 million people, something inconceivable to most U.S. citizens. Their umbrellas formed a multicolored patchwork quilt. On that Saturday, as word emerges that internationally all leads in the tragedy are pointing to Al Qaeda, the Spanish government still refuses to call into question its own hypothesis that the bombing was the result of Basque separatists, thus inciting growing anger. This evening—the night of "Cecilia Rossetto in Madrid," angry crowds demonstrate in front of government buildings, "¡Que nos digan la verdad!" [Tell us the truth!] they shout. Just before the show begins, a video is found in a garbage can near the city's main mosque. A voice speaking in Arabic claims responsibility for the bombings, and says it was the direct result of Spain's support of the U.S. invasion of Iraq. It is beginning to dawn on people that blaming ETA had been a shrewd attempt to retain power by the Spanish government. The presidential election is slated for the following day and their party's candidate, Mariano Rajoy, had been leading in all of the polls prior to the bombing. In the city there is a mix of emotions; fear, anger, confusion and profound sadness. It is in the midst of all of this that Cecilia Rossetto takes the stage at 10:30 pm.

THE SHOW

Not surprisingly, the theater is mostly empty. The silence weighs heavy among the few of us who have gathered. Surely the majority is doing the same thing I am, using the night to be transported somewhere else, in this case, specifically, to Buenos Aires. The air inside the Sala María Guerrero in the basement is thick. It is unnerving. There is almost complete stillness before the show begins, no laughing, nor conversation amid the audience members who have gathered. She emerges from a cloud on stage, all spiked heels, fishnet stockings, and push-up bra. "¡Soy una mina de café concert!" [I'm a chick from the café-concert!] she sings to us, "¡Soy un pedazo de tía!" [I'm a piece of woman!], she sings brazenly, hips undulating, legs kicking.

There are shouts from her pianist: "¿Cómo estás? Ceci?" "Estoy muy bien, Che. Estoy rebién" [How are you doin' Ceci? I'm really well, Che. Really well]. She rolls the rrrrr suggestively and casts a flirtatious gaze his way. We don't believe her. She isn't, in spite of her wide smiles and high kicks. Neither are we. She tries to cajole the audience into playing with her but it isn't working. We are a mute, sullen bunch. She goes into her routine, talking of the "nightmare" of the Argentine economic crisis."Ayyyy . . . ¡qué susto! soñé que el país se iba a la mierda, pero en realidad en la Argentina no ha pasado nada, ¿no?" [Ayyyy . . . what a scare! I dreamt that the country was going to hell, but, in reality in Argentina nothing has happened, right?], she implores her piano player, continuing, "no ha sido más que una pesadilla" [it was only a nightmare].

The words sound odd in their new context. A few polite chuckles, scattered, but for the most part we remain silent. The original meaning of the signifier "pesadilla" [nightmare] the Argentine economic crisis of 2001/2002, now has another layer of meaning, one much more relevant to the audience at this given moment, that of the train bombings. The reception and interpretation are overshadowed by the tragedy.

From the moment of her stage entrance, Rossetto attempts to engage her audience directly with her "teatro frívolo" [frivolous theater]. Her feminist camp cabaret is characterized by jokes, confessions, family stories, humor, political commentary, and sexual innuendos directed at the male audience members in the front row. She plays her role with an agile corporeal expression that reveals her formal training as a dancer and 25 years on stage. Given Argentine history, the hysteria-inflected monologues make sense, as Leslie Damasceno reminds us; "[t]he hysteric feels her/himself to have no history, or at least no integrated personal history that can be the basis for dealing with the demands placed on him/her" (158). The second half of Rossetto's show is more traditional theater, when she transforms into the morbidly shy, awkward, and unattractive Alicia, performing her award-winning monologue about a woman whose macho husband, a man who consistently humiliated her in public, has left her for another woman. This show, "Alicia, la separada" [Alicia, the Separated Woman] won the Sabastiá Gasch award for "Mejor monólogo" [Best monologue] in Barcelona in 1995.

Rossetto, embodying the stereotype of the Argentine cabaret diva in the first half, does not produce a show in which her spectators are expected to do much intellectual work, nor question how culture is produced for and consumed by European audiences. But she does require that we play with her. She tells us she "just arrived." Her show was elaborated for a Madrid audience—in it she self-tropicalizes and changes her language to fit their understanding, "Soy un pedazo de tía!" [I'm a piece of woman!] she shouts, using a colloquial register particular to Spain, and not Argentina. She is playing the "sudaca," to use the derogatory term Spaniards use for Latin Americans, but her words so often register Spanish colloquialisms that they strain her credibility, even in as much as they represent the fictional character that she has created. The actress has lived principally in Barcelona for the last 15 years. Thus her initial monologue is disingenuous, as are the wide-eyed innocent questions she asks her audience about Spanish life and customs.

Rossetto has been performing Argentina, and by extension, Latin America, for European audiences since 1990. It could be argued that her shows in many ways can be seen as the result of global influences and economic necessity that require her to "perform" her country in a way that is in accordance with her audience's frame of understanding, taking part in what Chilean critic Nelly Richard has called the "culture-spectacle"(73).[3] Her shows invariably include tangos, often boleros, and she also displays her linguistic dexterity by singing and speaking in *lunfardo* (a colorful argot of Spanish used in Buenos Aires). In her show "Resiste Rossetto" [Rossetto Resists] in Barcelona in 2003, she showed up on stage wrapped in the Argentine flag. She was asked to perform Argentina in her depiction of the character Jenny in Bertolt Brecht's *La ópera de los cuatro cuartos* by acclaimed European director Calixto Bieito in 2005 in France and Germany. She played the lead in Astor Piazzolla's one opera, *María de Buenos Aires* in France in 2006. It is clear that playing the tried-and-true Argentine role for European audiences has allowed her to make a living, not a bad situation to be in compared with that of many others from her country.[4]

Playing with the notion that she embodies the exotic and erotically charged excitement of her native country, her program also states she is: "del 'reservorio' de la pasión, vengo para hacer lo que más me gusta y que mejor hago" [from the center of passion, I have come to do what I like and what I do best]. She talks to everyone, learns names and will return to these audience members time and time again. They have become characters in her show. The jokes she tells them (often at their expense) are filled with sexual innuendos. Rossetto plays preying mantis, enticing the male only to rip his head off and eat it after copulation. Her shtick is not about food, exactly, it is about the woman who devours men, the vamp, the chew-em-up-and-spit-em-out kind. The stories she shares while on stage refer to the political situation in Argentina, her life as—she jokingly refers to herself—a "diva sex symbol."

Cecilia is trying to get us to laugh but the interaction with the audience and her humor feel forced. The best jokes that poke fun at Argentines are usually told by Argentines themselves, ruthless and unsparing in their self-analysis. But her humor is not effective with us that night. She asks if anyone has seen her before. When one man says yes, she continues,

> "Papi, hace quince años, contále, contále a la gente, hace quince años las tetas las tenía aquí arriba a los ojos. Nos mirábamos. Mis pechos no son posmodernos, son históricos. ¡¡Estos pechos han amamantado a una hija que ahora tiene veinte años y a dos o tres inmaduros como tu marido, también!" [Papi, fifteen years ago, tell them, tell the people, fifteen years ago, I had the tits right here, above my eyes. We would look at each other. My tits aren't postmodern, they are historical. These tits have breastfed a girl who is now twenty years old and two or three immature men like your husband!] she tells a woman.

We are still not laughing, so she tries harder, playing the Porteña stereotype to the hilt: "¡Me agarró un melodrama porteño, una tragedia argentina!" [I have been gripped by a porteño melodrama, an Argentine tragedy!] she wails overdramatically, the back of one hand placed theatrically on her forehead, inciting us to smile slightly but little else. The word that she uses to describe the Argentine economic collapse, "tragedy," is now robbed of its original semiotic punch and thrust into the new context: the Nuevo Teatro Alcalá, where we are gathered, is only a short walk across Retiro Park from the Atocha train station where many of the 191 victims lost their lives two days before. The "tragedy" of Argentina now seems far away and irrelevant.

After September 11 in the United States the sentiment was similar. Exactly when is it okay to laugh again? When can one do so without being immediately consumed by guilt and remorse? When is it acceptable?

Rossetto's show works with the established repertoire of signs, the tropicalized image of Latin American woman as the exotic cultural Other for First World entertainment.[5] She exaggerates gender and nation, her words are melodramatic, her hands fly in the air as she talks. In contrast to the short clipped sounds that characterize Castilian Spanish, Rossetto draws out the syllables in each word in almost a wail—"pero Che, ¿por quééé?" [but Che, whyyyyy?] She is an Argentine product re-packaged for Spanish consumers, reminding us at every turn, almost apologetically, "Es que así somos los argentinos" [It's just that this is the way we Argentines are]. She plays her exoticism well.

And who can blame her? "No fue mi intención establecerme en España. Fui a buscar sustento para mí y para mi familia" [I never had the intention of staying in Spain, I came to find sustenance for me and for my family], Rossetto tells an interviewer in the Spanish press. This is how she makes a living. She gives the public what they want and what they expect, playing the *sudaca* for them with the unspoken subtext: "buy me," or perhaps even more desperately (and accurately), "love me."

El maestro me dijo una cosa, "Pero,¿por qué venimos aquí Cecília! Para que venimos a Europa? ¡No nos van a comprender, Cecília! Además, ¡en Madrid hay 14,542 bares!" Me decía el desgraciado, "¡van a venir todos en pedo!" Pero usted no me comprende a mí, maestro ¡Esto es lo que me calienta! Este puñado de desconocidos en la oscuridad, ¡No sé cómo me van a reaccionar! Mira éste que tiene cara de cabrón, ¡pero cómo me mira! Eso me calienta, ¡¡sí!! ¡Qué me miran con malaleche! ¡Esto es lo que hace que mis hormonas juegan ping pong en la cabeza!

[Maestro said to me, "But Cecilia, why did we come here? Why did we come to Europe? They aren't going to understand us, Cecilia! Besides, in Madrid there are 14,542 bars!" The shameless one said to me "They are going to show up drunk!" But you don't understand me, maestro—this is what turns me on!!! This handful of unknown people in the darkness, I don't know how they are going to react to me! Look at this guy, with the face of an asshole, look at how he stares at me! This gets me hot!! Let them look at me with their nasty looks, this is what makes my hormones go ping-pong in my head!]

"Cecilia Rossetto en Madrid" breaks no new ground, artistically speaking. The theatrical code that is required by camp—the humor and complicity on the part of audience members—is not honored that evening of March 13, 2004, a night when spectators are not willing or perhaps not able, given the circumstances, to engage Rossetto. It is obvious that most of them, most of us, just want to be left alone, passive, quiet, to watch and listen. One nonparticipant she jokingly calls the "filósofo" [philosopher] for his brooding silence but she doesn't press him further, understanding the new boundaries that the last few days have created. People are fragile. The new context means she must work within the different interpretative codes that the circumstances require. She tries and is only marginally successful.

That is, until the bolero.

THE BOLERO

Cecilia tells us she wants to share a bolero. She says that it always brings to mind the face of someone she knew, one she would never see again, and sings to him. Rossetto's husband "disappeared" in El Vesubio, one of the notorious detention centers, during the Proceso de Organización Nacional from 1976 to 1983. She doesn't mention this, and probably the majority of the audience members do not know (not having been mentioned in any of the critical notes regarding the show). She begins to sing the song "Cuenta conmigo." Her voice, full of emotion, conveys a sweetness and sincerity that fills every space in the darkened room.

It happens. A damn has burst. People begin to cry. For some, the tears fall down their faces, while for others their eyes merely glimmer as they listen. Some cannot contain themselves. The woman sitting in front of me is sobbing. She is so overcome by emotion that she must temporarily leave the theater.

An immediate, visceral connection with the public is established. "Cecilia Rossetto" the character, full of sass and sexual bravado, has become Cecilia Rossetto, the woman living in Madrid who, like us, is just trying to make sense of all that is happening. She says that standing on stage that night is the most difficult professional moment of her life, outweighing the performances done in prisons, in convalescent homes, in orphanages, and in hospitals. Her responsibility is to alleviate our pain. She knows that. And she does. The shock of the previous two days that had manifested itself in the audience's silent stupor and tension throughout the first half of her performance is unleashed by the power of an Argentine bolero.

As Carlos Monsiváis has said: "Songs add psychological credibility to cabaret . . . collectivities gathered in bars and cafes hear songs that make intimate history a public concern—the autobiography of everyone and no one" ("Bolero" 318). In this case, Rossetto's bolero made public history an intimate concern, a sadness felt deeply, silently, and collectively in that moment, in a common bond forged in grief between audience members and performer. If there were ever any doubt about the power of popular culture and its importance in everyday life, it could be dispelled in that moment. Although the show did not work as an example of comedy, or of feminist camp cabaret that particular evening, for the audience, it nonetheless achieved a lasting transcendence.

The Cartoonist: Maitena

Although Rossetto is the cultural ambassador of Argentina in Spain, odds are, most people have never heard of her. The case is radically different for her compatriot, Maitena, full name Maitena Burundarena, who might be the most widely known Argentine in the world. Not Borges, not Cecilia Rossetto, but Maitena, the cartoonist whose strips now appear in newspapers around the globe. Maitena originally drew erotic comics for European magazines, but in 1994 the women's magazine in Argentina *Para ti* asked her to do a weekly humor section. This is how *Mujeres alteradas* [Altered Women] was born, the series that is now published throughout the world. From 1998 to mid-2003, Maitena published a cartoon daily in the Argentine newspaper *La nación*, under the title, *Superadas*. In 1999, the strip began to appear in the Sunday magazine of Spain's most widely read newspaper, *El País*. From that time on, Maitena became internationally famous. Her strips for *Mujeres alteradas* have been reprinted in five books, published in both Spain (Lumen) and Argentina (Sudamericana). Her cartoons continue to be published in other newspapers in Argentina and in twenty countries around the world. Several book collections of her work, including *Women on the Edge*, *Curvas peligrosas* [Dangerous Curves] and *Mujeres Alteradas*, have sold about a million copies combined around the globe and have been translated into French, Italian, Portuguese, Greek, German, Turkish, and English. In Argentina, her popularity has reached sing-name stature, like the soccer star Maradona.

When her compilation *Curvas peligrosas* came out in Spain she went on a publicity junket to that country. For four days she saw the fascination with which people greeted her satiric vision of gender. Her decidedly Argentine "tics" are recognized and identified with by people around the world. As Juan José Millás said: "Hay páginas de revista que uno lee. Y otras que, al recorrer-las con la vista, en realidad te leen. Entre todas las que tienen ese don, la mejor es la suya" [There are pages in magazines that one reads. And there are others that, glancing through them, in reality, read you. Among those that have this gift, hers are the best] (Pisani). While famed writer Rosa Montero has stated:

> Leer a Maitena es una auténtica experiencia. Sus viñetas son como un espejo de la vida cotidiana, pero hay algo más, lo que hace de ella una artista de genio: te hace pensar, y esa es la finalidad del arte. Todo arte es un intento de entender cómo somos, y Maitena es una artista en el

sentido más profundo y absoluto de la palabra" [Reading Maitena is an authentic experience. Her cartoons are like a mirror of quotidian life, but there is something more that makes her an ingenious artist: she makes you think, and this is the goal of art. All art is an attempt to understand how we are, and Maitena is an artist in the most profound and absolute sense of the word]. (Pisani)

But perhaps the highest accolade came from another Argentine cartoonist with a well-known name, Quino, best known for his comic strip *Mafalda*. "*Maitena*," he wrote in an introduction to one of her books, "doesn't aspire to be a mirror reflecting reality." Instead, he says, she grabs reality, mirror and all, "and throws it at our heads" (Rohter).

Maitena's strips are infused with humor and honesty, her panels have an almost "Sex in the City" feel to them. They speak to many women in Latin America and the world. She has said, "Women are not all the same, but the same things happen to us, I talk about solitude, separation, falling in love, anguish, failure, success, children, universal themes that everyone experiences" (Rohter). When Rohter asked her why she married so young, she replied, "Because he understood my jokes." He continued, "She then waits two beats just as a stand-up comedian would, and delivered her punch line: 'Unfortunately, that's the only thing about me that he understood.'" In a review of the *Altered Women* series published in the French newspaper *Libération*, it was stated, "It all takes place in Buenos Aires, but it could just as well be Paris, Madrid or Rome" (qtd. in Rohter). While this might be true, one cannot ignore that Maitena speaks to a very specific woman, a heterosexual woman, and one wealthy enough to have a maid. It is perhaps because of this audience that it is hard to find anything approaching controversial in her comics. Early on, Maitena became known for her drawings in erotic magazines with names such as *Sex Humor* in France, Italy, and Spain. But none of that bawdy humor is obvious in *Maitena*.

In her first volume of cartoons, as Cynthia Tompkins has shown, Maitena (b. 1962) identifies with the feminist movement when she says that she discovered early on that "para la vida de ama de casa era demasiado feminista" [she was too feminist to be a housewife] (*Mujeres* I, 5). Tompkins makes a point in discussing the audience of *Para ti*, primarily middle class, a fact that will naturally play into the formulation of the cartoons themselves (Wainerman 118).

According to Tompkins, Maitena's attitudes may be seen in the following recurring themes in her work: (1) implied criticim at the purported evolution of women's condition; (2) doubts; (3) feminist proposals; (4) double standards; and (5) typical, even stereotypical attitudes: in heterosexual relations and among friends, her homophobia, relations with gay men, attitudes towards lesbians, transvestites, psychoanalysis, virtual reality, and plastic surgery.

While women's lust isn't a central topic in Maitena's cartoons she does touch upon the subject of sex, albeit lightly: "Cuando tenés mucho sexo, te sentís un objeto" [When you have a lot of sex, you feel like an object] one character laments. The cartoon is of a naked woman on a bed, her legs in the air, thinking "I am also a person! I have a brain!" The next panel shows a woman sitting at a desk, wearing glasses, next to a stack of books and a type-writer: "Cuando tenés poco sexo, te sentís un insecto" [When you have a little sex, you feel like an insect]. This time she is thinking "I am also a woman! I have a body, no? "Algunas razones por las que a las mujeres nos llaman 'la gata flora'" [Some reasons why women are called indecisive] (*Mujeres alteradas 3*, 26).

In Maitena's *Curvas peligrosas*, she speaks to the theme again in "Círculo vicioso con poco vicio" [Vicious circle with little vice]. The character laments, staring in the mirror, "Si no tengo sexo me siento fea [If I don't have sex I feel ugly]. In the next panel, she continues, from bed, "si me siento fea no tengo ganas de tener sexo [if I feel ugly, I have no desire to have sex]. In the next frame, she is watching TV, clicker in hand, eating chips and having a pop, "si no tengo ganas de tener sexo, no me depilo" [if I don't feel like having sex, I don't shave me legs]. Finally, in the last panel, the character is in her under-wear, staring at her hairy legs, "si no me depilo, no tengo sexo" [if I don't shave my legs, I don't have sex].

In one cartoon, she divides men in bed into four categories: (1) the exhi-bitionist who keeps the lights on, opens curtains, brings mirrors, and wan-ders around naked (the character says "Cover ourselves? Why?" She says "Because I'm cold!"); (2) The talker (he tells you good things, he tells you dirty things, he asks you questions); (3) the nonaesthetic one, he keeps his glasses and socks on and is watching TV (the Female character asks, "Would you mind if I turned down the volume of the game?"); (4) the uncoordinated one, who squishes you, sticks his finger in your eye, and falls off the bed (she is screaming "Ayyyy!" He asks if he is driving her wild. Her response? "No, you are stepping on me") (58).

None of these above possibilities allow for much pleasure on the part of the females, much less lust, something echoed in "Four Sad Reasons to Fake an Orgasm": (1) because it is easier than explaining your lack of desire; (2) because it is easier than asking for what you like (in the panel, she is saying "yes, like that, but more. . . . less. . . ." He says "More or less?"); (3) because, in any event, he doesn't really care (the male is saying "oh, okay, can you pass me the clicker?"; and (4) because it is easier to fake one than to actually have one (he says "You liked it?" She answers, "I love you so much") (59).

This depressing view of sexuality is repeated in, "A few reasons why you haven't had sex in a year": (1) Because you don't feel like it (the first panel shows a business woman talking on cell with laptop, "I sleep 5 hours work 18, and I'm involved in a thousand projects"); (2) Because you don't have anyone to do it with; (3) Because you don't have a husband (two friends are talking, one says to the other, "I swear that until I get married I will not let another man touch me." Her friend says, "You act like you are a virgin but you've had more boyfriends, lovers and sex than Truman Capote." Her friend replies, "Yes, but what's missing is for me to try a husband." Her friend answers, "Of your own."); (4) Because you do have a husband (she is laying next to her husband in bed, he is reading, and she is thinking, "Uff, having to take off the pajamas that I just put on, try to start everything, manage to finish, go back to the bathroom, wash myself again, put my pajamas on yet again . . . how exhausting! Better yet, isn't there something to watch on TV?" (41, all translations are my own).

It seems that in the cartoons of *Maitena*, women are condemned to live lives without any sexual satisfaction at all. One cartoon, taken from *Superadas 1*, shows two old women talking; one says to the other, "You know every couple has its good times. My husband and I understand each other sexually perfectly, in twenty years we haven't argued one single night." Her friend says, "What?? You mean you have sex every night?" Her friend replies, "No. Never" (61). The one sexually adventurous female found in five volumes of *Maitena* is seen as somewhat psychotic, grabbing the pink collar of the man across the table, saying to him, "Look, I'm not an idiot, I know exactly what I want and how I want it, got it? So don't worry, eh?" He is panicked, sweat coming from his face, eyes bulging, "I'm not worried. I'm terrified!!" (*Superadas* 84).

Far from the lusty go-get-em approach of the stand-up comediennes discussed earlier in this chapter, oddly, Maitena's characters show no lust at all. The vast majority of the cartoons that treat the theme of sex, such as those listed above, have to do with the male appetite and the woman having to go along with it, resigned. Is it due to where her cartoons are published, publications aimed at a general population—is that the factor that makes them so tame? She did, after all, draw erotic cartoons before turning mainstream. Her cartoons do not deal with appetite either, though they show women who are forced to have plastic surgery, one supposes, to meet the ideal of feminine beauty. Christianity has identified gluttony and lust as two of the classic "seven deadly sins." Taboos, moralizing, and laws have historically been imposed to control and "civilize" the drives. And yet, even when laws are abolished, the residual guilt seems to remain. And while "good" women are not supposed to openly speak of sexual appetite, they are expected to fill male appetites both for food and for sex. This contradiction has been blamed by some feminists for the preponderance of low sexual desire and eating disorders among women. In Maitena's strips, similarly, as Tompkins points out, there is little mention of lesbianism, and none whatsoever of bisexuality. While sex is discussed almost exclusively in terms of male desire, and strictly the heterosexual flavor, and food is barely mentioned, the single most repeated theme in Maitena's cartoons relates to women's negative body image and the need for plastic surgery, or excessive exercise.

One might ask, at this juncture, if, by examining *Maitena*, I wasn't looking for lust in all the wrong places. Perhaps. And yet, Maitena is probably the most recognizable name from Argentina, male or female. Her critics constantly point out how "real" the characters in her strips are, and she has achieved worldwide recognition for her "universal" themes. If, for whatever reasons, be they external forces of newspaper editorial boards or internalized notions of taboo, she is constrained in her representations, this is valuable for readers to know. It shows that however far women might think they have come, it isn't far enough. And this, as Tompkins reminds us, is one of the recurring themes in her work. The abiding ideas concerning what a "decent" woman may publish in a respectable newspaper will always prevail. It is important to show that such taboos remain. The audience for our earlier examined comediennes or even for our science fiction writers to come is self-selecting, Maitena's is not. Her art and her success are very rooted in Argentine women's lives of the here and now, a world of e-mail, plastic surgery, and cell phones, also, specifically in the history of graphic humor in her own country.

In Maitena's universe, for whatever reason, sexual fulfillment and lust are virtually impossible. So it may come as no surprise that in alternate universes, as found in science fiction, the last popular culture side dish we will examine, women are able to embrace the full force of their lust—there are no taboos, nor societal contraints to inhibit them.

The Science Fiction Writers: Adriana Simon, Simone Saueressig, Daína Chaviano, Angélica Gorodischer, and Ana María Shua

Science fiction has been called the perfect genre for feminists because it enables writers to imagine freely alternative universes of greater sexual freedom. Like comedy, like cartoons, science fiction may be said to encapsulate the concerns of our times, take the pulse of a given society.[6] Joanna Russ observes that science fiction, what she calls "'What if' literature," is "the perfect literary mode in which to explore (and explode) our assumptions about 'innate' values and 'natural' social arrangements, [. . .] about differences between men and women, about family structure, about sex, [. . .] about gender roles" ("Image" 79–80). Although science fiction will present other worlds, they must be framed within a grid of intelligibility. And yet, while we understand the imagined world based on our understanding of the real world, Albert Wendland makes the point that science fiction authors ask their implied readers to become intellectually engaged because the stories will challenge their reality, forcing them to re-evaluate their convictions, gender expectations, and social contexts (51–52).

There are three points of differentiation between science fiction of the Spanish- and Portuguese-speaking worlds and their more well-known cousins in the English-speaking world: (1) It is "soft" in nature with an orientation towards the social sciences more than the "hard" sciences; (2) it often examines Christian symbols and motifs; (3) the stories are often humorous (Bell 14). Beyond that, as Darrell B. Lockhart has pointed out, in Latin America science fiction is a discourse of social protest (xii). He goes on to say, "The reader may journey into the future or the past, to utopian paradises or hellish worlds of cataclysmic disaster, to the outer reaches of space or the center of the earth, through time and parallel universes, meet alien races or the humans of tomorrow, enjoy the comforts or suffer the consequences of advanced super technologies—but all-the-while be looking in a mirror of the present" (xvi). According to Andrea Bell, another difference is that in Latin American science fiction protagonists are "young loners, alienated but resilient drifters on society's margins who, in spite of everything, retain a sardonic wit, occasional sensitivity, and, if they are men, a penchant for macho cockiness" (443).

Science fiction in the Spanish- and Portuguese-speaking worlds dates from the eighteenth century, and the largest production may be found in the traditional publishing centers of Argentina, Brazil, Cuba, and Mexico. Prior to the 1960s, it involved isolated efforts of writers who, for the most part, had no particular devotion to the genre but who found it a useful means of critiquing society (Bell 441). The first real wave of science fiction in Latin America was from the 1960s to mid-1970s in Argentina, Brazil, Chile, Mexico, and Cuba. At that time there was an emergence of magazines that would publish local writers and translations of foreign writers. It was a time that also saw the emergence of fanzines and conventions.

It is perhaps not a surprise that this dovetails with a time in which there was heavy censorship on all forms of writing, television, and in the arts. Writing science fiction provided writers with a way to make biting social commentary, thinly disguised. Science fiction has always served as a metaphor for issues rooted in a particular time and place. Authors had a safe zone, a place of comparative freedom, from which they could comment on life and imagine alternative worlds. An alien who criticizes a dictator, as opposed to a person, even a fictional character, somehow seems less dangerous.

The subgenre has proliferated in Latin America through a strong following of loyal writers and readers, through journals and fanzines, workshops, conferences, and literary awards, but, perhaps, most importantly via the Internet. The science fiction Web sites are numerous throughout the Spanish- and Portuguese-speaking worlds. These sites regularly publish new stories by authors, include interviews, articles on the topic, a calendar of events for enthusiasts, have chat rooms, and sponsor contests. In terms of specifically feminist science fiction, while there are no sites on that particular topic in Latin America, there are regularly international participants in the annual WisCon conference, the first and foremost feminist science fiction convention in the world. WisCon, first held in 1977, focuses on issues related to feminism, gender, race and class in science fiction. When it first began, only 200 people attended; it has since grown steadily. Perhaps the most interesting dimension is that it has two tracks, one academic and one for aficionados and writers. Jane L. Donaworth and Carol A. Kolmerten have found that in much of women's science fiction there are common themes such as the concept of collectivism versus hierarchy. In women's science fiction, men are often converted into the "traditional" feminine role, and there is creation of a new mythology related to women's identities and a valorization of experiences central to women such as motherhood (12–13). There is also often a valorization accorded to partnership as opposed to romance (13). Sarah Lefanu has also found that an in-depth presentation of sexuality is one of the primary characteristics of science fiction written by women. It often undermines the concepts of compulsory heterosexuality as well as celebrates lesbianism (Lefanu 71).

Stories and essays written by women have won many of the most important science fiction prizes in Latin America, including the "Más Allá" (Argentina), "David" (Cuba), "Nova" (Brazil), and "Puebla" (Mexico) prizes. Women regularly publish in anthologies and magazines. Women are also active in fan clubs, judge competitions, and produce fanzines. The Internet sites offer a place to publish new science fiction as well as a means of dissemination of useful information. It provides a sense of community among readers of different countries of the Spanish- and Portuguese-speaking worlds, listservs, and chat rooms. Rede Global Paraliteraria (RGP) has participants on several continents that discuss science fiction. Other fan sites include AMCyF and CIFF in Mexico, UBIK in Venezula, CACyF in Argentina, Sochif in Chile, and Clube de leitores de Ficção Científica in Brazil.[7]

Elizabeth Ginway, in her book, *Brazilian Science Fiction*, explored the interaction between typical science fiction icons and Brazilian cultural myths and expressions in three groups of writers: those from the 1960s predictatorship, from 1974 to 1981, and from 1985 to 2000. She argues that science fiction written in the third world requires critical tools different from those typically applied to European and Anglo-American science fiction. She uses cultural myths, ecofeminist studies, postcolonial studies and theories of globalization to do just that. The cultural myths of Brazil that she examines include that it is a green tropical paradise, that Brazilians are sensual nonviolent people that there is racial democracy and great potential.[8]

In the 1970s, Ginway shows how Brazilian science fiction depicts female characters in conventional stereotypes and demonstrates a desire to return to a preindustrial paradise, connecting women with nature (474). The 1980s and 1990s brought globalization and postcolonial realities, and with that growing numbers of women science fiction writers. Women authors contributed one-third of the stories to Gérson Lodi-Ribeiro's 2002 anthology *Como era gostosa a minha alienígena* [How Tasty Was My Little Alien], a collection of erotic short stories. The stories by the women contributors won first, second, and third prizes in the Brazilian Argos competition for best fiction (Ginway "Working" 485). Other contemporary Brazilian science fiction writers include Michelle

Klautau, who has written two novels *Crepúscuplo da Fé* [The Twilight of Faith] from 2001, and *A Legendária Hy Brasil* [The Legendary Hy Brasil] from 2005, both of which may be considered feminist. In 2003, Helena Gomes published *O arqueiro e a feiticeira* [The Archer and the Enchantress], the first of a three-part fantasy series.

Ginway examines two of the short stories written by women from *Como era*, both of which deal with female sexuality, Adriana Simon's "Dainara" and Simone Saueressig's "O Ano da Lua" [The Year of the Moon]. The protagonist of "Dainara" is suffering from a crisis in self-esteem that leads her to enter into a sexual relationship with an alien (and who hasn't been in that situation?). The alien eventually attaches itself to her head, much like a wig. Understandably, having an alien attached to her head creates an impediment to her relationship with her lover. As Ginway points out, "On the one hand, it makes it easier for her to tolerate his absences, since she no longer fears abandonment, and on the other, it heightens his [the alien's] sexual enjoyment, making him less willing to be apart from her" (485). The alien restores the protagonist's self-confidence enabling her to have uninhibited sexual satisfaction. Better yet, the alien's interest in the protagonist serves as a catalyst for a renewed interest on the part of her male lover (after all, if an alien finds her desirable, she must be hot). Her male lover recognizes that he should place her above his career. Happy ending. That is, for everyone except the alien.

In Saueressig's "O Ano da Lua," the protagonist is a female werewolf who falls in love with a human male, has a child with him, and then loses him when his own father kills him. The werewolf takes revenge on the father and then kills her lover's three half brothers as well as a priest. Ginway notes that the woman-as-werewolf "inverts our associations with the tradition of male sexual desire and physical power" (486). She is the aggressor, the predator. She kills both the father and a priest, but she is not just a beast, she can show compassion, as she does when she spares the life of a woman carrying the baby of her ex-lover. The werewolf also experiences profound sexual and maternal love. Ginway explains:

> The female authors of both of these stories allow their characters to share their passions, bodies, and minds with the Other: in the first case it is a human female with an alien, and in the second, a female werewolf with a human. The stories accept the male as sexual partner and lover at the same time that they question traditional gender roles. (486)

Daína Chaviano (b. 1957) is another important science fiction writer. She won Cuba's first award given to science fiction, the David award, while still a student at the University of Havana. Her winning entry was a collection of stories, *Los mundo que amo* [The Worlds I Love] (1980), and it was a best seller in Cuba. Chaviano also wrote *Fábulas de una abuela extraterrestre* [Fables of an Extraterrestial Grandmother], considered a "masterpiece of Latin American science fiction" (Toledano 55), and she won the Anna Seghers International Prize from the Academy of Arts in Berlin in November 1990. She became the first Cuban writer and science fiction writer to win the international award.

Her 1983 story is in the anthology *Cosmos Latinos*, "The Annunciation." The story is an odd combination of science fiction, Harlequin romance, and the New Testament and gospels. She asserts that fantasy and science fiction were a natural, given the fact that she lived in a totalitarian state (201).

In Chaviano's story, Mary is visited by an alien who is the sexy, strapping Angel Gabriel, "He was tall, and luminous white hair fell freely on his chest [. . .] he wore a tunic tightly fitted to his chest and fastened by a gold belt" (202). The angel is sent to Mary to tell her she is to give birth to a son. When she explains that she has never had sex, he tells her that he was anxious to be the one sent to earth to tell her the news. What follows is a somewhat clichéd seduction, with Gabriel taking the lead. Talking about her dress, he tells her "you should take it off, it's hot." "His hands delicately undid the ties of her dress and it fell to the floor" (206). Then Mary recounts her orgasm, "For the first time she realized that the angel's glittering clothes lay on the floor and that she . . . she . . . Mary shut her eyes tightly. Something incomprehensible was happening. Her entire body was trembling in the bed" (207). Finally, "She felt a sweet sharp pain that made her shiver from head to foot [. . .] she shook to her innermost core, as if a hot spring shower had bathed the deepest part of her seed" (207). From the center of the mist she could hear his voice "Blessed are you, Mary and blessed be the fruit of your womb! May the glory of the world be with you!" (207). For anyone who read Chaviano's story, I'm sure they never again heard those words uttered in church without imagining the real blessing that the angel Gabriel bestowed upon Mary.

Angélica Gorodischer (Argentina, b. 1928) is widely known for science fiction, and while her stories rarely have a religious inflection, they similarly revolve around sex with aliens. Gorodischer has been called not merely the greatest known science fiction writer of her country but also of Latin America (Urraca 85). She has also been referred to as "el Borges femenino" (Dellepiane

634). "The quality and quantity of her science fiction short stories have made her one of the most prominent science fiction writers in Argentina and arguably in the Hispanic world today" (Molina-Gavilán 402). In 1977, Gorodischer's *Casta luna electrónica* [Electronic Caste Moon] introduced the reader to one of the most widely known characters in Argentine science fiction: Trafalgar Medrano, an intergalactic traveling salesman from the city of Rosario, Argentina. Trafalgar will sell everything and anything except weapons and travels the universe, always returning to Rosario, where he sits in a bar, the Burgandy, and tells his companions of his exploits (574). According to Jerry Hoeg, when the author published *Trafalgar* in 1979, "both the protagonist's and Gorodischer's place in science fiction [were] sealed" (95).

Trafalgar's Rosario friends are listed in the beginning of her next text, *Trafalgar*, in a biographic sketch of the character taken from *Quién es quién en Rosario* [Who's Who in Rosario], published in 1977. Among his friends is Gorodischer herself (14). She, in fact, has referred to the character as "tan poderoso que me voy a topar con él en cualquier momento en la calle, o va a venir a tocar el timbre de casa y me va a invitar a tomar un café" [so powerful that I'm going to run into him at any moment on the street, or he is going to come and ring my doorbell and invite me to go have a coffee"] (Vásquez 574, my translation).

In one adventure, titled "A la luz de la casta luna electrónica" [By the Light of the Electronic Caste Moon], Trafalgar travels in the world of Veroboar, and "aristomatriarcado" [artistomatriarchy], a place where wealthy women have replaced men with machines. One thousand beautiful women are the leaders of the world, everyone else lives in squalor. The millar [thousand] are not born into their position but rather must earn it by securing a certain amount of money and possessing a degree of beauty that would deem them worthy of integration into the group. Once they become one of the group, they rule everything and everyone: "Ellas solas tienen un puño a todo Veroboar. Y qué puño! No podés ni estornudar sin su permiso" [They alone have their fist on everything in Veroboar. And what a fist it is! You can't even sneeze without their permission] (23).

It seems that the Governor, "rubia, ojos verdes, muy alta, con unas piernas que si las ves te da un ataque" [blond, green eyes, very tall, with legs that if you saw them would give you a heart attack] (24) is upset with the work that Trafalgar is doing on the planet. He sold some comic strip magazines to a man, who, in turn, sold them to the public. The millar confiscated his magazines and promptly executed him. The Governor has initiated an investigation into

Rosario's activities and Trafalgar is under house arrest, ordered to remain in his fleabag hotel until their work is completed. He is not to sell anything or go anywhere without authorization and he will be informed of when he will be able to leave, if, in fact, he can leave at all. Trafalgar, however, becomes tired of his predicament and sneaks out with the help of a hotel worker. He decides to plead his case with one of the members of the Central Government, Guinevera Lapislázuli.

When he arrives at her palace he finds it deserted, except for Guinevera herself, naked on her bed with a machine next to her that shines with a fluorescent light and has numerous buttons that would turn on and off (29). Trafalgar turns off the apparatus, undresses rapidly and begins to mount her when she calls him by the name of Mandrake, the name of a hero from one of the comic books that the women had confiscated. Soon after their lovemaking she realizes he has turned off the machine and she begins to scream. In a panic he rapidly dresses and leaves.

As it turns out, the 1,000 women rulers of Veroboar, when they become one of the group, are forced to leave behind everything, their families, their past, and their social class. It is expected that they remain virginal; they are never to have children. As compensation, however, they do have sex officially once a year with the help of machines such as the one Trafalgar saw,

The machine is able to give them two things. The first is a fantasy made real in which the mate of their choice will appear to be real in every dimension for one night. The model and programming are determined by the machine itself, although not limited in any way, she or he can be real, a fictional character, or the millar member may invent her own.

The second thing the machine provides is an orgasm. The "romance" between character and machine in the form of the hallucination goes on for days and when the women return they are "muy campantes a gobernar y a pasarla como reyes. Como reinas" [very cheerful to govern and to live like Kings. Like Queens] (35).

Trafalgar, shaken by the entire experience, enlists the help of a hotel worker and is able to find a cab to take him to the port of Veroboar immediately. He just barely makes his escape before the women arrive in a rush of sirens and machine guns and searchlights, firing at Trafalgar as he departs (36).

It is interesting in this feminist text to see how the use of the machine to bring a woman to orgasm independent of a man in and of itself does not seem to engender any panic on the part of our protagonist (unlike the reactions the same topic seems to incite as noted in our first Side Dish, Lust). In fact, when Trafalgar finishes his story, he comments that Veroboar is

> Miseria, mugre y barro y olor a enfermedad y a podrido por todos lados. Eso es Veroboar. Eso y mil mujeres espantosamente ricas y poderosas que hacen lo que quieren con el resto del mundo" [Misery, filth and dirt and the smell of sickness and rot everywhere. That is Veroboar. That and one thousand frighteningly rich and powerful women that do whatever they want with the rest of the world]. (33)

The narrator comments, "No se puede confiar en las mujeres" [You can't count on women] (33). Trafalgar's response must have had most women-readers cheer, "Por algunas cosas que he visto, en los hombres tampoco" [From some things that I've seen, (you can't count) on men either] (33).

The use of technology to reconfigure sex, gender, and sexuality is of paramount importance. In the case of Gorodischer this is somewhat ironic given that the famous science fiction author herself has admitted to deploring electric appliances and fast cars (Vásquez 572). After *Trafalgar*, Gorodischer enters into another phase but continues to write science fiction. The publication of *Kalpa Imperial. Libro I: La casa del poder* [Imperial Kalpa. Book I: The House of Power] (1983) and *Kalpa Imperial. Libro II: El imperio más vasto* [Imperial Kalpa. Book II: The Grandest Empire] (1984) marks another phase in her literary evolution. *Kalpa* concerns an empire and the humans that determine its history. While the world of Kalpa is fantastic it is also rooted in contemporary human society and social commentary abounds.

In 1991, Gorodischer returns to science fiction, after a brief interlude in which she published detective fiction. She now combines science fiction with the fantastic in *Las repúblicas* [The Republics] (1991). The five stories that comprise this collection all bear the author's unmistakable feminist approach, one that questions the validity of the binary model at all in the understanding of sex and gender.

Our final science fiction writer, though she is better known for her non-science fiction, is Ana María Shua, Gorodischer's compatriot. Shua's "Viajando se conoce gente" [Traveling One Meets People] from the 1988 book of the same title, was the author's first foray into the subgenre.

As Darrell B. Lockhart says, "Viajando se conoce gente" is "highly erotic and quite graphic in its elaboration of sexual desires and satisfaction, which are presented as a tourist commodity" (191). The story's female protagonist,

Marga Lowental Sub-Saporiti, is bored of travel on earth. She feels the need to go to other worlds, and so routinely catches a spaceship to another planet. A perk on the ship is that male stewards routinely bring their passengers to orgasm in order to help make the difficult journey more bearable. The protagonist, understandably, likes to take these trips because "después de todo, en los viajes, decía Marga a quienes inquirieron sin comprender las causas que la llevaban a atravesar una y otra vez el negro punto que se extendía entre las estrellas, en los viajes se conoce gente" [after all, on the trips, Marga would say to those who asked without understanding the reasons that would cause her to cross over and over again the black point that extended between the stars, traveling you get to meet people] (127). On this trip, she meets Carlos on the planet Mieres.

Carlos can change his shape into anything he wants, and so, clearly playing to his audience, he becomes a handsome man, capable of singing even better than Gardel. They are approached on the street by a hustler who wants to know if they would like to see a porn event, a live sex show, three aliens fornicating. Marga is unsure, but Carlos is interested. The alien orgy they witness lasts from pages 136 to 140 in one breathless sentence.

> Cerrar los ojos, sentir: ese excesivo número de lenguas entrando en sus orejas, deslizándose húmedas por su vientre, haciendo vibrar sus pezones, simultáneamente envolviéndola, húmedas lenguas, sentirse penetrada por algo frío, escamoso, fingidamente sex, un láser helado y diabólico, demasiado grande, doloroso, con móvil protuberancias bailando adentro de su cuerpo y de golpe, en la violencia del orgasmo infinito, la inesperada punzada en el ombligo, la fuera del dolor sumándose al placer en una sensación destructora, feliz.
>
> [Close the eyes, feel, this excessive number of tongues entering her ears, sliding wet over her stomach, making her nipples quiver, simultaneously wrapping her, wet tongues, to feel herself penetrated by something cold, scaly, a fake sexual organ, a frozen and diabolical lazer, too big, painful, with movable protuberances dancing within her body and all of a sudden, in the violence of infinite orgasm, the unexpected prick in the belly button, the strength of the pain adding itself to the pleasure in a destructive sensation, happy.] (140)

Phew. It ends when Carlos, overcome with desire, impregnates Marga with his own eggs. We learn he is both female and male. He impregnates her so that she can care for his offspring. It was spring in Buenos Aires when the larva begin to feed inside of Marga, and the author tells us that now Marga will begin a new trip, a real trip.

We close this side dish by moving from Argentine space traveler Marga Lowental Sub-Saporiti to spacey stand-up comedienne Marga Gomez in order to end where we began, with food, sex, and stand-up comedy. On her April 2, 2007 vlog, Marga talks about the LPGA tour, "Nabisco is sponsoring the Dinah Shore golf classic! Nabisco is trying to woo lesbians! I'm trying to woo lesbians, too!" She imagines the marketing executives: "How can we get more lesbians to buy more cookies? I know! We'll give them gift bags, with Are-Oreo-las and Clits-A-Hoy."

Food and sex have always been big issues for women, something easy to ascertain by visiting the psychology section of any bookstore, where titles populate the shelves on both themes, and both, it seems, are inextricably tied to addiction. Some titles include *Breaking out of Food Jail: How to Free Yourself from Diets and Problem Eating*; *Women, Sex and Addiction: A Search for Love and Power*; *Please Dear, Not Tonight: The Truth about Women and Sex, What They Want, What They're Not Getting, and Why*; and best of all, *The Sex Life of Food: When Body and Soul meet to Eat* by the improbably named Bunny Crumpacker. Our next side dish is not about pop psychology issues, but rather it delves into the literal and figurative issues both in print and in online journals of women from Argentina, Brazil, and Mexico.

3

⁂

ISSUES

From the North, Latin America is seen as a homogeneous block, unified by a mysterious and lush exoticism or a passion for political turbulence, or identified as a place where artists lack the capacity for abstract thought and "Western" logic.
—Francine Masiello, *The Art of the Transition*

She should have known. Or rather, she should have realized it the moment he said "Eu te vou comer" [I'm going to eat you]. Only, he never actually used those words. He said "Voce é um prato cheio" [You are a full plate] and she understood by this that he wanted to eat her. He did. He devoured her. Not sexually, though it was a seduction. Meeting the approval of the therapist she saw twice a week became her obsession. In each session he let her know that she didn't measure up to his standards for being a "real" woman. A real woman wore high heels. She tried, but teetered precariously, unable to keep her balance. He said her "problem" was that she didn't know how to relate to men. She found herself trying desperately to contort herself to fit into the mold that he had made for her, but each week she failed and became more despondent. This story of the abusive relationship between analyst and patient was told by Sandra Maria da Mata Azeredo, published in the Brazilian feminist journal, *Cadernos Pagu*, in 2003 under the title "Era uma vez . . . uma análise" [Once upon a time, an analysis]. It was one of a series of articles grouped around the theme "Eroticism, pleasure, and danger" that I discuss in this chapter.

This side dish extends the examination of sexuality in Latin American women's intellectual production to move beyond lust into other areas connected to the subject such as that explored in the story above. I investigate how the myriad topics that are connected to sexuality including sexual harassment, rape, incest, sexual tourism, contraception, prostitution, pedophilia, and abortion, are examined in specific issues of three feminist journals from Latin America from the early 1990s to the present, *debate feminista* from Mexico, *Feminaria* from Argentina, and *Cadernos Pagu* from Brazil. All three journals juxtapose articles by U.S., European, and more recently, by other Latin American scholars working in gender studies with writing by local scholars or activists. The chapter finishes with a brief discussion of some of the most popular online sites currently available in which feminist activists meet, exchange information, share ideas and advice, and publish critical, activist and creative writing.

This side dish is essential to our examination of understudied areas related to Latin American women's cultural production for exactly the reason that Francine Masiello mentioned above in her 2001 book, *The Art of the Transition*. Feminist journals, in fact, feminist intellectuals, have received scant attention in courses or texts on Latin American women in the United States. In general, there is little information disseminated about researchers in the region. This is problematic, for while the intention may be otherwise, the result is that Latin American women's cultural production becomes reduced to its literary production, the modern day raw materials sent to be processed in the critical writings of scholars in the north. Or as Masiello has framed the problem,

> From the site of the metropolis, where avid readers elevate the writings of Isabel Allende and Laura Esquivel to the top of national best seller book lists, where Rigoberta Menchú is a cause célèbre and her autobiography (although now under question for its claims to the veracity of horror) continue to be required reading in many university settings, North American academic critics also lament the poverty of intellectual reflection offered by their Latin American peers. (25)

It is for that reason that in this chapter I seek to provide one small sampling of the intellectual production of Latin American women and a few men in three journals with regard to our secret ingredient, sex. I do this to demonstrate that far from a "poverty" of intellectual reflection, feminists in Argentina, Mexico, and Brazil have been able to address issues related to sexuality in ways that are specific to their own context while at the same time selectively assimilating the ideas and perspectives from other countries that they found useful while adding them to original, local contributions. It is beyond the scope of this side dish to examine in-depth the entire range of topics addressed by these (mostly) women academics and public intellectuals on the pages of these journals, including, to name just a few, sustainable development, economics, politics, class privilege, globalization, the rights of indigenous women, and issues of racial inequality. The history, sociocultural factors and demographics of each country, as well as the editorial policies of each journal, have guided the prioritization of concerns related to sexuality found on their pages. This side dish also seeks to underscore the tremendous heterogeneity of Latin America, something often overlooked in academic institutions in the North that seek to homogenize the region.

One of the reasons that so little attention has been paid to the topic of women's magazines or journals in the past is that they have not usually been seen as cultural artifacts worthy of analysis, as Janet Greenberg notes (181). There are other factors as well, but perhaps the most important one, prior to the advent of the World Wide Web, was accessibility. Many of the journals could only be found in archives in Latin America or in individual's private libraries. Journals, magazines and especially newsletters do not have long life spans and often times are not saved. Many have not been microfilmed or scanned for scholars and it is difficult to get entire collections of even contemporary journals (Greenberg 181).

I seek to answer the following: where do themes and interests overlap between the countries with regard to the issues surrounding gender and sexuality? How do the editors address matters of differences of opinion among women, for example, regarding abortion or pornography, or prostitution, even as they defend the interests of women as a group? Beyond these questions, though related to them, I seek to examine to what extent discussions on sexuality from the United States and Europe or from other Latin American countries have resonated with the journal editors in each of these three countries. What has been translated on the topic? What, if anything, was adopted, adapted or ignored?

One of the problems with the notion of a indigenous criticism "uncontaminated" by European and U.S. theoretical debates is that it presupposes an essentialist condition for the developing world critic. As the group of feminist scholars from Stanford and Berkeley attest, even historically:

Latin American intellectuals, male and female, were well aware of the women's movement in Europe and the United States; the international

exchange of ideas was particularly important to the earliest propo-
nents of women's rights in Latin America. However, the acknowledgement of the influence of intellectual currents should not be allowed to
obscure the fact that a feminist inquiry of society arose out of a distinctive experience of Latin American women themselves. (Introduction. *Women, Culture* 1)

I am in agreement with Micaela di Leonardo that culture is not a fixed form,
frozen in time, but rather it is flexible and adaptable. It is important to
underscore, as Tim Hodgdon does in his study of Mexico's *fem* magazine, that
there is not a single culture, but rather many cultures in each country, "dif-
fering according to generation, gender, race, class, region, and personal experience" (83).

Francesca Miller has demonstrated that considerable exchange of ideas
and information among women's groups throughout Latin America dates
from the nineteenth and early twentieth centuries. Most specifically, this
took place via their participation in the annual Inter-American conferences,
where women were able to meet with other feminists and form a united front
with regard to issues such as suffrage and other legal and civil reforms (Introduction. *Women, Politics*, 10). Miller uses in her study documentation of Latin
American women's involvement in the development of the international
feminist movement from 1880 to 1948 (ibid. 11).

Brazil was the origin of some of the earliest feminist print activism in
Latin America, including the journal *O Sexo Feminino*, which first appeared in
1873 on the 51st anniversary of Brazil's independence from Portugal, a volume
that included the statement, cited by Greenberg, that it expressed "America's
will to give a cry of independence for women" (186). At the turn of the century
more and more women in Brazil became involved in movements for social
change. One journal, the *Revista Feminina*, published from 1914 to 1927, was
considered an important "organ for intellectual communication" according
to Susan Kent Besse, having printed 20,000–25,000 of each issue (32).

*Politics and Scholarship: Feminist Academic Journals and the Production of
Knowledge*, remains the touchstone for any approach to understanding contemporary feminist intellectual production in the realm of journals although
it does not include any discussion of Latin America. Patrice McDermott frames
her analysis by asking; "[I]n what manner do the journals contribute to the

construction, negotiation, and legitimization of feminist discourse in the academy, the contemporary women's movement, and the larger society?" (2).

Yet another important foundational source for research on this topic is Janet Greenberg's "Toward a History of Women's Periodicals in Latin America: A Working Bibliography" taken from the text *Women, Culture and Politics in Latin America*. She offers perhaps the most comprehensive index to date of women's periodicals, in which 377 periodicals were documented. The list, however, only goes to 1988. The article, therefore, predates the appearance of *debate feminista* in Mexico and *Cadernos Pagu* in Brazil, though it chronicles the founding of what was at that time, the new Argentine feminist journal, *Feminaria*, in 1988. Not surprisingly, the majority of the journals Greenberg found were in Mexico, Argentina, and Brazil: "The publication of women's magazines in Argentina has been consistent every decade since the 1830s, and in Brazil since the 1840s" (ibid. 173). Furthermore, by 1920, Greenberg shows how every country in Latin America, except in the Guyanas, carried at least one women's magazine (ibid. 173).

Greenberg was able to document the active, yet mostly unheard of, history of women's journalistic production in Latin America, though she does not include the production of scholars focused on Latin America and/or Latinas in the United States into her categorization. She based her own scholarship on a foundation already well established by such scholars as Argentine Lily Sosa de Newton and Jane Herrick of the United States (whose works chronicled Mexico City). Susan Kent Besse also provided vital information on the topic with regard to Brazil, information she uncovered while documenting the history of the women's movement in that country (181). Similarly, Meri Knaster, Silvia Arrom, June Hahner, and Asunción Lavrín have also done substantial work documenting the history of women's periodicals (Greenberg 181). As mentioned previously Tim Hodgdon examined the topic of sexuality in the Mexican magazine *fem* from 1976 to 1987. Finally, also previously mentioned, Francine Masiello discussed the North/South theoretical debates about gender found on the pages of *Feminaria* and *Revista de crítica cultural* in her 2001 book *The Art of Transition: Latin American Culture and the Neoliberal Crisis*. Feminist journals in Latin America were also special topics treated in dossiers in both *Feminaria* and Brazil's *Revista de Estudos Feministas*.

The history of women's journalistic participation dates from the second half of the 1600s in Mexico, at which time Señora de Bernardo Calderón is listed as a writer and publisher of *hojas volantes* [Flying Pages] (Anderson 315). In the nineteenth century, Spanish-American and Brazilian women:

> [. . .] forcefully entered the debate about women's role in politics and culture. Editors of pamphlets and periodicals, frequently writing under pseudonyms, often defended the political power of domesticity. They insisted on the rights of women to better education or to be heard in the public sphere; they expanded the definition of mother-hood to include devotion to the pen, they opened discussion with influential women in others nations. (Greenberg 174)

Of course, a significant difference exists between journalism devoted to what were considered "women's" issues, such as beauty and housekeeping and those journals that deal specifically with the needs for women to have a greater polit-ical voice and to address gender inequities or issues of sexuality. In the United States perhaps, the best illustration can be seen if comparing the differences between *Good Housekeeping* and *MS.* magazines, although it must be noted that the lines are often blurred in more recent journals, such as *Self* or *Real Simple*. Even the most traditional of the historically "girlie girl" rags, such as *Glamour*, have demonstrated much greater concern with feminist causes and have devoted segments to honoring women activists in the United States. Greenberg maintains that such divisions in Latin America were largely based on whether women or men ran the magazine. Men seem to be concerned with providing women with the journals and newspaper sections that center on the "trivial" such as cosmetics and fashion (or, not surprisingly, focused on pleasing men, sexually or in the kitchen, something that hasn't changed much in the format of contemporary newspapers, magazines or popular Web sites). Women-run magazines were more likely to be feminist and focus on the greater participa-tion of women in the public sphere, voting rights, and education.

One of the most surprising things Greenberg found, in addition to the large numbers of women writing and publishing in Latin America (the circu-lation of *La Semana de las Señoritas Mejicanas*, for example, had a subscription base of nearly 1,400 in 1851–52), was the startling array of cross-fertilization of ideas between feminists in these various countries (Greenberg 175). Long before the Internet, email or even consistent mail service, women were trav-eling in order to connect with others in nearby countries.

Oftentimes women made these connections as a result of political exile or economic unrest such as is the case for many of the participants in the three journals examined in this chapter who were Latin American-born but U.S.- or European-based scholars. In other instances the connections were due to the concerted efforts to meet and form Pan-American alliances in the early twentieth century. Most of the women who participated in journalism in the late nineteenth and twentieth centuries were of the elite class, while others were of the newly emerging educated class of women who oftentimes became schoolteachers. Still, by and large, the women that created literary or journalistic texts were small in number, and even then, it was limited to those who had money to travel and study. It can be argued that these urban, educated women in these various countries probably had more in common with one another than they might with a rural woman from their own country of origin. The same might be said today of the women who are involved in the writing or production of *Feminaria*, *debate feminista* or *Cadernos Pagu*, in spite of each one's attempts to address societal inequities.

The journals examined here enable us to take the pulse of primarily urban feminism in the countries examined during the time frame treated. They demonstrate the evolution of ideas regarding sexuality and work against what Masiello has called "the illusion of a unified Latin American feminist subject that has been the focus of theory abroad" (*The Art* 120).

In keeping with Rebecca Biron's scope of feminist journals, the periodicals examined are those that consider themselves to be "feminist." By this I mean that the women who produce them are in favor of reproductive rights and the rights of sexual minorities. They consider themselves antiracist and defenders of human rights in general. They see the need to report on and foster women's activism and to encourage women's creative expression. Finally, they all express concern with the need to stimulate debate on issues of sexuality, feminist theory, and practice (Biron 152).[1] The comparatively quick turn around of a journal article as well as the more overtly collaborative nature of its production, in comparison to a full book, make the journals particularly relevant in terms of current discussions of feminism.

In terms of the feminist journals examined here, *Feminaria* in Argentina was mainly associated with women's literary production and literary criticism. *debate feminista* in Mexico is more political in focus, although again, a substantial amount of the journal chronicles women's literary production both in Mexico and elsewhere in the Spanish-speaking world and to a much lesser degree in Brazil. *Cadernos Pagu* is one of the most popular journals dealing with gender studies and feminism in that country. Like the feminist journals

in the United States, there are some critics who have published or participated in all three. The cross-fertilization (and solidarity) is sometimes apparent, even as the priorities with regard to issues treated may be different.

debate feminista

For many women in Latin America, as perhaps in the United States, the idea
of focusing on sexual pleasure seems frivolous when sexual violence, in the
form of assault, battery, incest, some forms of pornography, and sexual torture of political prisoners are a greater concern. Tim Hodgdon showed how
Mexican feminists developed their own discourse on sexual violence on the
pages of *fem*—the country's first feminist journal, founded in 1975—during the
first ten years of its existence (94).

One element unique to the discussions of sexual violence on the pages of
fem that would also appear in *Feminaria* had to do with sexual torture of
women as part of state violence under authoritarian regimes, something that
was prevalent throughout Latin America, especially during the dictatorships
of the 1960s, 1970s, and early 1980s in Brazil, Argentina, Chile, and Uruguay.
This state terrorism was "a danger that their contemporaries in the US did not
face on a comparable scale" (99).

Debate feminista was founded fifteen years after *fem* and by many of the
same women who had been associated with the pioneer journal. It first
appeared in 1990 as the *Journal of Feminist and Cultural Theory* and had a read-
ership from the academic and political communities. The journal carries
international feminist thought by women and men and relates it to the political dilemmas particular to Mexico. Marta Lamas, founder and director,
explained the rationale for her decision to begin the journal:

> La razón para publicar *df* [*debate feminista*] tuvo que ver con cuestiones
> personales y políticas. Unos años antes había proyectado hacer un
> suplemento feminista en el periódico *La Jornada*, que sirviera para
> abrir el debate feminista con figuras intelectuales y políticas que no
> eran del movimiento feminista. Ese proyecto fracasó y entonces
> emprendí el de *debate feminista*. Esto fue a finales de los ochentas,
> cuando las publicaciones feministas existentes eran básicamente de
> difusión y lo que se necesitaba era algo más reflexivo. No hubo ni
> resistencia ni obstáculos (más allá de los económicos, que dificul-
> taron, pero no impidieron, su salida).

[There were personal and political reasons for starting *debate*. A few years before there was supposed to be a feminist supplement to the paper *La Jornada* that would serve to open feminist debate with intellectuals and politicians who weren't from the movement. The project was a failure and I started *debate feminista*. This was at the end of the 1980s, when the existent feminist publications were basically those of mass diffusion and what was needed was for something more reflective. There was not any resistance, nor obstacles (beyond the economic, which made its emergence more difficult, though not impossible). (e-mail to author January 28, 2002)]

The journal publishes between 1,000–2,000 copies of each issue, depending on the topic. Complimentary copies are provided to political groups or individuals. It has a subscription base of 19 universities in the United States, along with individual subscribers in this country as well as in Canada, Chile, Brazil, Argentina, Peru, Honduras, Guatemala, Spain, Austria, England, and Japan.

Funding for the journal has always come from Lamas, from advertising, and the small subscription base. It regularly includes feminist theory and politics as well as translations of international essays juxtaposed with essays from intellectuals, activists, and creative writers. It offers leftist political theory but also attempts to foster debate on international thought on philosophy, sociology, and politics, always using feminism as a context and point of departure. The publication comes out twice a year. Each issue is a book-length anthology, usually more than 400 pages, with a distinct theme.[2]

In the inaugural issue, Lamas stated that the journal was born out of the need to bridge the academic and the political. She rejected the separation between women's studies and feminist activism, and made a point of saying that *debate* was meant to build upon the foundation already established by the widely circulated feminist journal *fem*, begun in the 1970s. She argues, as did *fem*, against notions of feminism that separate it from larger contexts of social inequality. Feminist theory must be understood in terms of political questions and concerns. To clear up any lingering doubts about what the journal is or isn't, Lamas presents the following definition:

No es ONG, no es revista académica, no es órgano de un grupo político. No recibe y nunca ha recibido financiamiento. No hace rendición de cuentas a nadie, no depende de ninguna institución. Es un proyecto independiente, financiado por una persona, donde se da una confluencia de intelectuales, escritoras, y activistas feministas con grandes coincidencias políticas, estéticas y literarias.

[It isn't a Non-Governmental Organization, nor an academic journal, nor the organ of a political group. It doesn't now and it never has received financing. It doesn't owe anything to anyone, it doesn't depend on an institution. It is an independent project, financed by one person, in which there may be found a confluence of intellectuals, writers and feminist activists with great political, aesthetic and literary commonalities]. ("*debate feminista* y el debate feminista" unpublished essay sent to author January 28, 2002: 1).

Lamas and the other editors worked to foster awareness of sexual politics by living up to their name. Any debate had to allow for differences of opinion. The journal presented diverse perspectives on topics related to sexuality such as pornography, lesbianism, prostitution, sexual violence, rape, sexual torture, and incest. While *debate* is about the open exchange between women it is not, nor does it pretend to be, for the masses. It is not accessible to the majority of Mexican women in terms of either the cost or the content. In a country in which the average salary places most women and men well below the poverty line, the cost of each issue, about $15, is prohibitive. The 400–500 page length of each issue is also daunting. The essays are often highly theoretical and perhaps too complex for readers unfamiliar with the themes addressed. It is clearly a journal for the university educated and financially sound. This, in and of itself, may be considered problematic. Lamas argues that inequities in society must be the first area of concern for any political theory or project and yet in many ways the journal can be seen to promote or sustain these same inequities because it caters to an elite. It may be said to underscore the divide between theory and practice and yet, at the same time, it is hard to envision how such a fissure could be avoided.

Debate inserts Mexico into international intellectual debates, analyzing most issues on the basis of how they may be understood within the context of Mexico. For example, a December 2001 issue devoted to racism discusses the global nature of the problem before looking within the borders of Mexico, within the feminist movement, and within the journal itself. The unflattering, unflinching gaze, an acceptance of responsibility and the affirmation to make an effort to improve is admirable.

Debate's insistence on being a voice for Latin American women is frustrating because the boundaries and historical differences between so many regions is blurred. For example, in spite of the focus on "Latin America," for the first decade there was very little inclusion of Brazil, the largest country in South America and one with a strong feminist tradition. Treatment of the Caribbean is also somewhat cursory. The works originally came primarily from U.S., Mexican, Argentine, and European women, especially French and Italian feminists, but this changed significantly through the evolution of the journal and it came to include a much stronger presence from other Latin American countries. In terms of international coverage, there is little in the way of Asian or African presence, the Occident is clearly privileged.

If one were to examine the themes in the "desde . . ." [from . . .] sections discussed from 1990 to 2005 years in *debate*, it would be noted that some elements remain constant. Space is always devoted to psychoanalysis ("desde el diván" [from the couch]). Each issue is concluded with humor, the song and theater of Jesusa Rodríguez and Liliana Felipe in "Argüende" [Argument]. A book review section, "lecturas" [readings], and segments devoted to literature and writing are also always included.

In terms of sexuality, the presence, and in some cases privileging, of male voices, particularly with respect to gay identity, has become more and more commonplace in the most recent issues of *debate*. It was in May 1994 that the editors realized there had been an absence of works dealing with sexuality in the previous ten issues. This changed markedly in the subsequent issues. In 1994 there was still a focus on the binary distinctions that would later become blurred, "Pareciera que nuestra 'verdad' parte de nuestra experiencia vital desde el cuerpo: como mujeres u hombres, como indígenas o blancos, como viejos o jóvenes, o como heterosexuales u homosexuales" [It would seem that our "truth" comes from our vital experience of the body: as women or men, as indigenous or white people, as young or old, as heterosexual or homosexuals] (ix). That particular issue (November 2000) deals principally with male homosexuality, as evidenced by the inclusion of Tony Kushner and essays on the Stonewall riots of 1968, often heralded as the beginning of the gay movement in the United States.

In the last fifteen years, a preponderance of articles related to gay identity has appeared, so much so that it is perhaps tongue-in-cheek that the "Interview with a Heterosexual" was published in July 1996. And yet, while homosexuality is discussed, it is male homosexuality, not female, that is privileged.[3] The majority of these articles is focused on gay men and in surveying their titles (see footnote). I am reminded of Janet Greenberg's findings that, "during the political upheavals in the early nineteenth century, the female voice and female print context were not infrequently usurped to express a masculinist critique of society and government in times of censorship and surveillance" (Greenberg 176). In looking at this growing trend of articles I am concerned that *debate* is moving in this direction, something we see echoed in *Pagu*.

An example of the journal's capacity to confront controversial topics related to class, race and sexuality is apparent in an issue from May 1994. The topic, censorship, was planned before the Chiapas conflict broke out.[4] A connection was established between the theme and the current events given so that many of the Chiapas women had felt silenced in the struggle. An immediate and heated debate ensued among the editorial board members of *debate*, an internal conflict among some women who, while wanting to be in solidarity with the women of Chiapas, nonetheless felt concerned about advocating the use of violence. Some of the *debate* women went to Chiapas, and realized, perhaps somewhat sheepishly, their own weaknesses and limited vision of the Chiapas movement as women from the capital, with "la Mirada idealizadora chilanga" [the idealized gaze of the Mexico City woman] compared with the difficult reality (vii). The Ley de Mujeres [Women's Law] written by the women in EZLN (Zapatista Army of National Liberation) was included in the issue (16), as well as a document written by Samuel Ruiz Garcia against abortion (published in its entirety) (435–56). Abortion itself remains one of the most polarizing issues for Mexican feminists. In the 1970s, the movement was seen almost exclusively with the decriminalization of abortion and as such many women did not want to be associated with it (de Barbieri and Cano 346).

Over the last fifteen years intellectuals publishing in *debate* have moved away from feminism and toward gender studies. As Lamas states, the distancing from essentialism has required the need "no sólo pensar en las mujeres, o dirigirse sólo a ellas: es pensar en cada circunstancia, en cada situación qué ocurre con los hombres y qué con las mujeres" [not only think of women, or direct ourselves only to them, but rather think in every circumstance, in every situation, what happens to men and what to women] ("De la autoexclusión al radicalismo participativo. Escenas de un proceso feminista" 37).

Lamas is quick to point out the weaknesses of feminist activism in Mexico, namely that militant feminists, filled with their sense of radicalism, have often chosen not to work or negotiate within a pragmatic framework and the existing system, instead preferring to set themselves apart and denounce convocations of women. One such event was the United Nations Year of the Women celebration in 1995 in Beijing. The militants said that these events had been usurped in an attempt to neutralize the activism of women (ibid. 9). Such an approach, argues Lamas, has ended up only making Mexican women disappear from all registers (ibid. 8).

In terms of sexuality, this militant attitude has manifested itself in the problem of politics of "all or nothing." When debates around abortion emerged in the early 1980s, some women argued that it should be available and free for women who were up to seven months pregnant (ibid. 24). In other words, there was no middle ground that would have offered a more viable possibility or entryway for real change to occur. It was only in January 2002 that criminal penalties for abortion in proven instances of rape or severe physical deformity were removed and the penalization for other abortions went from five years in prison to three. Abortion remains the fourth highest cause of maternal mortality in Mexico.

Feminists in Mexico who wrote in *debate* (or for that matter *fem*) had to fight against the cliché that they were all lesbians or abortionists. In a country in which the foundational national fiction for women is rooted in motherhood, it was, in some cases, even dangerous to argue otherwise. Many women might perhaps privately have accepted feminism, or for that matter legal safe abortions and freedom in terms of sexual orientation, but they could be afraid of doing so publicly in a country in which the Catholic Church is still so important. Connected to this, political parties did not, and do not want to speak out against the Catholic Church (ibid. 24).

In spite of such difficulties, the conversation about sexuality has broadened over the years. In 2003, the entire issue, volume 29, was devoted to "Las raras" [The Rare Ones], subtitled "la inquietante decisión de no ser madre, las agallas para ser distintas, la fuerza del deseo prohibido, el objeto del goce de las sospechosas" [the unsettling decision to not have children, the guts to be different, the force of prohibited desire, the suspected one's object of pleasure].

In that issue, the editors underscore their commitment to queer studies, and topics included lesbianism in Mexico in the first two decades of the twentieth century, as analyzed by Robert McKee Irwin in a short story by Heriberto Frías, the queer and the state in the work of Chilean Gabriela Mistral and hate crimes committed due to sexuality in the United States (in which the author, María Mercedes Gómez, makes the distinction between violence that is hierarchal, perpetrated against women and racial minorities, and a violence of exclusion, as is the case with sexual minorities). Lawrence La Fountain-Stokes introduces the topic of *sexilio*—when someone is forced to leave their own country to live with greater sexual freedom somewhere else—in his analysis of Puerto Rican and New York queer culture, while Carlos Monsiváis focuses on gay and queer marginal communities within Mexico and the struggle for visibility.

The editorial states that the need for a special volume on the topic emerged when editors realized the need to focus on the many women who do not fulfill the role required by society, "para realizar su verdadera femininidad" [to realize her true femininity]. What was never taken into account, according to the study published in that issue by Cécile Dauphin, "Mujeres solas," [Women Alone] were the many women, historically, in Mexico who never had children due to demographic reasons such as the different ratios of male to female in some towns as a result of wars or migration for work to the larger cities or to the north. According to conventional morality, if a woman did not marry she could not become a mother, so oftentimes being single meant celibacy, at least in eighteenth, nineteenth, and a large part of the twentieth centuries. Women who did not have children were often considered pariahs, as were women who were sterile. This is not even taking into consideration women who make the decision not to have children, something that remains an oddity to this day.

This topic of "the strange ones" included discussions of women who elected to join monasteries or even the suffragists who decided not to have children. With the arrival of contraception in 1960, women were not only able to decide when to have children; for them it also became easier to opt out of motherhood altogether. The difference this generation of Mexican women had with their foremothers is that they refused to renounce their sexuality (x). The editors decided to elicit responses to the topic online from some of the women who had collaborated with the journal over the course of a few months, after which, it was decided to share some of the stories in the dossier.

In examining the trajectory with regard to sexuality of *debate feminista*, perhaps one of the best indicators of change may be simply to purvey the advertising and announcements posted on the final pages, often some 25 additional pages, in two specific volumes. In volume 25, from 2005, this includes an ad for the gay magazine *Boys and Toys*. The photo is of a handsome fellow with moussed hair sitting and staring at the camera, with an older man behind him, his arms placed on the younger man's shoulders. Among the topics listed in the advertisement included in *Boys and Toys* we find "derechos humanos" [human rights], followed by art, erotic photography, interviews, chronicles, music reviews and the like, obviously demonstrating a prioritization of these topics. In other pages, one can find contact information to learn about laws pertaining to abortion and reproductive rights and another ad, this one for *Queer* magazine, a journal put out by the Asociación de Investigaciones Queer in an effort to "promote issues of concern for gay and lesbian communities as well as working on strategies within Mexico to fight for respect, recognition, protection and the free exercising of human, sexual and reproductive rights." Another page offers information about the center Províctima that aids with legal information and psychological counseling those who have been victims of violent crimes. This particular issue includes in the final pages an alert from the National Commission on Human Rights regarding crimes of intolerance, xenophobia, and homophobia. Finally, there is a manifesto by a group called Catholics in Favor of the Right to Decide about their concerns regarding the new pope and his history of silencing dissident voices. The group also expresses concern regarding sexual abuse by clergy and AIDS, two of the greatest challenges facing the church in the twenty-first century.

The ads ten years earlier were significantly different. Volume II was an issue that carried the theme "sexualidad: teoria y práctica."[5] The advertising section begins, as always, with information about Jesusa Rodriguez's Bar El Hábito Teatro la Capilla, but it includes nothing related to sexual minorities. The majority of the information is related to rural women and nutrition, such as an ad for the group Semillas [seeds] that works to help women achieve economic independence with various projects and in need of donors. It is clear to see that the shift has gone from the "women in development" that occupied much of the first issues to a greater presence of issues related to dissident sexualities, framed as an issue of human rights.

When asked if the journal has had an impact on the lives of Mexican women, founding editor Lamas was characteristically honest:

No lo creo. Tal vez ha tenido impacto en el debate intelectual de las académicas feministas, y en el debate de los líderes feministas.

[I don't think so. Maybe it has had an impact in the intellectual debates among feminist academics, and within the debates of feminist leaders.][6]

She addressed in a more systematic fashion four areas of impact in a formal presentation during 2001:

1. Entre nuestros 'pares' en A.L. (en Perú y Brasil han reeditado nuestros trabajos) [Among our colleagues in Latin America (in Peru and Brazil they have re-edited our work)].

2. En academia gringa, latinoamericana y cultural studies [In U.S., Latin American academia and cultural studies].

3. En academia mexicana y latinoamericana de estudios de género [In Mexican and Latin American gender studies].

4. Entre cierto mundo intelectual y político [In a certain intellectual and political world].

Unfortunately, within the feminist movement itself, Lamas admits uncertainty. Activism in some cases precludes reflection and registering what has been lived. Some feminist groups have refused to have any connection to the journal at all, undoubtedly due to the perception that it is elitist (Lamas "*debate*" 7).

To close, I would like to return to the most impressive feature of *debate*— its capacity (or perhaps that of its founder Marta Lamas) to self-interrogate— "Sólo un proceso autocrítico que hasta la fecha el movimiento feminista no ha realizado favorece la construcción de una práctica política digna de ese nombre" [Only a self critical process that until this time the feminist movement has not realized will favor the construction of a practical politics worthy of this name] ("De la autoexclusión" [From self-exclusion] 40). *Debate feminista* constantly examines its own problems, blind spots, and difficulties in addressing Mexican feminism. Are there problems and inconsistencies in the journal? Yes. Does that mean one should cease in the attempt to foment social change via the space for debate that the journal fosters? Absolutely not. Is it U.S. and Eurocentric? Yes. Are there over generalizations regarding Latin America? Routinely. Are some men given privileged space within the framework of the content, without having to do the thankless labor associated with journal production? Apparently. Is it too theoretical for the vast majority of the population? Probably. Too costly for most Mexican women? Undoubtedly. Did it take too long to finally address the issue of sexual minorities? Yes. But all of these things notwithstanding, *debate feminista* remains a remarkable artifact, one that overflows with ideas, humor, and open debate.

Feminaria

Francine Masiello has maintained that one of the most distinctive features of *Feminaria*[7] similar to *debate* was the way that it sought to foster conversation and open intellectual exchange among women. The journal received many prizes, as did its editor, Lea Fletcher, who, much like Lamas, managed to almost singlehandedly keep it afloat since the first issue published in 1988 until 2002.[8] *Feminaria* "gathered in its pages the most complex and rigorous critical, social, and literary works about women in developing countries. The lasting power of this publication, the seminars and discussions conducted by Fletcher represent, in many cases, true pioneer efforts in the world of Latin American women writers."[9]

Fletcher explained that with the return to democracy in 1983 feminist activities flourished in Argentina. There was, however, no publication with broad circulation that reflected this nor [feminist] theory elaborated on both the national and international fronts. Although the supplement "La Mujer" in the newspaper *Tiempo Argentino* (1982–86) didn't contain theory, it was a source of constant information about, and reflection on, women's issues. By 1987, when the idea of *Feminaria* came about, the only way to get books on feminist theory was from abroad and this was difficult because of the inflationary spiral the country found itself in. Facing the above situation as well as a crucial need for creating strong and extensive networks among women, *Feminaria* set about to create a pluralistic space for feminist thought and discussion and to share feminist theory produced at home and abroad.

The primary obstacle Fletcher and the co-founders encountered was financial. During the times of the restoration of the democratic process, in the mid-1980s, funds for many sociopolitical projects were available. However, there were none for strictly intellectual feminist projects. *Feminaria* was always an independent journal, that is, it was not the house organ of any group. It began with a staff of four women and grew to seven women by 2002, all of whom shared an interest in a journal that would provide a broad spectrum of viewpoints of the national and international feminist debate.[10]

According to Marifran Carlson, the opening of university preparatory schools for women in 1905 marks the beginning of the feminist movement in Argentina. It was in that same year that the Manuela Gorriti Center was founded in order to provide services to women and a meeting place for feminists to discuss issues of political and social reform. In 1918, Julieta Lanteri founded the National Feminist Party (155). Argentine women were granted the right to vote in 1947, thanks in large part to Eva Perón's effort to increase voter support for the Peronist Justicialista party, not due to her particular affinity for any notion of a "feminist" consciousness (189). Divorce was finally legalized in 1986 (Mercer "Feminism"). As Masiello states, on the pages of *Feminaria* Fletcher and her colleagues revisited many early feminist activists in an effort to show "continuity between women's movements of the contemporary period and earlier historical moments" as well as to establish the historical moorings of Argentine women's struggles (*The Art* 121).

Feminism in Argentina, especially during the 1970s, is quite different from that of Mexico. Part of the rhetoric of the Process of National Reorganization (1976–83) was that women were to adhere to traditional patriarchal models of femininity. The extensive propaganda campaign that was mounted in the country was to ensure that they did not deviate from their roles. There was no room for the heady activism of other countries but rather the period was characterized by great fear and uncertainty in which demanding women's rights seemed trivial given the larger concerns of the reported 30,000 "disappeared" in the country. During that period overt demonstrations of feminism became less visible in the country and it wasn't until the dictatorship ended that women were able to take up again many of the movement's issues that had been put aside in 1976.

The circulation of *Feminaria* at its zenith was 1,200 copies. Each issue contained articles on feminist theory, literary criticism, creative writing, and poetry. Half of the articles submitted for consideration were published. *Feminaria*, while not as unwieldy as *debate feminista* because it was typically a mere 100 pages, nonetheless suffered from some of the same defects as the Mexican journal. It was overly focused with women's urban experience at the expense of the rural areas. In terms of cost, *Feminaria* was also out of reach for the average Argentine woman, as was *debate feminista* for the average Mexican woman. The unemployment rate rose steeply in Argentina in 2000 and 2001 as the country suffered the worst economic crisis in its history at the beginning of this decade. What little extra cash women had was diminished significantly, while the costs of production rose. If, in the last chapter, the analogy was made between pop culture and fast food, in this chapter, a more useful food analogy would be between Latin American feminist journals and organic food—something that, while undoubtedly healthy, because of cost, can only be consumed by the wealthy.[11]

Feminaria survived during those lean years thanks to various means, among them, the women who invested their own money in it. Collaborators did not charge to reprint their articles. Some loyal patrons also supported the venture. In the first issues the presence of numerous members of Fletcher's own family may be found among the "patrocinadares/as" [patrons], along with U.S. professors and frequent contributors such as U.S. scholars Gwen Kirkpatrick and Francine Masiello. The editor, Fletcher, did all design and layout, and the executive committee decided on the content. Unfortunately, but perhaps inevitably, the country's financial problems became impossible for the journal to surmount. The last print issue appeared in 2002, although a new issue for 2007 was produced and is available if one requests it online.

The inside cover explained that the name of the journal was taken from the title of the book of women's culture and wisdom found in French writer and theorist Monique Wittig's *Les guèrrillères*. The editors further clarified that while the journal itself was considered feminist, it did not seek to limit the concept of feminism to one particular definition. On the contrary, they considered any essay worthy of publication as long as it was not sexist, racist, homophobic, or in any other way discriminatory. Additionally, the editors reserved the right to "emancipar el lenguaje" [free language] of any sexist elements found in articles, such as that of using "man" as a synonym with humanity. "Consideremos que la relación entre el poder y el saber también se expresa a través del ejercicio del idioma." [We believe that the relation between power and knowledge is also expressed through the use of language] (inside cover). The back cover of each issue, a rough correspondence to the "Argüende" section of *debate*, had a touch of humor, generally in the form of a cartoon.

Like *debate feminista*, extensive sections dealt with the issues of sexual violence and abortion. Topics related to homosexuality were given much less attention than they received in *debate feminista* though they became a larger presence over the years. Virtually no studies were included that focused on masculinity, and for that matter there was little (though some) inclusion of essays written by men.[12]

The journal was divided into two parts: *Feminaria* and *Feminaria literaria*. In *Feminaria*, the ratio was usually one article from a non-Spanish source to two from Latin America, including Argentina. The rest of the section was almost entirely made up of Argentine events, material, interviews, bibliography, etc. In *Feminaria Literaria*, the articles were written almost exclusively by Argentines but also incorporated literature from any country. Two exceptions were the "dossiers" which were on, of, and by authors from other Latin American countries and the poetry and short stories sections, which were usually from Argentine authors, though not always.

Like *debate*, *Feminaria* also sought to provide multiple perspectives on issues regarding sexuality, as was the case in 1994, issue 13, when many pages were devoted to the topic of abortion and viewing the debate from every vantage point. The sections were succinct, occupying no more than one complete page or two at most, but covered the legal, medical, religious, and ethical dimensions to the debate. Other examples of issues related to sexuality were special sections that were devoted to prostitution (22/23) and Lesbianism (5, "Acerca de las relaciones de poder entre feminismo y lesbianismo" [About Power Relations between Feminism and Lesbianism] and 6, "Mes de la historia y el orgullo gay y lésbico" [A Month of Gay and Lesbian History and Pride]), and transvestites have also been given some attention (24/25) though less than that found in *debate*. Sexual violence was present from the first issue in 1988 in "El mito del cazador "cazado" en los discursos de la violación sexual" [The myth of the "hunted hunter" in discourse about rape] and in the last issue in 2002, "Políticas públicas, violencia de género y los nuevos retos para el feminismo: El ejemplo de México" [Public politics, gender violence and the new challenges for feminism: The example of Mexico]. The topic was also addressed in various issues through the journal's history. Pornography was the focus of volume 7 in "Nosotras, los objetos, objetamos: la pornografía y el movimiento de las mujeres" [We females, the objects, object: Pornography and the Women's Movement]. Like *debate*, an entire issue was devoted to maternity in volume 15 (1995) and reproductive rights were discussed again in volume 26/27, 2001, framed, as in Mexico, in the context of human rights.

Unlike *debate*, *Feminaria* never attempted to present itself as the "voice" of Latin American feminism, even while acknowledging the commonalities. On the contrary, it was intentionally and specifically rooted in Argentina and the balance of material included demonstrated this in every issue. When the focus was extended beyond their borders, more often than not it was the United States, Italy or France that was mentioned, while there is little discussion of Brazil, in spite of their common border, that country's own history of feminism, and the fact that it is the largest country in South America.[13] Perhaps in large part this was due to the Argentine immigrant heritage or is a reflection of the deeply rooted Francophile tendencies in the country. In terms of the inclusion of other countries of Spanish-speaking South America, *Feminaria* published poetry of women from Peru, Chile, Guatemala, Mexico,

Bolivia, and Colombia, though little in the way of critical theory. There was an entire section devoted to Latin American women writers living in Europe or the United States such as Helena Araújo, Marily Martínez de Richter, Alicia Kozameh, and Diana Raznovich.

State-sponsored sexual terrorism was explored in issue 17/18. Editor Lea Fletcher contributed her own essay on the topic of sexual violence of political prisoners, "Un silencio a gritos: tortura, violación y literatura de la Argentina" [A silence that shouts: Torture, Rape and Literature in Argentina], while another essay dealt with the language employed by the military during the dictatorship regarding women, "De mujeres y discursos: veinte años es mucho" [Of Women and Discourses: 20 Years is A Lot]. Claudia Laudano from la Universidad Nacional de La Plata demonstrated in that essay how women were relegated one of three roles during the repression, "defensoras, contro-ladoras y educadoras" [defenders, controllers and educators] in terms of the patriarchy and family and later "colaboradoras" [collaborators]. Women were supposed to keep in check the behavior of their children, to educate them properly in order to defend the interests of the nation (Laudano 24). The rhet-oric of the epoch also focused on the woman who chose to work as being a threat to the well-being of her children. This same rhetoric was used against the Mother of the Plaza de Mayo in order to declare them unfit because they had failed in their above roles by raising terrorists (24):

> Tal como afirmamos anteriormente, alrededor de *la maternidad* y el lugar de la madre en la sociedad se configure para los militares *el núcleo central de las significaciones imaginarias para las mujeres*, el lugar deparado por el destino y si bien se proporcianan otras opciones posi-bles, éstas indefectiblemente se anundan y subordinan a la construc-ción de la maternidad como la principal. [As we affirmed earlier, the military saw *maternity* and mother's place as the *central nucleus of the imaginary significance for women*, a place determined by destiny and if other possibilities for life were available, these are unfailingly subor-dinate to the notion of maternity as the central one.] (25 original emphasis)

As Masiello points out, *Feminaria* sought to call into question binary models for understanding sexual difference, as seen in a mid-1990s contribution of Diana Maffia about Marisela, a transsexual whose children were taken away from her because she was deemed unfit. "Maffia reflects on natural categories of gender identity and on the shifting relationships between sexuality and political power in Argentina" (Masiello *The Art* 122–23).

In terms of the possible impact that the journal has had, Fletcher is very proud to note that the impact has been not only in the literary realm, in which it is cited in almost every article or book dealing with women's or feminist issues in Argentina, but also in terms of the journal's use in some university classes on the topic of women in Argentine history and literary studies. "It appears that the journal was able to garner the cloak of respectability in its maturity," she said, "at a time when feminism was no longer perceived in most circles to be a threat to national security.[14] Unfortunately, we are unable to see where that line of thought would have gone, the "red thread," to use Masiello's term, that connected all issues together and dealt with the "full span of political and legal claims as well as women's access to public culture."

Cadernos Pagu

The problem of funding was not as grave of an issue for *Cadernos Pagu: Revista do Núcleo de Estudos de Gênero*, the feminist journal we examine from Brazil. Of course *Pagu*, which began in 1993, is connected to an academic institution and gender studies programs, something that ensures publication. *Pagu* has often received international funding for the journal, unlike *debate feminista* and *Feminaria*, which chose to remain independent. I have chosen to limit my discussion of Brazilian feminist journals and sexuality to *Cadernos Pagu*, and not to its older sibling, the *Revista de Estudos Feministas*, only because the journal has had a greater range of topics related to the theme of sexuality and several special issues dedicated to sexual issues related to Brazil.

Pagu was named in honor of the Brazilian avant-garde intellectual of the 1920s, Patrícia Galvão (1910–1962). The journal covers roughly the same time frame as *debate* and *Feminaria*. It began in 1993 with the idea of contributing to the topic of gender studies in Brazil, through the diffusion of articles on the topic from national critics and a critical reading of international literature on the topic.

Pagu has a sophisticated Web site[15] that includes the indices from the history of the journal, where one can trace the trajectory from the initial issue in 1993 (volume I), one that contained a mere seven articles, all of which centered on women in Brazil, to the latest issue from 2007 (volume 29) that included a dossier of eleven core essays related to the theme of family arrangements and migration, five additional essays connected to the themes, and four book reviews. This growth has been steady over the years, though the content has remained, for the most part, devoted to Brazil, with roughly 50–75 percent of all articles dealing with that country. Although the journal is purportedly devoted to "gender" studies, a mere 5 percent to 10 percent of the essays specifically treat the theme of masculinity. The majority of *Pagu*'s essays have been focused on women.

A watershed year for *Pagu* was 1998 because it was the first time in which a subcategory of the issue was devoted specifically to "Feminismo(s) contemporâneo(s)" [Contemporary Feminisms] and includes an extended essay by American critic Judith Butler. The majority of the essays in that issue deal with the topic of gender studies in terms of an area of research and three deal with specifically the constructions of masculinity, which is to say, it is the first time in which a balanced assessment of constructions of gender is included. Prior to this issue, "gender studies" as we will see in Chapter Five, had seemed almost a coded way of referring to "feminist studies." That said, in the last few years the journal has focused more than ever on the instability of sexual identifiers and the problems with binaries of any sort that try to contain the vast array of possibilities for sexual, gendered, and national identities. There is now a greater focus on transnational movements, sexual and ethnic minorities within the country as well as abroad. This parallels what was seen in later issues of *debate feminista*, and it is unfortunate that we are unable to see if *Feminaria* might have evolved in the same direction.

Cadernos Pagu does not have a general editor and each issue is usually listed as coming from the Comitê Editorial, although dossiers are organized around specific themes by one or two members. From the inception of the journal, the ongoing presence and contributions from Adriana Piscitelli are noteworthy and most of her interests are related to the topic of sexuality. She organized four of the issues, including the inaugural issue, "De trajetórias e sentimentos" [Of Trajectories and Feelings] (1: 1993), as well as "Gêneros, narrativas, memórias" [Genders (Genres), Narratives and Memories] (8/9: 1997), "Corporificando gênero" [Embodying Gender] (14: 2000), and "Mercado do sexo" [Sex Market] (25:2005).

In issue 14, "Corporificando gênero" was one of the first to treat the theme of sexuality exclusively. It includes essays related to race, power, violence, and prostitution. Of particular note are the photos that accompany an essay written by Miguel Vale de Almeida concerning "Corpos marginais: notas etnográficas sobre páginas 'de policia' e páginas 'de sociedad' [Marginal

Bodies: Ethnographic Notes on Police Pages and Society Pages]. This unusual essay on visual culture is a comparative analysis on the presentation of convicts and socialites in a regional newspaper of Brazil, images that "allow identifying representations of social inferiority based on race, gender, class and sexual classifications" (130). Almeida argues, "in the process, the body and its exposure to the observer's eye play the role of elements that objectify social expectations" (130).

Gay and lesbian issues in Brazil have been examined on the pages of *Pagu* throughout the history of the journal, in articles dealing with the formation of families, legal rights, adolescent sexuality, and the medical establishment: the topic of intersexuality is introduced in volume 24 (2005), with an article published directly in Spanish "Cuando digo intersex: un diálogo introductorio a la intersexualidad" [When I say intersex: an introductory dialogue to intersexuality].

Brazil is, of course, connected to the image of the hyper-sexualized woman, particularly the *mulata* that is prevalent in popular culture and media in general. Increasingly, *Pagu* carries essays that treat topics related to this mass media version of sexuality that, while not unique to the country, are certainly a greater concern there, such as sex tourism. "Exotismo e autenticidade: relatos de viajantes à procura de sexo." [Exoticism and authenticity: tales of travelers in search of sex] by Adriana Piscitelli, was the first to treat the topic in volume 19 (2002). The author later devoted an entire issue to the topic of sex workers, in volume 25 (2005), around the theme "Gênero no Mercado do sexo" [Gender in the Sex Market].

Piscitelli makes the argument in the opening editorial section of volume 25 that the focus of intellectuals has usually been on supply, as opposed to demand, and the special issue would like to change that focus. That issue discusses, among other things, the trafficking of women, sex workers in the nineteenth century, transvestite prostitution, and sex tourism on Copacabana beach and in Vila Mimosa. What is unique about the presentation of the topics is that it is not done from the perspective of repudiation of such activities. There is no moralizing. On the contrary, this conceptualization of sexual labor, as framed by the article by Guyanese-born scholar Kamala Kempadoo in the lead essay, suggests that there is nothing inherently violent or abusive about sex work (although it is widely acknowledged that sex workers can be victims of rape and sexual harassment on or off the job). Kempadoo argues that it cannot be construed as a universal or a-historical category, but rather acknowledged as something that is subject to change and redefinition through time.

In both the dossier, written by Piscitelli, and Kempadoo's "Mudando o debate sobre o tráfico de mulheres" [Shifting the Debate about the Trafficking of Women] the women argue that there is the need to broaden the discussion to not only think of prostitution in terms of women, but also in terms of often young men and transvestites; and to not think exclusively of their clients as men, but rather acknowledge that in sex tourism, the clients are also women, in an economically advantaged position vis-à-vis the "natives."

Kempadoo discusses the roots of the anti-trafficking movement, showing that it emerged from condescending middle-class feminist groups in the United States and Europe, intent on saving their "poor sisters" (59), and shows how "much of what is pursued in the name of a war on trafficking and fear of transnational organized crime and porous borders has troubling consequences for poor communities around the world and has both gendered and racialized implications." Kempadoo connects the topic to international migrations, something beyond the control of local governments, and argues that it only serves to reinforce the hegemony of the strongest over the weakest.

Kempadoo's argument, one that is later explored in articles related specifically to Brazil, is that international anti-trafficking laws are treating the effect as opposed to the causes for sex trafficking, among which she includes: globalization, patriarchy, racism, ethnic conflicts and wars, ecological devastation, and religious and political persecution.

Piscitelli argues that part of the problem with the configuration of many strands of feminism from the United States and Europe is that prostitutes are always seen as victims. Alternatively, the distinction is made between women who "choose" to become prostitutes versus those that are sold into sexual slavery without acknowledging that a woman who makes such a choice may not have had any viable options for sustaining her family. Patriarchy is not the only relation of domination, or even the most important one that these individuals face. Racism, imperialism, and international inequality also play a part in their subjugation. Contributors argue that instead of viewing prostitution as inherently violent and anti-women, it is rather the working conditions that are the real violence, the informal circumstances of their employment that violate the rights of these individuals. This position isn't "pro" prostitution as much as it a way to defend it as a choice and understand it from the standpoint of human rights or social justice.

Discussing the "demand" side of the prostitution equation, sex tourism is explored not merely as that done by men to women (or girls) but also by European or American women with boys in the Caribbean. Buying and selling sexual services is discussed in terms of transnationalization. The mobility, in terms of tourists, immigrants, refugees, exiles, and workers, affects the political relations between countries in a way that is without precedent. The sex market is connected to transnational networks and international pressure to control the market has had a disproportionate negative effect on undocumented workers, usually women of color living illegally in countries.

Piscitelli argues that the articles in the issue of *Pagu* that she edited all demonstrate that, "o sexo é visto como uma táctica cultural que pode tanto desestabilizar o poder masclino, como reforça-lo" [sex is seen as a cultural tactic that is as likely to destabilize masculine power as it is to reinforce it]. Prostitution needs to be understood in ways that are more complex than good/bad, either/or. It may be seen as a space of agency in which women are just making use of the sexual order that exists.

The dossier of issue 21, was devoted to "Erotismo: prazer, perigo" [Eroticism, pleasure, danger] (2003) and includes the essay "Couro imperial: raça, travestismo e o culto da domesticidade" [Imperial Leather: Race, Cross-dressing and the Cult of Domesticity] by Anne McClintock about the different ways that sadomasochism practices may be understood. It is clear that *Pagu* seeks to explore issues of gender and power in the global market by examining the ways in which race, nation, region, age, class, gender affect visibility and erotic consumption. Another concern expressed is with the processes of self-exoticization in the country to cater to the clients from the north. How are places, their habitants and cultural production turned into goods for consumption by a wealthy clientele?

In *Pagu*, even dossiers not necessarily connected to sexuality will usually have one or two articles that make the connection. For example, in issue 26 (2006) "Repensando a infância" [Rethinking childhood], there were discussions on pedophilia, incest, prostitution, child pornography, and sexual violence against children. One article discusses issues surrounding the adoption of Brazilian children from the poor slums of Porto Alegre by wealthy U.S. clientele and Europeans, while another examines the way that children learn gender and sexuality.

In 2007, for the first time, *Pagu*'s dossier was organized by two men, Richard Miskolci and Julio Assis Simões, on the topic of "Sexualidades disparatadas"

["Dissident Sexualities"].[16] This particular issue uses a translated excerpt of Eve Kosovsky Sedgwick's *Epistemology of the Closet* as a point of departure. Other essays included revolve around gay marriage and moral panic, one on male homosexual identity in Brazilian anthropology, a discussion on Judith Butler, an article on "Queer theory and the intersex" by Nadia Perez Pino. Discussion of gay ghettos and gay and lesbian socialization, and finally on GLBT (Gay Lesbian Bisexual and Transgender) film festivals were also highlighted.

What has been easy to trace in these three journals is the way in which globalization and technology has radically transformed their content and the way in which they are published. An attempt to create a transnational feminist network was made in 2001 with the establishment of the International Association of Women's Studies Journals. The women who attended the first meeting in Canada were editors of journals published by universities, conglomerate publishers, nongovernmental organizations, and small groups of dedicated feminists with whatever resources they could find. They came together to explore ways the journals can work together in a collaborative manner. Participants also agreed on the need to promote action-oriented research activities and studies. The new organization created a statement of principles, saying that the members sought to:

1 Enhance communication between editors and managing editors of women's studies journals around the world, whether they are primarily academic, policy oriented or community based;

2 Share resources and strengths and to overcome weaknesses, especially to share the resources of northern based journals with journals in the south;

3 Develop collaboratively effective and accessible web and Internet resources, resulting in shared marketing, editing and dissemination resources for all the journals;

4 Pioneer collaborative electronic publishing within a feminist framework. INWSJ achieves its objectives through: list serve; workshops; research; seeking funding for journals to participate equally (Meyer 149).

While the goals were laudable, the challenges were almost insurmountable. For one, not all of the editors present had the means or the political freedom to express their views on women's lives and women's writing. In fact, the issue of writing itself and the conditions in which writing takes place in global feminist contexts became a topic of discussion. In the South, in general, women writing about gender and feminism faced many problems, including censorship, lack of funds, and poor distribution. In some cases even engaging in such an activity was dangerous. This was in sharp contrast to feminist journals in the North that generally had better funding, were more established, and whose editors' greatest concern was one of greater legitimacy. How could such obstacles, and such a chasm, be overcome?

The possibilities for Web publishing were considered very important, but this brought up the issue of accessibility, social class, and privilege. How many people have access to computers in developing regions of the world? Virtual space, however, it was agreed, for those who had access to it, encouraged free speech and the empowerment of women. Yet another topic that came up was the need for the inclusion of different kinds of articles, profiles, interviews, and debates along with more traditional academic articles. Creative writing, activist and academic writing were all deemed worthy of inclusion. In 2003, INWSJ comprised 32 journals in 18 countries in the North and South, of which only two were from Latin America. More disheartening, after that year, and after having had two previous meetings, the first in Canada and the second in Africa, the organization appeared to have disappeared altogether. Still, the issues the women raised were important and deserve consideration.

My final curiosity in this side dish is to see if, in fact, technology has been able to provide a space for women in Latin America, something that requires knowing how many people regularly access the World Wide Web. The latest figures may be found in Table 3.1, though there is no way of knowing what the percentage of women is for each country of Internet users, nor, for that matter, the purpose of those who use it.

It is not surprising that the countries with the highest literacy rates are also those with the largest percentage of Web users. Still, with the exception of Costa Rica, at best only roughly 20 percent of the population uses the Internet. This means that in the same way that the journals catered to a primarily wealthy reader, Internet sites will also touch this same demographic. But then, what sort of Web sites have emerged in the last ten years? Have they, in fact, addressed the issues of inclusivity raised by the INWSJ? I begin by examining the Web sites for three journals discussed in this side dish.

While *debate feminista* has a Web site, it has not been updated since 2005.[17] An active page still remains where you can subscribe to the journal, and images from the 2006 and 2007 covers are available. There is a link to see online "previews" of the journal through 2005; however, the links to the previews

Table 3.1 Statistics about Latin Americans and Access to the Internet CIA World Factbook

Field Listing	Internet Users	Percentage of Total Population
Argentina	8.184 million (2006)	20%
Bolivia	580,000 (2006)	6%
Brazil	42.6 million (2006)	22%
Chile	4.156 million (2006)	26%
Colombia	6.705 million (2006)	15%
Costa Rica	1.214 million (2006)	30%
Cuba[1]	240,000	2%
Dominican Republic	1.232 million (2006)	13%
Ecuador	1.549 million (2006)	11%
El Salvador	637,000 (2005)	9%
Guatemala	1.32 million (2006)	10%
Honduras	337,300 (2006)	4%
Mexico	22 million (2006)	20%
Nicaragua	155,000 (2006)	3%
Panama	220,000 (2006)	7%
Paraguay	260,000 (2006)	4%
Peru	6.1 million (2006)	21%
Uruguay	756,000 (2006)	22%
Venezuela	4.14 million (2006)	16%

Note 1. Private citizens are prohibited from buying computers or accessing the Internet without special authorization; foreigners may access the Internet in large hotels but are subject to firewalls; some Cubans buy illegal passwords on the black market or take advantage of public outlets to access limited e-mail and the government-controlled "intranet" (2006).
Source: www.cia.gov/library/publications/the-world-factbook/fields/2153.html

after 2003 are not functioning. *Feminaria*, meanwhile, has not had a print issue since 2002, but a 2007 issue is available if one orders it online. No previews are available. *Cadernos Pagu*, like its sister publication *Revista de estudos feministas* is available in print form by subscribing or for free online through www.scielo.br.

It should be noted that SciELO (Social Science English Edition) is a project online that provides free access to texts in English published by social science journals in Latin America. The site has some 30+ journals available from Argentina, Bolivia, Brazil, Chile, Paraguay, and Uruguay.[18]

I will provide a brief overview of four Web sites that relate to feminist and gender studies, one that originates in each of the countries discussed.

My emphasis was to find comprehensive sites, those focusing on feminist activism, academic research or study, organizations and associations, government and business resources, discussion lists, and online journals. My interest was also to find sites where subscribers are able to post their own creative and intellectual work, in the hope that this will be helpful for scholars and students.

Artemisa Noticias—Periodismo de género para mujeres y varones was founded in Argentina by Sandra Chaher and Sonia Santero in 2005.[19] Their intention was to have a site that would further knowledge regarding the impact of gender on women and men. Specifically, the creators seek to examine the norms and values that mold identity into either masculine or feminine and how this plays out in terms of discrimination in families, in communities, and in politics. They seek to decipher these established norms and analyze the effects that these have in the lives of women and men. While gender is something often seen in the mass media as something that is only of interest to women, Chaher and Santero wanted to call attention to the ways in which concepts of gender affect both men and women and underscore how it is in the interests of both to fight for equality in terms of defining their work and responsibilities. They chose the goddess of hunting, Artemisa, because they felt she was the personification of an independent feminine spirit.

Artemisa has articles concerning health, entertainment, culture, and, most importantly, gender equality. Readers also can contribute articles to the site as well. There is also an online store and links section. Although there are no chat rooms, women routinely post comments to articles. Most comments posted are reactions to articles published by the site or to current events that concern the above topics. There is a section of "webs recomendadas," which includes links to sites from all over Latin America that concern women or feminism; for example, Cima Noticias (Mexico), Feminaria Editora (Argentina), and Mujeres Hoy (Spain). It is difficult to know exactly how many women subscribe to the site but it gets approximately 50,000 hits per month, of which 90 percent are from women.

Creatividad Feminista—un espacio donde ser mujer no es un dato indiferente [Feminine Creativity–A Space Where Bring a Woman Is Not an Unimportant Fact][20] was founded in 1998 in Mexico, although "Se inicia en México pero se hace en el lugar en que nos encontremos ya que su equipo es de diferentes países de Latinoamérica (México, Bolivia, Chile)" [It starts in Mexico but is done wherever one happens to be because our team is from different countries in

Latin America (Mexico, Bolivia, Chile)]. *Creatividad Feminista* has feminist
articles, poems, art, radio, recommended books, an online store, and a chat
room, everything revolving around issues of feminism from all around the
world. Posted articles mainly concern facets of the contemporary feminist
movement. The stated purpose of the site is "Comunicación y reflexión desde
una perspectiva feminista autónoma" [Communication and reflection from
an independent feminist perspective] and 3,562 women subscribe to the site.

Cimac Noticias—Periodismo con perspectiva de género [Cimac News: Journal
with the Gender Perspective]. Organización de Comunicación e Información
de la Mujer[21] started in 2007 and is based in Mexico. The articles (written by
the site's creators and staff writers) are for Latin American women and concern health, well-being, entertainment, culture, and, most importantly, gender equality. However, subscribers can contribute their own editorial articles
to the site as well. There is also an online store, weekly and monthly publications, and links section. Topics addressed include women's health, well-
being, daily activities, entertainment, culture (popular fashion, restaurants,
etc.), employment, crimes against women, and issues of gender equality. The
stated purpose of the site is:

> Nuestra misión es generar y publicar información noticiosa, asegurar
> que las y los periodistas incorporen los derechos humanos de las
> mujeres en su trabajo cotidiano, así como promover los medios como
> una herramienta de transformación educativa y social que sirva como
> estrategia para que las organizaciones civiles transmitan sus activi-
> dades, demandas y propuestas. Nuestra visión es contribuir al cambio
> social y a la democratización de los medios. Buscamos influenciar las
> agendas nacionales y globales a favor de los derechos humanos y la
> equidad social. [Our mission is to generate and publish news informa-
> tion, to make sure that journalists incorporate human rights for
> women in their daily work, as well as to promote the media as a tool
> for educational and social transformation that serves as a strategy so
> that civil organizations transmit their activities, demands and propos-
> als. Our vision is to contribute to social change and the democratiza-
> tion of the media. We seek to influence national and global agendas in
> favor of human rights and social equality.]

Cimac has a section with links to other sites, including feminist/journalistic
Web sites such as Mexico's *Red Tamaulipas* and *Mujeres de Sociedad y*

Política, and Argentina's *Artemisa Noticias*. More than 2000 women subscribe to the site.

CFEMEA (Centro Feminista de Estudos e Assessoria) was established in 2003 in Brazil and provides news about the women's movement in Brazil, legislation affecting women, articles posted by subscribers, the feminist journal published by *CFEMEA*, a calendar of *CFEMEA* events, and a links section.[22] There is also information on events and movements affecting the social, economic, and political rights of women in Brazil. The stated purpose of the site is the following:

> CFEMEA Feminist Center for Studies and Advisory Services is a non-governmental, non-profit organization that works for the citizenship of women and gender equality. It fights for a just and democratic society and State in an autonomous and non-partisan way. Founded on feminist thought, CFEMEA actively participates in the national women's movement, and integrates with international feminist networks, especially in Latin America. It also participates in different initiatives against racism.

A series of "Commitments" are also listed that include: "to defend and broaden democracy; to overcome gender and racial/ethnic inequality and discrimination; to affirm liberty, autonomy, solidarity and diversity." Links are included of other mostly Brazilian organizations that promote women's rights, help women find work, and help those that are victims of sexual abuse or violence, for example: *Confederação Geral dos Trabalhadores*, *Central Única dos Trabalhadores*, *Campanha da Não-Violência contra a Mulher*, *Comitê Nacional de Vítimas da Violência*, *Conselho Nacional dos Direitos da Mulher*, among others.

Artemisa Noticias and *Cimac* are Web sites that are predominantly news sources for women. They publish stories that affect women and have to do with gender equality. While they offer places on their Web sites for the public to comment or blog, they mostly publish stories written by their own staff. *Creatividad Feminista* is a website where a majority of the articles, essays, and art is contributed by the public. While the content is similar to the previous three Web sites mentioned, it is more of a creative outlet for Latin American women instead of a news source. *CFEMEA* is more of an informative Web site about the organization itself and its activities to promote women's rights in Brazil through fundraising, awareness, and other events.

All of the Web sites have in common their mission to provide a journalistic source for women. They all respond in some way to the primary issue raised by the gathering of feminist journal editors, how to bridge the gap between intellectuals and activists. Some focus on fostering women's creativity and opportunity for expression such as *Creatividad Feminista*, while others are concerned more with expanding the political and economic rights of women through articles, essays, and so on. Either way, they all are about women and for women.

Conclusion

What I have sought to do in this side dish is to show how Latin American intellectuals from Argentina, Brazil, and Mexico combine local and imported knowledge to create a discourse on sexuality that is unique to their own circumstances.

This has not been an exhaustive account of feminist journals but merely an inroad in which I have attempted to trace some salient themes among the three journals discussed with regard to sexuality. The many areas that remain to be studied with regard to feminist journals and feminist Web sites include globalization, race, poverty, critical theory, technology, cultural studies, legal issues, economics, and environmental issues, each of which could warrant a book unto itself. Beyond this, it must be recognized that this is a small sampling of feminist journal production in Latin America. Many other journals could have been examined, such as *Mora* (Argentina), *Nomadías* (Chile), *Revista de Estudos Feministas* (Brazil) or even those that carry overwhelmingly "feminist' or gender studies-related themes, such as Chile's *Revista de crítica cultural*, and yet do not identify themselves as such.

Clear trends are apparent in all three journals discussed in this side dish. The inclusion and analysis of Web sites and the option to contact contributors and editors via e-mail have heightened the connectedness of those devoted to feminist and gender studies. The journals also, to varying degrees, include more men and studies of masculinity. Editors seem to have accepted that the construction of masculinity or the oppression of some men under patriarchy is a viable area of analysis. With regard to differences, *Feminaria* demonstrated much less concern in terms of content with regard to racism and indigenous issues as compared to its Brazilian and Mexican counterparts, perhaps due to the comparatively homogeneous population of mainly European descent. Although Brazil, like Argentina, suffered through dictatorships through the 1970s and early 1980s, the mark seems more indelible on the Argentine psyche, as evidenced by the essays in *Feminaria*. In all three journals the devastating impact on women of neoliberalism and globalization has made itself apparent in the most recent issues.

While *debate feminista* and *Feminaria* do include other Spanish-speaking countries in their conceptualization of Latin America, there is very little mention of Brazil. *Cadernos Pagu* has demonstrated a much more concerted attempt to be inclusive of Spanish-speaking countries, by offering more essays in Spanish and extended dossiers that illustrate partnerships with women from other Latin American countries who are working together to combat racism and violence against women, and to fight for reproductive rights. Latin Americanist scholars living in the United States such as Francine Masiello, Nora Domínguez, Mary Louise Pratt, Marta Savigliano, and Sonia Álvarez have been a presence in all three venues. However, as mentioned, the inroads tend to be mostly in the direction of the Spanish-speaking regions into Brazil and not the opposite. When the insights of Brazilian scholars such as Claudia Lima de Costa and Adriana Piscitelli make their way onto the pages of *debate feminista* or other journals in the Spanish-speaking world, to be read by Spanish speakers in their original Portuguese, as the Spanish language contributions are provided in *Pagu*, I believe it will signal a change.

This ongoing omission and, I would argue, marginalization of Brazil has also been felt by U.S. scholars working with the Spanish and Portuguese-speaking regions of the world as evidenced by the fact that the panel proposed for the 2003 Modern Language Association to be sponsored by *Feministas Unidas* had originally been called "Bridging the Gap: Feminist Theory and Hispanic Women's Writing," proposed by Lisa Vollendorf. It was changed "after considerable discussion" to read "Bridging the Gap: Feminist Theory and Hispanic and Luso-Brazilian Women's Writing," co-chaired by Vollendorf and Brazilianst feminist scholar Peggy Sharpe, a presence in both *Pagu* and *Revista de Estudos Feministas*. Indeed, it would appear that this is a critical "gap" that should be addressed, in order to insure that the women who are "unidas" are, in fact, united at all.

Identity is an enticingly intricate issue. It seems that one overriding commonality in each of the journals discussed is this sense of moving away from strictly discussing feminism or feminist criticism based on biology to acknowledge and incorporate a compendium of hegemonies that serve to circumscribe identity formation for everyone, the multiple intersections of power abuse that cross with class, age, race, sexual orientation which sometimes make it difficult to talk in terms of a unified category of "women" or "men" at all.

The most important observation with regard to the topic of sexuality in the three journals treated is that there was not an attempt to follow ideas from the North, but rather to evaluate the relevance of the theories in a different context. While there are topics that overlap with regard to certain issues such as abortion, prostitution, and rape, there is also variation, whether it is discussing the sexual torture of women prisoners in Argentina under the dictatorship, the effect on rural women in Mexico of the migrations to the North, or the sex tourism on the beaches of Rio de Janiero. Perhaps more important, there is greater cohesion than ever before in terms of the content of the journals, reflecting a greater presence of articles by critics and public intellectuals from other parts of Latin America and even Africa, as opposed to offering (and privileging) essays by European or U.S. scholars. What Masiello perceptively found with regard to *Feminaria* may also be applied to *Cadernos Pagu* and *debate feminista*:

> A revised cartography emerges to destabilize the North/South crossing. Debates about the artificial nature of frontiers, the boundaries between self and other, the restrictions between public and private identities, between individual and collective endeavors are the repeated subject of interest in *Feminaria*. As if to override the dominance of the North and move towards alternative configurations of the collective, attention frequently moves toward the value of feminist conventions. Inquiring about the possibility of alliance, rethinking the global and local paradigms, the north/south axis is displaced in order to interrogate the force of the global. (Masiello, *The Art*, 121)

The journals display a range of theoretical concerns about sexuality and gender. They also demonstrate the ongoing projects of Latin American intellectuals (118). Most importantly, all three journals underscore the need for open conversation and debate among women as much as the development of a sense of community.

At the beginning of this side dish, we read the story of the woman who refused to be swallowed up by her powerful interlocutor, her male therapist. In the same way, the Latin American intellectuals profiled in this chapter have not been "swallowed up" by their more powerful neighbors to the north. They have defined their own issues of importance, and charted their own intellectual course on the pages of these journals, in accordance with the particular sociocultural milieu in which they live.

"Eu te vou comer" [I'm going to eat you], the Brazilian woman at the start of this side dish had been convinced her analyst had told her. She didn't let him. She walked away.

4

❦

FLICKS

I'll have what she's having.

—*When Harry Met Sally*

The conjugation of food with sex in films over the last 25 years has led to some memorable scenes, including the above quote from *When Harry Met Sally* (1989, dir. Rob Reiner, written by Nora Ephron). Lust and food were also central themes in the UK/USA film *Chocolate* (2000, dir. Lasse Hallstrom), based on the book by Joanne Harris, about a woman who opens a chocolate store in a French village. From Latin America, *Like Water for Chocolate* (1992, dir. Alfonso Arau), based on the book by Laura Esquivel, set the food-equals-sex standard, while it was also paramount in the Latino remake of Ang Lee's *Eat Drink Man Woman* (1994), *Tortilla Soup* (2001, dir. Maria Ripoli, screenplay by Brazilian Vera Blasi), and *Woman on Top* (2000, dir. Venezuelan Fina Torres, screenplay by Brazilian Vera Blasi).

The sexuality discussed in the films here does not always or directly connect to food. A few caveats before taking that first bite: although my reading of the films is feminist, I do not make the assumption that the directors themselves were intentionally trying to make "feminist" films. I do not seek to "prove" that these films, nor their directors, are feminist, but rather I seek to point to a feminist aesthetic, as I address the treatment of sexuality and desire as it is visually and thematically composed. I am also not making the argument that a feminist aesthetic is rooted in biology. By that I mean to say that while the majority of the films I talk about were written and/or directed by women, there are many examples of male feminist filmmakers in Latin America, one of whom will be discussed at the close of this chapter.

While there are many films in the last 20 years that have been directed by women in Latin America, compared to earlier decades, most of these films have had limited distribution and are not available in the United States. One reason is that there are so few women directing films to begin with. As cited by the Guerrilla Girls and Alice Loca on their "Anatomically Correct Oscar" billboard displayed in Los Angeles on the eve of the Academy Awards in 2004, women still account for only 4 percent of all working directors internationally (Dorsey "Women Making Movies").

Until recently, films directed by Latin American women were often only available in video format, and in a system, PAL, which cannot be recognized by United States VCRs. While the temptation to examine these lesser-known films is great, I have limited my selection based on what is readily available on DVDs so that readers/students may have a chance to obtain and judge the films for themselves.

Although critics have written about some of the directors discussed here, they have done so primarily through a study of the themes in their films, which, while important, are only part of what must be considered when doing filmic analysis. I am more interested in the manner in which form under-scores content. How do filmic techniques such as the framing of shots, edit-ing, color palette, the pacing of the film, and the lighting reinforce a film's message about women's (or in some cases, "feminine" male's) sexuality?

This chapter also provides an overview of Latin American women's con-tributions to the film industries in their respective countries with particular emphasis on the time since 1980, when there has been a veritable explosion of women's participation in all facets of filmic production, particularly in Argentina, Brazil, and Mexico, but also in other countries. This new presence is documented in the chart found in the Appendix that traces the recognition of Latin American women directors and screenwriters in the top 15 inter-national film festivals since 1980. This overview of Latin American women's film-making is followed by a more specific treatment of feminine sexuality in three films released since 2000: *La niña santa* [The Holy Girl] (2004), directed by Argentine Lucrecia Martel, *Sin dejar huella* [Without a Trace] (2000), directed by Mexican Maria Novaro, and *Antônia* (2007), directed by Brazilian Tata Amaral. The chapter finishes with a discussion of sexuality in the film, *Eu, Tu, Eles* (2000), which was directed by a young Brazilian male, Andrucha Waddington.

While there has been a growing recognition of international films by women directors, it still remains a fact that males direct most films that get distributed in the United States. Accessibility within the countries in which these films were made is another thorny issue. While it is understood that independent films in the United States and Europe are seen by a minority of film viewers to begin with, those who have in most cases the disposable income to go to the theater, when one adds to the mix the limited economic resources of many individuals in Latin America, as well as the preponderance of films that come from Hollywood and are the central point of filmic reference for most of the population, then the number of individuals who have ever seen these films becomes small indeed.

The idea is that this chapter may serve as a blueprint for scholars interested in offering a course on contemporary Latin American feminist film. In the foreground is the representation of the female body and themes connected to sexuality. Necessarily, the discussion is focused on the countries that have historically had the greatest filmic production: Argentina, Mexico, and Brazil, each of which has experienced a veritable "boom" in recent decades on the part of women filmmakers. And it wasn't just that they were making films, some of these films were also financially successful when released in their own countries, something exceptionally difficult in places where the majority of screen space in theaters is devoted to showing American-made movies. Although films made by women from the other countries will also be addressed, whenever possible, it must be understood that many, if not most, Latin America countries simply do not have the funding available to keep a film industry running.

On Definitions

For a number of reasons, any discussion of Latin American feminist filmmaking is vexing. How to define either term—Latin America or feminist? To begin with, it is difficult to cast a blanket over an entire region when there are certain countries that have had no significant film production ever, such as El Salvador or Guatemala, or minimally, such as Paraguay. Inevitably, these countries get subsumed under a category that then comprises the four major film-producing countries, Brazil, Argentina, Mexico, and Cuba. Then again, other factors come into play. For example, Argentine film production over the last 15 years has leaned heavily on Spanish funding or in some cases that of other European or U.S. sponsors, thus producing a series of co-productions. Does that problematize the notion of a film's "latinamericanness"? Can countries as diverse as those listed above even be considered in relation to one another when their own histories differ greatly?

To define Latin America as though it were a monolithic entity is always the burden for those of us who work in area studies, and yet this is how, in fact, our courses are defined in the curriculum and taught, with Spain usually occupying its own domain while the 19 Spanish-speaking countries of Latin America are thrown together in the same pot. This is less the case with Portugal and Brazil, the smaller country almost swallowed up by its enormous former colony. Brazil, as Latin America's largest country, however, given that it also has a Latin-based language very similar to Spanish, must be brought into any discussion of the region.

Moving on to the equally sticky issue of defining feminist film, what exactly may be said to constitute it? According to David William Foster, the following factors must be evident: (1) it must tell the story of women's lives; (2) while it doesn't have to be told by a woman, as not all women tell stories in a feminist way, it needs to be acknowledged that generally the most believable stories are those told by subaltern groups about something they have lived; (3) women must be involved in all aspects of the filmmaking and production at all levels; and (4) the film should break with the narrative conventions of masculinist filmmaking.

In other words, stories need to be told in a different way, resisting openly the horizon of expectations of the viewer (indeed calling into question the "naturalness" of the standard U.S. filmic construction to begin with). In Foster's eyes, a feminist film is that which does the unexpected, scandalizes, perturbs, make uncomfortable, decentralizes, and inverts what is seen as "natural" or "normal."

But these demarcations only lead us to greater confusion. Does this mean that a film by a male director and primarily male crew may not be considered feminist, even if it has a women-focused content? Does any rupture in traditional filmic technique mean that a film is necessarily feminist? For example, would the films of Pedro Almodóvar fall into this category and be considered feminist, even when the film is one that has few women personages, such as *Mala Educación* (2004)? Can a film entirely about men and directed and produced by men ever provide a feminist aesthetic? Conversely, can or does the presence of women directors, producers or filmic crew ensure any connection to what may be termed a feminist sensibility?

In an essay on early Brazilian women filmmakers by Elice Munerato and Maria Helena Darcy de Oliviera, "When Women Film," the authors found in their overview of the early history of women directors in Brazilian film startlingly few divergences from typical themes and filmic techniques used by males. This, of course, begs the question: was this an intentional adjustment on the part of directors to cater to the reality of audience interests and tastes? Or was it the result of the internalization of masculinist models and/or masculinist gaze on the part of the filmmakers? Does the lack of such a corpus indicate a sell-out of sorts on the part of the women involved, or was their mere presence and their work during those early years enough to consider their work "feminist"? There are no simple answers.

Feminist Film Criticism and Women Filmmakers in Latin America

Before turning to the films, it is important to understand some of the touchstones of feminist film criticism and to have a general understanding of the historical roots of women's filmmaking in Latin America.

The first project of feminist film criticism, initiated during the 1970s, involved primarily a recuperative effort. There was a need to go back through film history and to examine women's presence on the screen as well as their participation in filmmaking. In a vein similar to what was found in the famed *Celluloid Closet*, there were studies that emerged that found some feminist subtexts in some early films. Furthermore, scholars also discovered that there was a central view of women in classic Hollywood films. These inevitably fell along the lines of the bad girl getting her due while the women characters more closely in synch to the masculine ideal reaped the rewards for doing so, usually marriage to the leading man.

These moralizing tales are due to the fact that, according to some feminist film theory, film is yet another technology of gender, to use Teresa de Lauretis's term, coined from Foucault's notion in which the power structure is maintained, transmitted, and internalized through various "technologies" of society, or institutions. Mas'ud Zavarzadeh echoes this, maintaining that no film is ever innocent; it is always clearly a site of ideological investment. In Zavarzadeh's opinion, in standard big industry films, this is always a one-way street from the powerful to the powerless, meant to preserve the status quo by making societal inequity appear "natural." De Lauretis and other feminist critics contend that film, thus, serves as yet another mechanism whereby gender and sexuality are regulated.

But then the question becomes, is the fact that a film is directed by a woman going to change this? Or are such notions so ingrained as to be inevitable in any filmic production? After all, one cannot step outside oneself and one's society. Furthermore, at least in the case of filmmaking, even if one were to attempt to do so, there remains the issue of audience accessibility and identification. Will anyone go to watch a film that falls outside of the standard grid of intelligibility? The display of dominant "truth," the filmic representation of the ideological production of the "real" ("experience") will always be present in contemporary film and presented as "natural." The task of the critic is to make visible this web of signification at work within the dominant ideology represented in a film's "reality." It must be denaturalized.

My use of women's cinema refers to films directed principally, though not exclusively, by women. Whether or not they were made primarily with a women-based audience in mind is usually uncertain (although it was the stated purpose of one of our directors in this chapter, Brazilian Tata Amaral). The use of the term feminist is also my own, as mentioned, and not, in many cases, theirs. It is reductive and impossible to account for the array of filmic representation and fit it all under a neat rubric. Like Judith Mayne, I do not mean to suggest, as it would seem, the essentialist notions that somehow films directed by women are in any way better or more "authentic" in their depictions of feminine sexuality (4). I have chosen films that run counter to the established filmic canon, but I do not mean to foist yet another absolute onto women's cultural production. As Mayne states

> [. . .] I do not think that feminist discussions of the works of women filmmakers is served by continued insistence upon the absolute division between classical Hollywood cinema and its alternatives. To begin with, such a division places a kind of utopian burden upon alternative filmmakers, to such an extent that any traces of dominant cinematic practice—lurking fetishism or shade of voyeurism, to be precise—would be seen as suspect. Given the institutionalized ways in which the cinema functions, and how individuals are acculturated to respond to the cinema, it is difficult to know just to what extent a truly alternative cinematic practice is possible. (4)

There is no way to underestimate or calculate the impact of Hollywood versions of women's sexuality on public expectations of the cinema. Similarly, there is no way to estimate or calculate the impact these versions have on filmmakers. What is clear, however, is that one falls into a trap of generalizing, and thus essentializing, women filmmakers and their products. Thus we become enmeshed in the binary, "classic" cinema portrayals of women's desire versus women created portrayals, somehow implied to be more "authentic." As Mayne points out, this is rigid, and problematic, in its own way (6).

The idea behind this chapter is to examine how pleasure and desire are represented filmically, the how as opposed to the "why." How is gender created and sexuality construed? How is it subtly inscribed into the filmic language? What are the ideological keys that we can detect in the construction of subjectivity and identity?

While films centered on women have achieved notable success in recent years, an examination of the top ten summer films from any given year will show that the majority of the blockbuster films will still be centered on males and be directed by males. So the question becomes, do Latin American women filmmakers share any characteristics at all? In Mexico, Alma Rossbach says, "Women's scripts are different because there are different themes. In my country it's often the story of a family—their habits and conflicts, the thoughts that women have about sexuality, or confronting men in relationships, or about children, or about being mothers" (Seger, *When Women*, 117). She argues that the films tend to be about the texture of daily life. The "heroes" in women's films tend to be quite "normal."

Many women are uncomfortable with the idea of singling out gender as a factor in their filmmaking. Even discussing women's voice can be problematic, or in the case of one filmmaker, Danish documentary filmmaker Johanna Demetrakas, whose ideas about how women's films are different, are at the very least open to debate:

> One of the things that interests me most is gender and how it manifests itself. When I started to write screenplays, I began to see subtle differences. Structurally, men seem to work in an Aristotelian way. I didn't invent this idea of comparing or associating male and female sexual rhythms with artistic modes of expression. From a male point of view, conflict is essential. Their stories have one conflict, which is always one clear piece of action that triggers everything and has to be overcome. There is one climax, and of course one denouement. That isn't necessarily so from a female point of view. That is a huge, fundamentally different approach. With the female approach, there are many conflicts, its multiclimatic, and often has many endings." (Seger 136–37)

Of course, one of the most limiting notions in classic Hollywood films is that women must be young, beautiful, and sexy to be in a film. This is less frequently the case in films directed by women, where the females on the screen are more likely to resemble those one would see on the street.

As David Harvey reminds us, "the eye is never neutral." Cinematic sexuality is essentially a set of representations, semiotic cues to the viewer. The result of this representation is situated somewhere between the real and perceived images. These images are cut up and rearranged according to the vision of the director, working closely with the cinematographer to present some sort of a coherent reality. As Lefebvre says, "The illusion consists in the failure to perceive this dismemberment" (96–97).

Sexuality is recorded and constructed, acquires meaning, and as a cultural creation, influences the reality it comes from as it helps to shape our perception of that reality. Through the selection, manipulation, and control of images the director and cinematographer create an imagined landscape. Meaning is made, legitimized, contested or obscured. Examining the production and consumption of the cinematic landscape of sexuality will enable us to question the power and ideology of representation, and the problems of interpretation (Hopkins 47). How are meaning and ideology constructed regarding sexuality in a film? What is the chain of signification? Looking beyond this, what are the global, political and economic issues at stake in the film's production, distribution, and consumption? Finally, who controls our perceptions of what constitutes the "real"? An important point to make is that those creating films in Latin America who are trying to sell their film to a North American or European market are often burdened with the need to self-exoticize in order to provide what is expected of them to film viewers. Another problem is that, according to Zavarzadeh,

> [M]any societies have access to film-producing technologies but are unable to make the texts of their films an effective part of the construction of the real simply because their texts are marginalized by the film and information texts of more powerful economic interests. This mode of neocolonialism attempts to make the world intelligible in terms that legitimate the dominant clearly seen in the post World War II expansion of the U.S. culture industries. (97–98)

Thus, the world becomes constructed through the eyes of the most powerful countries, primarily the United States, creating a north-to-south flow of representations, values, images, and ideas. Films produced in the South that do not conform to these values, images, and ideas are often ignored. Another factor to take into consideration is that even when a given country in the periphery produces its own films about its own cultural, historical and sociopolitical reality, it is often not taken into consideration simply because the filmmakers will rarely have the capital to circulate it internationally.

Film scholar Zavarzadeh has pointed out that "the spectator chains together the film's signifiers on a cultural grid of intelligibility—an ensemble of assumptions and presuppositions about the 'real' into an account that makes the film socially intelligible" (II). This grid of intelligibility is also there on the part of the film's director, whether it is consciously or subconsciously utilized. For the cultural critic, then, deciphering the film can lead to a chicken-or-egg dilemma. Do filmmakers present such images by unwittingly replicating their own frames of intelligibility for others who are like them, or do they do so consciously because movie audiences are so conditioned to seeing things in a particular way that they will not go to a film that does not conform to their cultural values and expectations?

I will be considering where the viewer's attention is focused on the screen. My interest is in examining as much the treatment of the themes related to gender and sexuality as the ways in which the director underscores these themes using filmic techniques. Do they complement one another or are they at odds? Do they represent interesting innovations? What is framed in each shot; what is the camera angle from which the spectator views the subject? How is lighting or shadow used? How do specific shots and the editing of these shots impact the meaning of the film? How does the director use the film's color palette? How is the film paced?

A Short History of Latin American Women Filmmakers

As documented in the text, *Cine y mujer en América Latina: Directoras de largometrajes de ficción* [Film and Women in Latin America, Directors of Feature Length Films] by Luis Trelles Plazaola, there has been a presence of women directors almost from the inception of film in Latin America. The problem is that it is difficult to detect and catalog because many women worked on films at the beginning of the industry but were not acknowledged as having done so, due to societal stigma attached to women working. Women were often in front of, and behind the camera, more often than not as the result of economic necessity—everyone had to wear more than one hat.

The problem, however, is that it was considered unfeminine to have names listed in the credits. Many women were involved in partnerships with their husbands or other males and it was he who got the screen credit (Trelles 2–4).

It was in 1896 that film arrived in Argentina, Brazil, and Mexico, the following year it was introduced in Cuba, Colombia, and Venezuela. Within a few years it also arrived in Peru, Puerto Rico, and Chile (6). Initially the films were of the news; it wasn't until 1910 that films with specific stories were introduced.

In Argentina, Emilia Saleny, an actress in the theater, was an early filmmaker, having done *La niña del bosque* [The Forest Girl] in 1916 and *El pañuelo de Clarita* [Clarita's Handkerchief] in 1917 (9). Maria V. de Celestini is another early filmmaker, having directed *Mi derecho* [My Right] from 1920. Little information is available on these early films. Plazaola was unable to find very much as there was no continued production on the part of either woman.

Before 1930, in Brazil, Georgina Marchiani was the only woman to be both in front of and behind the camera in *O Guarani* [The Guarani] (in 1916). She said that she was the camera- person only because they couldn't afford to pay someone else to do the job. In Brazil, until 1930, there is no record of any woman director. It was in that year that a Brazilian woman directed the first film, *O Mistério do Dominó Negro* [The Mystery of the Black Domino] by Cléo de Verbena. It is known that she was forced to sell what little she had to finance that one film. Meanwhile, fellow Brazilian Carmen Santos, in 1932, established her own film company, Brasil Vita Filme.

In Mexico, during this same time frame, up until 1930, there were two women directors. One was Mimí Derba (María Herminia Pérez de León), Mexico's first film star, who was both an actress in theater and singer of zarzuelas (Spanish musical theater). Derba, along with Enrique Rosas, founded Azteca Films in 1917. The company lasted only one year but it produced five feature films that were written by Derba. She was the first female director in Mexico, with *La Tigresa* [The Tigress], a film she neither acted in nor wrote (Garcia 107). The other Mexican director from that time frame was Cándida Beltrán Rendón. With little economic backing, she directed, starred in, wrote and did the scenic design for the one film, *El secreto de la abuela* [Grandmother's Secret], from 1928 (Trelles 11).

The economic and political instability of the other regions of Latin America made any film industry almost impossible, but, in 1929, with the introduction of talking films in Latin America, this changed, if ever so slightly. Film industries were established in Brazil, Mexico, and Argentina and consisted principally in three genres, melodrama, comedy, and musical, all local in content. As the demand grew so did the number of directors in each country. It was a filmic production aimed at the masses and not intended for documenting social injustices or fomenting activism. While women were often the focal point of these new films there were still comparatively few women working behind the camera. At this time, three Mexican women became known for their directing skills.

The first was Adela Sequeyro, "Perlita," who had been a popular radio personality. Although she began as an actress, after working with some of the most important filmmakers in the 1930s she turned her attention to directing three films, starting with *Más allá de la muerte* [Beyond Death] in 1935, for which she was a writer, actress, and producer, later for *La mujer de nadie* [Nobody's Woman] in 1937, and finally with *Diablillos de arrabal* [Little Devils from the Arrabal] in 1938. Sequeyro was also a writer. These films were produced by the company she cofounded, Producciones Carola. *La mujer* was considered a melodramatic comedy and *Diablillo* was focused on child characters. The second Mexican film director of the 1930s was Chilean-born Eva Limiñana, or the "Duquesa Olga" (Trelles 17). Limiñana earned credits as producer, writer, screen adapter, for ten films in which José Bohr starred in the 1930s.

In the 1940s, two Brazilian women became famous for their film work: the Portuguese Carmen Santos and the Paulista Gilda de Abreu. Carmen Santos had been a star of silent movies, many of which, unfortunately, were either lost in a fire or simply never exhibited. Another version is that the man in her life, who had financed the films, decided to destroy them.

Carmen Santos was the producer of two of the most important films in Brazilian history, *Sangue Mineiro* [Blood from Minas Gerais] and *Lábios Sem Beijos* [Lips Without Kisses], both from the same year, 1930, and both directed by Humberto Mauro. In 1932, Santos founded her own production company Brasil Vita Filme, and Humberto Mauro again was prominent in the films that were produced. As a director, Santos put most of her energy over three years into the filming of *Inconfidência Mineira*, about the attempt at insurrection in Minas Gerais in the eighteenth century, which was an early attempt for Brazil to assert its independence from Portugal. Santos was the producer, director, screenwriter, and one of the leading actors. She died in 1952 at the age of 48. Fellow Brazilian Gilda de Abreu was a singer, composer, writer, radio personality,

theater, and film producer. She was well known for her work in musical theater. Married to a famous singer and actor, Vicente Celestino, she had her
directorial debut in 1946 with the film, *O Ébrio* [The Drunkard], a film based on
one of her husband's songs. The film was a hit. The success enabled Abreu to
continue her work. She directed *Pinquinha de Gente* [Pinquinha of the People]
(1947) but the film didn't achieve nearly the same success as *O Èbrio*. In 1951,
she did a third film, *Coração Materno* [Maternal Heart]—a sentimental drama
centered on maternal conflict. While fellow Brazilian director Carmen Santos
was interested in the historical epic, Abreu wanted to direct sentimental
films. Abreu, like Santos, also formed her own production company: Pro-Arte.
In 1973, she adapted one of her novels, *Mestiça* [Mestiza], into a film that was
directed by another woman, Lenita Perroy (27). She continued to work in filmmaking until her death in 1979.

Meanwhile, in Mexico, the 1940s were considered the Golden Age of cinema. The genre was dominated by nationalistic themes that were exhibited
primarily in melodrama and "Churros," or formulaic movies. It was at that
time that the most important woman director would emerge, Matide Landeta.
She didn't direct her first feature film until 1943, a time in which the Mexican
film industry was in expansion. Before that, Landeta had worked as a script
girl for some of the most important figures in Mexican film. It was in 1945 that
she served as the assistant director for her first film, in collaboration with
Cuban Ramón Peón, with *Espinas de una flor* [Thorns of a Flower] (19). She
would go on to collaborate with other filmmakers including José Díaz
Morales. In 1948, she directed her first film, *Lola Casanova*, which "traces
Mexican culture to its pre-Colombian roots through the desires of a white
woman." This was followed by *La negra Angustias* [Black Angustias] from 1949,
about a *mulata* colonel in the Mexican revolution who exerts power outside
the confines of gender, only to face racial conflict with her male literacy
teacher, and finished with *Trotacalles* in 1951 (19). As Trelles points out:

> *Lola Casanova* y *La negra Angustias* son películas contrastantes en ambi-
> entes y protagonistas pero que comparten varias notas comunes. Son
> ambas adaptaciones fílmicas de obras de Francisco Rojas González.
> Revelan ambos filmes, en cuanto al tema, una preocupación por el
> interior de México puesto que las tramas de *Lola Casanova* y *La negra
> Angustias* se sitúan respectivamente en Sonora y Jalisco. Sus personajes
> femeninos se mueven en un trasfondo de mestizaje, abuso de poder,

explotación del pobre y grupos marginados. [*Lola Casanova* and *La negra Angustias* are contrasting movies in terms of both the settings and the protagonists, but they share various similarities. They are both filmic adaptations of works by Francisco Rojas González. In terms of themes, they both show a preoccupation with the interior of the country given that the stories in both *Lola Casanova* and *La negra Angustias* are situated in Sonora y Jalisco. The feminine personages move in a backdrop of miscegenation, abuses of power, exploitation of the poor and marginal groups.] (19)

Although Landeta stopped directing after *Trotacalles*, she continued working on filmic adaptations throughout the 1950s.

Originally from Chile, Eva Limiñana arrived in Mexico as a pianist and became known for her adaptations and screenplays. She directed one film, codirected with Carlos Toussaint, in which she also wrote the screenplay. It was titled, *Mi Lupe y mi caballo* [My Lupe and My Horse]; it was filmed in 1942 and opened in 1944.

The film was a "ranchera," starring popular singer María Luisa Zea, but there were many problems in the production and it ended up being the only film ever directed by Limiñana.

In Argentina, after a couple of decades in which women were not very active in filmmaking, a new phase of women's activity was initiated in the 1960s with Vlasta Lah and her two feature films, *Las furias* [The Furies] (1960) and *Las modelos* [The Models] (1963). Lah is the only woman Latin American filmmaker during the 1960s, a period in which women in Brazil and in Mexico were working more behind the scenes. *Las furias* was almost entirely female in its cast, with Mecha Ortiz, Aída Luz, Alba Mujica, Olga Zubarry, and Elsa Dabiel.

The rise of the Independent film movements in the 1950s and 1960s in Latin America, the *Nuevo Cine*, was very important for women. Other important developments include the founding in Mexico of the University Center for Cinematographic Studies (CUEC) in 1958.

From 1960 to 1990 Argentina, Mexico, and Brazil all suffered from economic crises. Argentina and Brazil also experienced a break in democratic processes and periods of military dictatorship, terror regimes, and repression. The external debt in each country grew exponentially and there were high rates of unemployment and collective poverty. In Brazil in the 1960s, there was only one feature length film directed by a woman, *As testemunhas não condenam* [Testimonies Don't Condemn] by Zélia Costa.

The film industries were hurt by this situation and yet, paradoxically, it also meant the creation in all three countries of official protection of national films, threatened by the impact and power of the U.S. film industry. National institutes were developed such as the *Instituto Nacional de Cinematografía* in Argentina, *Embrafilme* in Brazil, and the *Instituto de Cine* in Mexico. Governments began to subsidize national filmic production, as well as enact laws to require showing national films. There was a desire to recapture the commercial success of the American films or to imitate the successful formulas used in Hollywood, in other words, more sex, and more violence (37).

The old guard in film began to die off, while the new filmmakers, including Arturo Ripstein, Jaime Humberto Hermosillo, and Felipe Cazals appeared on the scene in Mexico. In Brazil at the same time were Bruno Barretto, Walter Hugo Khoury, and Carlos Diegues, as well as the filmmakers associated with the *Cinema Novo*, most notably Glauber Rocha and Nelson Pereira Dos Santos. In Argentina there was the *Generación del 70*, led by Raúl de la Torre as well as figures such as Eliseo Subiela and Carlos Sorín. Argentina's representative to the *Cinema Novo* movement was Leopoldo Torres Nilsson, who owed a great deal of his early creative impulse to his wife, novelist Beatriz Guido (38–39). Many of these filmmakers would serve as mentors to the women filmmakers who would later emerge in all three countries in the 1980s and 1990s.

The creation of the Colectivo Cine-Mujer in the 1970s in Mexico was an important move in the direction of a specific path for Mexican women filmmakers. It was a group that explicitly had an activist agenda and was against oppression of any kind against women under capitalism. It attacked the dominant attitude that censured female pleasure; it did not accept the "expropriation of the female body by the law or the Church" (Millán "Género y representación" 45). With the inception of Cine-mujer there was also the rise of independent feature cinema. "The Colectivo, an essential chapter in the development of the documentary genre, saw itself as part of the greater movement of feminism in international cinema" (Blanco 447–48).

There was a desire to speak about women's experience, about taboo subjects such as abortion, sexual abuse, and rape as well as labor conditions and class issues. Sexuality was also a major theme. The women in Cine-mujer sought to have a distribution outside of the usual venues, opting for places such as "schools, factories and hospitals" (Millán 45). Their stories revolved around their personal experiences and in doing so, found their voice (45). Cine-mujer dissolved in the 1980s but the impact is undeniable (254). Almost a decade later women directors of feature films would emerge working primarily within the industry.

In Brazil, three woman filmmakers emerged in the first five years of the 1970s. Lenita Perroy premiered *Mestiça* [Mestiza] (1973) and *A Noiva da Noite* [The Bride of the Night] (1974), Vanja Orico directed *O Segredo da Rosa* [The Secret of the Rose] from 1973, and Tereza Trautman had her first feature film, *Os Homens que Eu Tive* [The Men I Had] (1973), a film that was censored due to its strong erotic content and as a result was not seen in the country until 1980 with the less suggestive title, *Os Homens e Eu* [The Men and I].

In Mexico, meanwhile, Marcela Fernández Violante was the first woman filmmaker to emerge from an academic program in film, the CUEC (Centro Universitario de Estudios Cinematográficos), part of Universidad Nacional Autónoma de México (UNAM). She was one of the first graduates of the program, one that she was a part of from 1964 to 1968. Her graduation film, a short about Frida Kahlo, won the Diosa de Plata award for experimental film in 1967. She also eventually became the director of CUEC (Trelles 47). Violante's first feature film was *De todos modos Juan te llamas* [In Any Event Your Name Is Juan], a film financed by UNAM, and as such on the margins of commercial film. It concerned the problems and conflicts of a macho general's family and the "Cristeros" movement.

In Cuba, only one woman produced a feature film from 1960 to 1989, Sara Gómez Yebra. Her film was called *De cierta manera* [In a Certain Way] (1974) and it deals directly with machismo. It is about a racially and socially mixed couple living on the fringes of Cuban society. Gómez did not see the completion of *De cierta manera*. Tomás Gutiérrez Alea and Julio García Espinosa finished the editing. She had left explicit instructions as to how she wanted it done.

It was still noteworthy that during this time women directors began to appear in countries other than Brazil, Argentina, and Mexico and that these directors for the most part had formal training in filmmaking. These women did not emerge from theater as their foremothers had done and their work was characterized by thematic similarities. Eva Landeck in Argentina tried to make a new kind of film, without famous actors, some that focused on atmosphere in a neorealist mode. Marcela Fernández Violante followed in the footsteps of her predecessor Matilde Landeta by working with very few resources, and dealing with the theme of the revolution (Millán 50).

From 1970 to 1985, perhaps the most well known filmmaker in Latin America was María Luisa Bemberg, with five feature films, followed by her fellow Argentine, Eva Landeck, with three films, as well as the Brazilians Ana Carolina, Tizuka Yamasaki, Susana Amaral, and Tereza Trautman. In Mexico there was Marcela Fernández Violante, with five productions, and Mará Elena Velasco.

The most important period in the development of women directors in Latin America was the 1980s. It was during that ten-year span that women directors began to gain prominence and international recognition for their work (see Appendix). In 1980, Japanese-Brazilian director Tizuka Yamasaki (b. 1949) won international critical acclaim for *Gajiin: Os Caminhos da liberdade* [Gajiin: The Paths of Freedom]. The film won the a Special Mention at the Cannes Film Festival, the Golden Kikito for Best Film and Best Screenplay at the Gramado Film Festival, and the Grand Coral for first prize at the Havana Film Festival. In 1983, fellow Brazilian Ana Carolina would win the Garamado Film Festival Award for Best Director for *Das tripas coração* [Heart and Guts] and, in 1985, yet another female director from Brazil would achieve international acclaim, Susana Amaral (b. 1932), who won the OCIC (International Catholic Organization for Cinema) award at the Berlin Film Festival with her movie *A hora da estrela* [The Hour of the Star], based on the story by the same name by Brazilian novelist Clarice Lispector.

Meanwhile, *Camila*, a film about early Argentine activist Camila O'Gorman, directed by María Luisa Bemberg (1922–1995) was nominated for an award in 1984 by the Cinematographic Academy of Arts and Sciences in Hollywood. Two years later, *La historia oficial* [The Official Story] (1985), a film written by Aida Bortnik and directed by her husband Luis Puenzo, received the Oscar for best Foreign Film. Fina Torres from Venezuela received the Cannes award for best film for a young director, the Golden Camera, for *Oriana* in 1985 and the Golden India for Best Screenplay and Best Film at the Cartagena Film Festival (51). Mexican director Maria Novaro also received praise at the end of the decade for her film *Lola*, recognized with the award for Best First Work at the Havana International Film Festival.

Videocassettes led to a greater dissemination of these directors' works in the 1980s. It was during this time that one can also note for the first time what may be considered a feminist aesthetic in the films, in which defiant, rebellious women were often the central characters, especially in the work of

Bemberg, Ana Carolina Teixeira Soares, and Tizuka Yamasaki. This is also the first time women are actually having a sustained filmic production.

Bemberg is without a doubt the most important figure that emerged at this time. She had been a part of the Teatro del Globo during the 1960s and in the 1970s worked often as a scriptwriter and on her own short films. Her first feature film was *Momentos* [Moments] from 1980, followed by *Señora de nadie* [Nobody's Wife] in 1982 and *Camila* in 1984, with *Miss Mary* in 1987. In August 1990, her last film, *Yo, la peor de todas* [I, The Worst of All], was screened. She founded her own production company GEA Cinematográfica. Her films show a clear feminist bent and all were well received both in her own country and internationally. Unfortunately, she died in 1995.

During this time, Brazil's Ana Carolina Teixeira Soares (b. 1943) made a trilogy: *Mar de Rosas* [Sea of Roses] in 1977; *Das tripas coração* [Sweat Blood] in 1982, and *Sonho de Valsa* [Dream Waltz] in 1987. Her films were known for their surrealist tendencies, and "anarquia maxima" [maximum anarchy], particularly *Sonho de Valsa* in which a woman evolves, gets married, and integrates into established society, then questions, rejects or attacks the most beloved notions of the upper and middle classes. The attacks leveled against society are apparent in all three films, but they become more difficult to understand in the final film.

Tizuka Yamasaka had studied with Nelson Pereira Dos Santos and Glauber Rocha before directing her first feature film, *Gaijin: Caminhos da Liberdade* [Gaijin: Paths of Freedom] in 1980. Gaijin has a strong feminist protagonist, a Japanese immigrant struggling in Brazil against prejudice. This film may be considered the first in a trilogy focused on the Brazilian woman in which there are also close ties to Brazilian history and national identity (Trelles 53). Her next film was *Parahyba, Mulher Macho* [Parahyba, Macho Woman], about the poet from the Northeast Anayde Beiriz, the lover of the lawyer João Dantas who assassinated João Pessoa, a contemporary of Getúlio Vargas in the 1930s (53). *Parahyba, Mulher Macho* told the story of a rebellious woman fighting against the dictates, attitudes, and conventions of society; she was a rebel in terms of fighting the dominant political class to defend her rights. In Tizuka's third film, *Patriamada* [Beloved Country] from 1988, the director explored a love triangle—a woman between two men. This takes places with a backdrop of the "abertura" in Brazilian politics after the end of the dictatorship in 1985, with mass demonstrations in Rio de Janeiro. It is a hybrid of documentary and fiction. The film was criticized for not balancing out these two sides very well.

In Mexico, in the late 1970s and 1980s, Violante continued to direct films, including *Cananea* in 1977, *Misterio* [Mystery] (1979), *El el país de los pies ligeros* [The Country of Light Feet] (1980) and, finally, *Nocturno amor que te vas* [Night Time Love You Leave] (1987). The 1980s also saw the emergence in Mexico of director María Elena Velasco, known as *La India María*. She was a popular film actress who later became a director with three films to her name: *El coyote emplumado* [The Feathered Coyote] (1983), *Ni Chana ni Juana* [Neither Chana nor Juana] (1984), and *Ni aquí ni de allá* [Neither Here nor There] (1987).

Joanne Hershfield and David Maciel show how a new generation of women directors emerged in Mexico in the 1980s and how women also took on a larger role in all aspects of filmmaking. As they state "[. . .] principally because of machismo and institutionalized sexism, women were excluded from other aspects of filmmaking, a situation that remained static until the 1970s. In the late 1970s and early 1980s women had become a visible and influential force within the film industry" (249–50).

The authors attribute this to three factors: (1) the changing roles of women within society with respect to the rise of feminism and the economic crisis that caused many women to enter the labor force and universities in the 1960s and 1970s; (2) the development of two film schools the Centro Universitário de Estudios Cinematográficos and the Centro de Capacitación Cinemtatográfica (CCC) that were evolving into strong programs, with a resurgence of interest on the part of students, many of whom were women, throughout the 1980s and 1990s; and (3) the ending of the unions within the film industry that had traditionally had male leadership and did not let women take part. "By design, their policies excluded women from participation" (250). One such rule was that which stipulated that a woman could not be an assistant director, a role critical to the development of professional directors.

In the 1980s, women directors also emerged in Peru, Venezuela, and Colombia. In Colombia, Camila Loboguerrero directed her first feature film in 1983, *Con su música a otra parte* [With Her Music to Another Part]. She later did *María Cano*, a biography about a Colombian labor leader from the 1920s. In Venezuela, Solveig Hoogesteijn (b. 1946) directed *El mar del tiempo perdido* [The Sea of Lost Time] (1981) and *Macu, la mujer del policía* [Macu, the Policeman's Wife] (1987). In Peru, Nora de Izcue (b. 1934), in 1982, directed a coproduction with Cuba, *El viento de Ayahuasca* [The Wind of Ayahuasca], a love story that deals with the magical religious beliefs of the Amazon region.

New Cuban women directors in the 1980s included Rebeca Chávez, Miriam Talavera, and Mayra Vilásis. Although women made up 55 percent of the technical and professional categories in Cuba in 1986, around the same time, there were no women at all in the more technically specialized positions of cinematographer, assistant cinematographer, or lighting technician at the national film studios (Zayas and Larguía 88, 91).

Due to the country's economic crisis, in Brazil in 1992–93 only four feature films were released. In 1994, ten films were released. Finally, from 1995 to the first half of 1998, the number rose substantially. Eighty-five films were released. While encouraging, it still does not reach the numbers that films in the 1970s did, when on average 80–100 films were released annually (Ramos 412). With the return came international recognition, including Walter Salles's *Central do Brasil* [Central Station] at the Berlin Film Festival, José Araújo's *O sertão das memórias* [The *Sertão* of Memories], and Oscar nominations for Fábio Barreto's *O quatrilho* [Foursome] and *O que é isso companheiro?* [What's This, Friend?], directed by Bruno Barreto. All of these films dealt specifically with Brazilian identity and history. In August 1998, *Cahiers du Cinéma* devoted an article to this theme, calling it a renaissance. A similar phenomenon occurred in Chile, in Argentina, in Colombia, and in Mexico (Ramos 104, 112).

In the 1990s, a new phase was characterized by the tendency to examine Brazilian reality and cinematography. Carla Camurati's (b. 1960) *Carlota Joaquina, Princesa do Brasil* [Carlota Joaquina, Brazilian Princess] was an epoch feature film but one that was a revisionist history of the common story known in Brazil about the Portuguese royalty. It was popular in large part because the audience was able to share in the private jokes about Brazilian identity. It was this film in 1995 that reawakened the interest of the Brazilian public and was seen in 40 film festivals and by 1.5 million spectators. The humor was often crass, popular in nature, but nonetheless did the trick in terms of getting the Brazilian public. In 1995, the comedies *Pequeno Dicionário Amoroso* [Little Dictionary of Love] by Sandra Werneck (b. 1951) had 400,000 spectators and *Carlota Joaquina* almost a million. Even more remarkable, in 1998, *O Noviço Rebelde* [The Rebellious Novice], directed by Tizuka Yamasaki, had almost 2 million spectators.

Meanwhile, in the 1990s in Mexico, Hershfield and Maciel note that the presence of women in every facet of film production distinguishes that country's cinema from "almost any other national cinema today" (251). "A record number of women directors have debuted with feature films within the last ten years [. . .]." Unique in the history of Mexico's cinema is the fact that over one-third of the directors of the generation of the 1990s are women, including María Novaro (b. 1951), Busi Cortés (b. 1950), Dana Rotberg (b. 1960), Sabina Berman (b. 1955), Guita Schyfter (b. 1947, Costa Rica), Maryse Sistach (b. 1952), and María Elena Velasco (b. 1940), all of whom have completed at least two feature films (251). At the same time, Matilde Landeta (1910–1999) and Marcela Fernández Violante (b. 1941) each made a narrative film and other women did shorts and documentaries. Still other women have had their scripts or novels produced, such as Laura Esquivel (b. 1950) with *Like Water for Chocolate*.

Hershfield and Maciel argue that the women directors who emerged in the 1980s and 1990s shared many characteristics, among them the fact that they were involved in many aspects of the film beyond directing, including screenwriting and editing; "collectively these women directors characterize their films as *cine de mujer* or "woman's cinema," which is to say that an overt feminist viewpoint has as much of a role in content as form; the women of this generation did their training in Mexico; the influence of documentary filmmaking is paramount, both in style and content. The techniques are evident; they are young; they have more control over all aspects of filmmaking, publicity and distribution" (255).

These similarities notwithstanding, there remain many differences in terms of approach, techniques, and individual style as well as narrative. "For example, Busi Cortés seeks to construct an intimate cinema with touches of magical realism within an innovative reading of family relationships. María Novaro defines her cinema as *cine de autor* that reflects her individual dreams and reality while addressing gender consciousness, Maryse Sistach attempts to combine a *cine de mujer* with a commercial film without losing emphasis on a solid narrative that incorporates a woman's perspective into the popular filmic discourse" (256).

According to Patricia Eren's Introduction to the section "Assessing Films Directed by Women" in the book she edited, *Issues in Feminist Film Criticism* (1990), there are certain questions that are fundamental points of departure when watching a film: (1) the position for female spectator—is it masochistic or compliant? (2) Is there an expression of women's desire and critique of male assumptions? Are women seen as objects of male desire? (3) Role of male spectator? (4) Are there any issues that might be threatening to male viewers?

and, finally, (5) How are gender, class, ethnic issues treated? (333–34). I will be examining some of these issues, and a sixth, the treatment of feminine sexuality, in three films.

Lucrecia Martel (Argentina, b. 1966): *La niña santa* [The Holy Girl] (2004)

Lucrecia Martel is one of the country's most acclaimed contemporary directors. She is the second internationally known female director to emerge from Argentina after María Luisa Bemberg, winning the 1999 Sundance Filmmakers Award for the script of her previous critical success, the film *La Ciénaga* [The Swamp]. The film's follow-up, *La niña santa*, was nominated for the Golden Palm award at Cannes. In the film she transmits this notion of fragmented body in both form and content. As the filmmaker has said, "Religion and medicine have the fragmented body in common. That's what interests me."

Martel came of age during the end of the dictatorship in the early 1980s and the country's subsequent return to democracy. The so-called "Dirty War" ended in 1983 after a seven-year period in which some 30,000 people "disappeared" and were presumably killed by the military government. After that, the country plunged into a series of economic catastrophes that characterized the late 1980s and 1990s, something previously mentioned in our discussion of Cecilia Rossetto in Chapter Two. In December 2001, when there were widespread protests throughout the country because the peso, no longer pegged to the dollar, fell to its true level, one-third of its previous value. Large segments of the middle class slid into poverty as the country tried to address its international debt. The causes of the country's decline were numerous: the rise of neoliberalism, foreign debt, and internal governmental corruption. The infrastructure came close to the brink of collapse. Streets, highways, public transportation, and all state-run facilities were in a state of decay. There was a profound sense of disillusionment that characterized the period from 2001 to 2004, leading to a massive immigration to other countries, primarily Europe and the United States.

The disillusionment, however, was at least in part a catalyst for some remarkable filmmaking. The Spanish government worked with the Argentine film industry on joint projects. *La niña santa* is just one example of this collaboration, and the film was also produced in association with Italy and the Netherlands.

Martel directed *La niña santa* and also co-wrote the script. It is not a film focused on dialogue, or for that matter even much narrative action. Instead,

Martel creates a visual (and auditory) work of art in almost a collage form. The storyline is about a devoutly religious girl Amalia (Maria Alché), who lives with her mother Helena (Mercedes Moran) and her uncle Freddy in a hotel that her family runs in the far north of Argentina. Amalia and her best friend Josefina go to Bible classes and are concerned with when or if they will ever receive their "calling" to serve God. At the same time, they spend a lot of time thinking and talking about sex. These two preoccupations of God and sex become fused when one day, in a crowd, a middle-aged man moves behind Amalia and presses his hard penis against her butt. It turns out that he is a doctor who is staying at the hotel where Amalia lives, and that he is in town for a medical conference of eye, ear, nose, and throat specialists. Amalia becomes obsessed with the doctor and is convinced that her calling is to "save" him from sin. She stalks him. She masturbates thinking of him, and then prays. She touches his hand in the elevator, stares at him in the pool, and follows him down the hallways of the hotel. At last she corners him in his room and tries to kiss him. He rebuffs her.

Amalia's mother also sexually desires the married doctor, and she is convinced that he feels the same way about her and that they are both just repressing their desires. And Josefina, Amalia's best friend, is having her own sexual encounters. Josefina has found a way to rationalize having sex by never doing it missionary style, nor talking during the act. The doctor's wife calls to tell him that she and the children have decided to join him, meaning to make his business into a family vacation. Amalia shares her secret with Josefina, and her friend later uses it to divert attention from her own sexual exploits when her parents catch her (she tells them that he is merely consoling her about the devastating news that her friend has been sexually molested). The film ends just when the doctor is about to be exposed for his act, and the audience is left in suspense as the final credits roll.

Martel is known for her use of symbolism and sound. It is clear that she is trying to convey a multisensorial experience for the viewer. The signs of decay are seen throughout the film. The hotel is run-down and crumbling. The chairs are rusty, the pool looks dirty, the rooms dark and seedy, and the personages, with the exception of Amalia's mother, all constantly look sweaty. In the scene in the beginning of the film when the doctors arrive for the conference, Amalia's uncle Freddy tells them that there have recently been "renovations." These appear to consist of a radio and a TV that does not work. Martel captures this ugliness with a yellowish-brown palette.

The fragmentation of body is transmitted visually through the use of certain shots in which it is cut either by clothing, furniture, lighting, scenery or the frame of the shot itself. Arms, heads, and legs are often removed from the shot completely and there is a focus on the mouth and ears, showing how Martel visually underscores the theme of the conference specialists in the way she frames each shot.

In terms of sound, the odd, mysterious, piercing sound of the Theremin playing on the street and later in the hotel is disconcerting and also reinforces the sense of strangeness and alienation that is a part of the theme. Obviously, the one element that would be most difficult to convey on film would be that related to the nose or olfactory sense but Martel does this masterfully by lingering on hotel workers as they spray for bugs.

Martel's treatment of the theme of adolescent sexuality is unusual for various reasons. First of all, her female protagonist, Amalia, is not an attractive girl. She is presented as an awkward child as opposed to a sexualized object. Sometimes she is backlit, and appears almost like an angel, while other times the camera sees her from below and she appears ugly, mean, and unkempt. There is no male gaze operative here, there is nothing titillating about the presentation of any of the scenes relating to her encounters with the doctor. While she is a child, she does not strike the viewer as a naive victim, she does not seem "innocent," something that would have been a filmic cliché. In this same way, the doctor is not demonized or presented as "guilty." More than anything he is seen as someone who is socially awkward and conflicted. Martel is very clearly moving away from any neat binary in showing the behavior of her personages. She does not sit in judgment. There is a lesbian subtext evident in the relationship between the two adolescent girls as they frolic in bed or in the hotel's pool. The playful touches, the steady gaze of the camera on their faces as they stare at each other, all point to this, and yet, again, there is nothing titillating about the presentation, their body parts are not focused on. The viewer is often unable to see the entire face, or in some cases to hear parts of conversations, and there are fragmented sounds and fleeting images. By showing us shading and darkness, by focusing on things that are only half seen, Martel underscores the ambiguity and the lack of ever having a clear sense of anything.

An additional theme in the film relates to the stories we tell ourselves to justify our own behavior when the motivations behind that behavior can be called into question. Martel seems to point to the fact that most people are engaged in forms of self-deception or revisionist history, reworking the narrative of their lives in order to see actions that were motivated by self-interest instead of motivated out of concern for others. When Josefina betrays her friend to hide her own sexual encounters from her parents, she tells herself that it is out of the desire to "protect" her friend. When Amalia stalks the doctor, she tells herself it out of the purity of her religious devotion instead of lust. So what is the "truth"? Martel's message is that it is impossible to ascertain. There is no neat binary. It is always just beyond our grasp—we are all capable of being both victims and victimizers, innocent and guilty, good and bad simultaneously.

María Novaro (Mexico, b. 1951): *Sin dejar huella* [Without a Trace] (2000)

Maria Novaro is the most important and successful woman director in Mexico. During the 1970s she was a part of Mexico's first feminist film group, the *Colectivo Cine-Mujer* [Women-Film Collective], an organization dedicated to telling women's stories on film. The group also sought to expand employment opportunities for women in the film industry. Novaro's formal cinematographic studies lasted from 1980 to 1985 at the University Center of Film Studies (CUEC) in Mexico City. Her most important feature films include *Lola* (1989), *Danzón* (1991), and *Jardín del Edén* [Garden of Eden] (1994). She is both director and scriptwriter for the majority of her feature films. *Danzón* received critical acclaim around the world, including at the Cannes Film Festival, where Novaro was nominated for her directing talents. Novaro's films have female protagonists and tend to involve a physical journey. The themes of motherhood, female friendship, and absent males are also constant throughout her work. The characters generally are from the working class; they are usually single mothers; and their primary solace comes from their relationships with other women. Men are frequently relegated to a marginal role or reduced to caricature. "A consistent feature of her work is her acknowledgment of the many complex sociological forces that influence women's lives, while simultaneously emphasizing the role free will and individual psychology has played in the unfolding of her protagonists' stories" (Sutherland). Novaro's film *Sin dejar huella* won the 2001 prize for Latin American film at the Sundance Film Festival.

In *Sin dejar huella*, Ana (Aitana Sánchez-Gijón) is a Mexican-born, Spanish-raised dealer of fake Mayan archeological relics. She crosses the border into Mexico from Arizona and is taken in for questioning by Mendizabel, an intimidating police officer determined to have sex with her. He releases her but she is destitute and she must make her way to the Yucatan. In a roadside cafeteria she meets Aurelia (Tiaré Scanda), a young mother who has run away from her drug dealer boyfriend Saúl after stealing his stash and selling the drugs to pay for her trip. Aurelia wants to work in Cancún instead of in the dangerous *maquiladoras* (foreign-owned factories) in Juárez, where women workers in the factories have been found tortured and raped in a series of unsolved murders. She has left her older son with her sister, giving him a plane ticket to Cancún and promising that she will be at the airport waiting for him with mariachis in a few months time. Ana and Aurelia make strange traveling companions. Ana appears wealthy, very white, and highly educated. Aurelia is the earth mother, baby at her breast, feisty and streetwise. Of course, fleeing an ominous red car forges a sisterhood between them. Both of the women are convinced that the occupants are after them. Ana, expecting it to be Mendizabel, while Aurelia is convinced it is Saúl. Through the course of the journey, a friendship gradually forms. One way that Novarro underscores this gradual transformation is through changes in their clothing and hairstyles. At the start of their journey Ana is in a pink dress and high heels, with her hair down, while Aurelia is dressed in jeans and tennis shoes, her hair pulled back tightly in a ponytail. At the end of the film they are dressed similarly, in jeans, and their hair is down. Although Ana leaves Aurelia, after stealing her money, Ana appears at the airport the day little Juan is to appear, though instead of mariachis, she has a traditional Mayan music ensemble.

The notion of border is at play literally and metaphorically throughout this story. The film is also unique for its inclusion of Mayan characters, language, and settings. When the women are on the road to Cancún inevitably there are very few other cars on the road, serving to emphasize their isolation. If there are any vehicles in sight, beyond the red car, they are filled with men, policemen, highway maintenance workers or truckers. Numerous semiotic cues are used throughout the film to signal the social class and personal characteristics of each woman. For Ana, it is the pink dress and the sunglasses. For Aurelia, it is her cigarette, tight jeans, and tied-up shirt.

Novaro closely corresponds the music to the various Mexican regions through which the two travel, beginning at the border with the *narcocorridos*. The lyrics (as well as the road signs, "Bump Ahead" and stores signs "The Friendship Store") are also used to underscore the particular situation of the women at a given moment.

In terms of Novaro's presentation of sexuality, it is not overt, but rather runs as an undercurrent in the homoerotic bond between the women. Both women are beautiful, in a conventional Hollywood sense, and the shots of them are sexualized, especially in the case of voluptuous Aurelia, whose breasts, waist, and buttocks are continually focused on. The women spend a lot of time wet, frolicking on the beach, or bathing in a watering hole. Towards the end of the film the two women have an argument that resonates more as a lover's quarrel and the camera moves from their faces to a painting in the restaurant that depicts two naked women, side by side. Aurelia looks at the painting and she ends the conversation abruptly. In the end, when Aurelia sees Ana at the airport, and Ana meets Juan, the happy little family walks off. No need for men. Novaro plays with this notion of expendable men one last time during the closing credits when Ana and Aurelia, with the baby and Juan, are having a idyllic day at the beach. There are cardboard cutouts of men that the women playfully pose with.

The film addresses different kinds of borders, linguistic, regional, gender-based, class-based. When Ana speaks in the language of the Maya indigenous people, there are no subtitles, placing the viewer most likely in the same state of non-comprehension as Aurelia.

One more point about sexuality must be made. The point of departure for Aurelia's journey is the city of Juárez. The phenomenon of the female homicides in Ciudad Juárez, called in Spanish the *feminicidios* [femicides], involves the violent death of hundreds of women. The bodies of over 400 young females have been found since 1993 and roughly the same number remain missing. The victims of these crimes were between 15 and 25 years of age. Many were students, and most were working at the maquiladoras or foreign-owned factories. There were signs of sexual violence, abuse, torture, or, in some cases, mutilation on most of them. Despite past and current unsolved murders, in August 2006 the Mexican federal government dropped its investigation. While it is an important issue, and one that deserves international attention, it is a strange element to be included in a film that is for the most part, a comedy. Returning to the distinctions made by Enrens and Foster with regard to feminist films, in terms of *Sin dejar huella*, the presentation of "rah rah" sisterhood and bad men seems dated and shallow, the gaze feels traditional, where the women are objectified. So while the content of the film may be connected to an overt feminist theme—the importance of female friendships—the form is not. It remains tied to the shoot-em-up brand of action films and a masculinist gaze. The theme of feminine frienship is also examined in *Antônia*, our final film by a women director.

Tata Amaral (Brazil, b. 1960): *Antônia* (2006)

Tata Amaral's film *Antônia* is about four friends who each, improbably, have a grandfather named Antônio. They are back-up singers for a rap group called *O Poder* [The Power], but dream of making it big without the boys. They call their group Antônia, in honor of their uncles. The film was a hit in Brazil and also became a television show of the same name, and starring the same four women. Amaral made the decision to allow TV Globo to make the film into a show in order to reach the sorts of poor communities that her films depicts, where there is often little disposable income that can be used to go to a movie theater, but almost everyone has a television set. Beyond that, she did not have money to finish the film. So the television series began in 2006, before the film came out. Almost 50 million people watched it (out of a total population of 180 million). It marked the first time four young black women who were positive role models appeared on Brazilian television. *Antônia* is the third film of Amaral's trilogy centered on women's lives that began with *O céu de estrelas* [Starry Sky] (1997), which was voted one of the three most important national films in the 1990s and won 18 awards. Her next film *Através da janela* [Through the Window] (2000) also won critical acclaim.

The four young black women are living in a favela outside of São Paulo and dreaming of becoming hip hop stars. Each of the four has a tragedy in her life. Preta (Negra Li), a single mother, leaves her husband because he is cheating on her. Lena (Cindy Mendes), when pregnant, is told by her boyfriend that she can only keep the baby if she leaves the rap group and agrees not see her family or friends. Barbarah (Leilah Moreno) has a brother who is attacked in the favela along with his gay lover. The lover is killed. Barbarah is imprisoned when she uses martial arts to attack a boy who attacked her brother, accidentally killing him with a blow to the head. Mayah (Jacqueline Simão) is thrown out of the group early on when Preta accuses her of flirting with her husband.

It was Amaral's decision to make a film that would show images of strong Afro-Brazilian young women and that would provide a different view of the favela than some of the shoot-em-up movies about favela drug culture and crime that have captured international attention, such as *Cidade de Deus* and *Orfeu*. She got the idea after doing a documentary on hip hop music in the favelas. When she worked in the favela of Santo André, Amaral realized that the inhabitants cared about their community and wanted to improve their neighborhoods. They were not all desperate to leave. This is an underlying theme of *Antônia*. Amaral is a white woman moved by the racist depiction of blacks. She intentionally used nonprofessionals, all rappers, and instead of putting words into their mouths via a script she presented them with scenarios and had them improvise; in other words, instead of the usual situation of actors molding themselves into characters, this worked in reverse, having the characters molded to fit the reality of the girls. This, by Foster's criteria, makes for a decidedly "feminist" film, one that changes the established paradigm for making films.

While this is a film about feminine friendship, a bit similar to *Without a Trace* in that almost all of the males are presented as cartoonishly bad, there is a marked difference. For while Novaro was often given to using a masculine gaze, one that objectified Ana and Aurelia's bodies, the most startling element about Amaral's film is that in spite of it being about four young women, at no time are the girls sexually objectified. In fact, sexuality has virtually no presence whatsoever in the film. While this is unusual in filmmaking in general, it is especially so with regard to Brazil, where the semiotic cues for the country have always been connected to mulata or Afro-Brazilian women and sexuality. The girls in *Antônia* are not conventionally beautiful by Hollywood standards. And there is never any homoerotic subtext between the girls in the story, as there is in both *Sin dejar huella* and *La niña santa*. That said, the fact that the catalyst that leads to Barbarah's imprisonment was the homophobic attack upon the singer's brother and his lover points to the literal danger into which that sexuality or the appearance of alignment with the feminine can place individuals.

The entire movie is based on the way that men, in particular men with exaggerated machismo, circumscribe the freedom of women and sexual minorities. Indeed, from the *Antônia* Web site, the tagline for the film is: "On the outskirts of São Paulo, four girls struggle against poverty, violence and male chauvanism to make their dream of living off rap music come true."[1] And yet Preta, clear to point out that she is not a feminist, raps, "I am a strong woman, I'm a proud warrior. I wasn't born to serve. Preta [is] loyal with active voice. Neither feminist nor pessimist, I'm satisfied." While Barbarah raps in a similar tone, "I'm Barbarah. Strong. Courageous, curious. Indian, African, European. Mixed blood. But don't confound! I'm not frivolous. I'll show my dagger."

While Amaral sought to make a movie about black women, those often excluded, in an affirmation of women's bonds and women's strength, it suffers from the same flaw as *Sin dejar huella* and feels clichéd. The women are too good, the men too bad. That said, the numerous filmic innovations Amaral used for *Antônia* point to a decidedly feminist aesthetic, one that defies the standard model of objectification of women's bodies or a glorification of heterosexuality.

While Martel, Novaro, and Amaral may all be said to present a feminist sexual aesthetic in terms of the three films discussed here, and in light of the parameters listed by David William Foster and Patricia Eren at the beginning of this side dish, perhaps the best example of a feminist sexual aesthetic in the last five years came from a young Brazilian director who happens to be male, Andrucha Waddington (b. 1970). This aesthetic was displayed in his film *Eu, Tu, Eles* (2000) with screenplay by Elena Soarez. The film was featured in the Cannes Film Festival in 2000 and was also an official selection for the Sundance Film Festival in 2001. It won the Grand Coral for best film at the Havana Film Festival in 2000.

The film centers on Darlene, who lives in a rural village in the northeast with her son. She accepts a marriage proposal from Osias, a much older man, in an effort to improve her precarious living situation. Darlene works each day in the field while Osias lies in a hammock. Darlene gives birth to a black baby, who looks very little like Osias but a lot like the black worker that exchanged glances with her over a well early on in the film. Cousin Zezinho comes to live with the unhappily married pair, and soon Darlene and the cousin are having an affair. Darlene gives birth to his child. Later, a handsome stranger, Ciro, begins to work alongside Darlene in the field, and he comes to stay with her and Osias and Zezinho. Soon they, too, are having relations and she becomes pregnant. Ciro wants to take her away from Osias' house, but she finds a way to have a room built onto the house just for him.

The reason that the film may be considered feminist has to do with the presentation of Darlene's lust. It is not sensationalized, nor titillating, such as in the gaze used by Novaro to frame Ana and Aurelia in *Sin dejar huella*. There is no religiously connected anguish associated with it, as in *La niña santa*. Darlene is not attractive in any sort of conventional Hollywood way. The men, with the exception of Osias, are not presented as the almost cartoonish brutes in *Antônia* or *Sin dejar huella*. Darlene's sexual relations with all three men are presented as though they were the most normal occurrence in the world, something predicated on logic. Osias owns the house; Zezinho occupies himself with the household chores and cooking, while Ciro is able to use the money he makes in the field to contribute to the household. When Zezinho tells Osias that Darlene is pregnant with Ciro's child, and that the young boarder wants her to run away with him, he appeals to Osias logic, "What will happen to us if the two of them leave? We will be left here alone." Screenwriter Soarez, and Waddington, show us at the end that, in fact, the liberal or progressive circumstances notwithstanding, Darlene is at the mercy of Osias. The movie ends with the homeowner taking the three children to be registered in town as his own. Darlene is trapped. Leaving now would mean leaving them behind, though admittedly she never showed much of a desire to leave to begin with, but rather, only to incorporate Ciro into their unusual household.

The early shots of the film show Darlene always alone, tiny on the screen with vast empty shots of the rural northeast behind her, no other figures in view at all. As the film progresses it becomes gradually populated with other figures. The light changes, she is surrounded by others and, in some cases, joy is reflected on her face and happiness seen in the unconventional family.

What this film demonstrates is a similar progression to that found in the last side dish on feminist journals and it is one that also correlates to Martel's film, *La niña santa*, which is to say, binaries are unsettled, denaturalized. This corresponds with one of Foster's notions that a feminist film is one that will subvert our expectations. There is a wider spectrum of representation of gender and sexuality, one that includes homoerotic intimacy as part of the fan of many possible conjugations for feminine sexuality, both for women and men. This new paradigm allows for women characters who do not fit a Hollywood standard of beauty, and includes men who identify with a feminine sensibility as part of the panorama for understanding "normal." It is an aesthetic that often defies the binary trap of either/or, while demonstrating, as in the case of *Antônia*, the consequences of not adhering to compulsory heterosexuality. And yet, within the language and the logic of these films, it is society that is at fault for requiring such behavior, not the characters in the film. In other words, if these films have a "technology" at work in terms of sexuality, to use De Lauretis's term later echoed by Zavarzadeh, the ideological subtext is one that denaturalizes standard paradigms, makes them appear to be at best off-kilter, such as Martel's Catholicism, and at worst life-threatening, as seen in the case of the thug who beats up Barbarah's brother and kills his lover.

To illustrate this expanded range of representations of sexuality, I end this side dish where I began, with food and sex. What is key in *Eu, Tu, Eles*, is that Zezinho shows his affection for Darlene by lovingly preparing her lunch, which he takes to her each day while she toils away in the fields. When Ciro begins to work alongside her, Osias instructs Zezinho to take Ciro his lunch as well, and Zezinho begrudgingly agrees. One bright blue day, Zezinho rides his bicycle to the fields with their lunches and is unable to find them. He wanders through the sugar fields, peering between the canes, only to finally catch a glimpse of the two making love. This feminist film is about tolerance, and Waddington, much like Martel, is a filmmaker who is focused on texture over dialogue, subtleties over grand gestures, poetic filmic composition instead of quick editing, and a dizzying rhythm. In short, the sexuality in *Eu, Tu, Eles*, much like *La niña santa*, is one that is not brisk as a boil, but rather a slow simmer.

5

❦

CLASS

Once you allow the students to laugh, it's all over.
—Stephan Greenblatt, "Me, Myself and I"

The cocktail of sexuality, gender, and academia over the last 30 years in Latin America and in the United States has been volatile and potent. More Molotov than Martini. That said, it has not been without humor.

In 1995, the Chilean parliament banned the use of the word "gender" in that governmental body (24). According to Kemy Oyarzún, the politicians were afraid that the concept of gender would act as a front to "smuggle" into Chile "aberrations such as the recognition of homosexual couples as families and the legalization of abortion" (24). One of the politicians at the forefront of the deliberations sent an open letter to the Women's Right's minister at the time, Josefina Bilbao, urging her to be "a faithful representative of the normal people of this country" (ibid. 24). Clearly, only the mentally ill could disagree with him. This absurd debate was going on at the same time the University of Chile was inaugurating its postgraduate degree program in Gender and Cultural Studies, which Oyarzún would go on to direct. Not surprisingly, the decision to have such a program was fraught with controversy, as Nelly Richard would later document in her book *Cultural Residues*.

In the United States, two years later in 1997, an academic conference on sexuality at the State University of New York New Paltz campus created an uproar when one of the university's trustees wrote an essay for the *Chronicle of Higher Education* entitled, "Revolting Behavior: The Irresponsible Exercise of Academic Freedom." The conference, she contended, was merely a "thinly veiled recruitment of students and other attendees into a sadomasochistic network named the Lesbian Sexual Mafia." She mentioned that the conference included: "proselytization for lesbian anal and public sex, as well as for bisexuality, female masturbation, and sadomasochism; [. . .] the demonstration and aggressive marketing of sex toys for women; the free distribution or sale of pornography and a 'how to' lesbian sex manual and a pervasive bias against mainstream heterosexual practices 'vanilla sex'" (De Russy 26).

Soon both the *New York Times* and the oldest and most respected news program in the United States, *60 Minutes*, joined the fray. The *New York Times* published a lengthy article in the Education section: "Furor Over Sex Conference Stirs SUNY's Quiet New Paltz Campus" while *60 Minutes* carried a segment called "Sexuality 101," about gay and lesbian studies. The segment began with senior journalist Mike Wallace providing a parental warning, "Some of what you're about to see, indeed, some of what is being taught on college campuses today, is for mature audiences only."

What is clear from these examples is that the academic study of gender and sexuality provokes great emotions. It is perhaps for that very reason that the topics are critically important to study. As my college women's studies professor, historian Mary Rothschild, used to say, "Your resistance is a measure of my oppression." Clearly, if the issue did not matter, everyone would be indifferent to it. As George Chauncey, one of the professors interviewed for the *60 Minutes* piece, later argued in the *Chronicle of Higher Education*:

> [T]he furor over college-level courses that teach the critical study of sexuality might seem surprising. There is little reason to think that a 20-year-old will be traumatized by references in the classroom to sex when the president's alleged sex acts are graphically described in the nightly news. Indeed our culture is so saturated with erotic images and talk about sexuality—in the movies, in advertising, on talk shows and on network news—that one might expect more people to recognize the need for serious study of the representation of sexuality and its place in our culture.

In both CBS and the *New York Times*, confusion reigned. They conflated sex education classes with gay history and gay literature classes. They confused academic conferences with required courses, and safe sex lectures by students with scholarly lectures presented by professors.

But I can see you shaking your head, thinking, "But, come on, this was a decade ago! Surely things are different now!" Think again. The issues of sex, gender, and sexuality in education continue to be deeply divisive at all levels in both Latin America and in the United States.

In an essay entitled "Me Myself and I" from the *New York Review of Books*, Stephan Greenblatt explains that when he tried to bring Thomas Laqueur, a professor at UC Berkeley and the author of *Solitary Sex: A Cultural History of Masturbation*, discussed in Chapter One, to give a lecture for his undergraduate students at Harvard enrolled in a course entitled History and Literature, there was "an outbreak of jitters":

> Panic set in not among the students [. . .] but among the core of instructors who lead the seminars and conduct the tutorials. Though sophisticated and highly trained, when they were faced with the prospect of discussing the history of masturbation with the students, many of them blanched. Coprophagia wouldn't have fazed them at all, sodomy wouldn't have slowed them down, incest would have actively interested them—but masturbation? Please, anything but that.

Greenblatt calls a meeting to discuss what he termed the "Great Masturbation Crisis" and goes on to recount what happened:

> The first thing that I noticed was that everyone had developed overnight an intense sensitivity to double-entendres, as if language itself had become feverish. "When is Laqueur coming?" (chuckles). "His visit raises a number of issues" (giggles). "What do we hope will emerge from this discussion?" (snorts). "I am sorry if his visit rubs some people the wrong way" (loud guffaws). Perhaps in response to this burst of silliness, an experienced and ordinarily quite sensible instructor got up and made an urgent speech. "I have taught sexually charged subjects before," she said gravely, "and there is one thing that I believe is absolutely crucial: there must be no humor at all. Once you allow the students to laugh, it is all over."

And it isn't just the higher education people who have the jitters.

In 2005, The Public Broadcasting Station, known for its educational programming, got into trouble when in the children's program "Postcards from Buster" the world-traveling animated bunny paid a visit to a friend who had two moms. The whole idea behind PBS's educational programming is to promote diversity, so this should have been seen as a perfect example of inclusiveness. But President Bush's Secretary of Education, Margaret Spellings, denounced PBS for spending public funds to create this segment of its children's show (De Moraes 7). Diversity is fine, but only within reason, or to return to the Chilean politician's words, only within "normal." PBS was forced to pull the show.[1] Buster got busted. Meanwhile, in Brazil, in an effort to combat the number of homophobic crimes committed in that country, the federal government formed an alliance with Lesbian Gay Bisexual and Transgendered Non-Governmental Organizations nationwide to support the program, "Brasil sem Homofobia" [Brazil Without Homophobia], launched in 2004. The initiative entailed training activists and developing materials to be incorporated into school curricula throughout the country in order to change perception regarding same sex sexual practices. While the public support was laudable, there was never any funding committed to implementing the ideals of the program.

In this side dish I seek to illuminate one final area with regard to Latin American women's cultural production, and that is the place of academic feminism, of which sexuality is only one dimension, though perhaps the one most emotionally charged. This final chapter is a companion to Chapter Three, "Issues," in that once again I seek to address the topic of women intellectuals in the practice of everyday life.

The establishment of women's studies programs in the United States in the 1970s, the hallmark of legitimacy, was never a particularly easy sell. Even in 1986 when I finished my undergraduate degree in women's studies, people who learned of my major often confused it with some sort of home economics program (obviously I went to college to get my "Mrs." degree, I was told with a wink). One day I realized that I had enough credits to get my BA degree in either Spanish or women's studies, but I was unable to afford the additional year of coursework required to finish with both. I decided to seek out advice from an academic advisor.

An imposing man in his late sixties, he stared at me without blinking from the other side of an enormous desk as I explained my situation. I asked which of the two majors he thought would be more beneficial for my future. He didn't hesitate. "Both of them are useless." He then paused, deep in thought; "but I suppose Spanish is slightly *less* useless." Not exactly a ringing endorsement.

I seek to point out some general but significant differences with regard to the evolution of women's studies and gender studies programs in Latin America, arguing that while the original inspiration to create women's studies programs may have come from the United States, the programs themselves have developed in ways radically different from their U.S. counterparts, and for that matter, from each other. The tremendous heterogeneity of Latin America cannot be glossed over or dismissed. My hope is that this chapter will whet the readers' appetite with regard to the array of materials available on the topic and invite future study.

The importance of knowing that such programs even exist is that this is one way to address the uncomfortable north/south divide that is mirrored in the classroom in which mostly Anglo North American scholars are the analyzers, while anyone south of the U.S./Mexican border (or within a minority or ethnic groups within our own borders) becomes an analyzee.

It is important to underscore that a similar binary exists within the countries of Latin America themselves, but it is framed according to a rural-urban divide, where the city slickers analyze the rural poor. As Claudia de Lima Costa notes, "In an edifying discussion on feminism, experience, and representation, Chilean cultural critic Nelly Richard (b. 1996) points out that, in the global division of labor, the traffic in theory to and from metropolitan centers and peripheries remains tied to an unequal exchange; while the academic center theorizes, the periphery is expected to supply it with case studies. In other words, it is reduced to the practice side of theory or, in another perverse binary opposition, to the concrete body as opposed to the abstract mind of metropolitan feminism" (Costa 740). In many countries, this periphery is not exclusively in the rural areas but rather also exists in the literal periphery of large metropolitan centers, where internal migration of rural poor to the cities has led to rings of poverty or squatter settlements.[2]

Such divides, north-south, rural-urban, and center-periphery within cities, do not acknowledge or allow into the fold the fact that there are women (and some men) writing and researching gender issues in these countries and teaching in gender studies and women's studies programs on both sides of the divide. For whatever reason, those individuals producing knowledge in these countries tend to be all but ignored when, usually with the best of intentions, scholars in developed countries set about to examine cultural production. It is essential, in order to round out the representation of Latin American women, to see them not as merely producers of artifacts that the scholar in the United States will greedily gobble up, but also as producers and consumers of intellectual knowledge in the practice of everyday life in their respective countries.

Academic Feminism in the United States and Latin America: Origins, Definitions, and Differences

In the United States, women's studies programs began in the late 1960s and continued to grow with the women's movement of the 1970s. Programs were modeled on the American studies and ethnic studies (such as Afro-American studies) as well as Chicano studies programs, all of which were the result of the sustained activism of the 1960s in the Civil Rights movement. The first women's studies program in the United States was established on May 21, 1970, at San Diego State College (now San Diego State University). Currently, there are 395 such programs in the United States and some 700 women's studies programs around the world.

At many institutions in the country, women's studies morphed into gender studies, essentially allowing men into the fold, a field that studies how femininity and masculinity are configured. The focus remained similar to women's studies in that it examined both cultural representations of gender and people's lived experience and also was meant to bridge feminist theory with activism. In the last ten years, men's studies has also emerged, analyzing how men have also been constrained by patriarchy. Women's studies, men's studies, and gender studies have sought to underscore issues of class, race, and location. Gender studies became connected to lesbian, gay, bisexual, and trans-gender studies that in some cases all of these disciplines were housed under the rubric of cultural studies.

Academic institutions, never known for their rapid adjustments to a given trend, accepted (at best warily, though sometimes with outright hostility) these changes, and configured departments and programs accordingly. Women's studies and gender studies programs in the United States have been particularly successful in the humanities, specifically in disciplines such as history, linguistics, literary theory, popular culture, film theory, art history, theater studies, and musicology. Theoretically speaking, there are three phases that have developed chronologically over the last 40 years and in some cases overlapped within women's studies: (1) theories of equality; (2) of difference, and (3) of deconstruction (Buikema 3).

As Derrida reminds us, weakening one hegemony can also mean reinstitution another, which is one reason that women's studies and gender studies have had a rocky history (Derrida qtd. in Richard *Cultural Residues* 84). The university machine is the dividing line between legitimate (authorized) and illegitimate knowledge. So how can one be simultaneously inside and outside? The only solution, according to Nelly Richard, is to remain critically vigilant so that one does not become co-opted into the system.

A second problem discussed by Richard, one that she mentions with regard to the establishment of the gender studies program at the University of Chile, but that is also applicable to programs throughout Latin America and the United States, is that academic authority demands that its subjects maintain a solid and sure (virile) discourse concerning the unique and final truth of meaning (88). This is clearly something at odds with contemporary theory that refuses to mandate a single voice of knowing, the "Master" narrative.

Both in Latin America and in the United States, women's studies may be seen as an attempt to bridge the gap between knowledge and politics, theory and practice. That said, the pairing has been far from idyllic. In addition to the problem mentioned by Richard above, academia is by no means an environment free of sexism, classism, homophobia, and racism. As Richard points out, women find themselves in "the paradox of being both caught inside the symbolic code and deeply opposed to it. The point is that, willingly or not, we are complicitous with that which we are trying to deconstruct" (*Cultural Residues* 185). The role of the academic activist then becomes one to question the artifices of dominant representation and thus provide alternative readings.

While the Latin American women's studies and gender studies programs started in the early 1980s were in large part inspired by the programs that emerged in the United States and Europe, they developed very differently. The programs, the obstacles women faced, and the socio-historical context in which these programs emerged, were radically diverse. Among the numerous differences between the Latin American programs that emerged in the 1980s and the United States programs we find the following:

1. The catalyst for most programs was the United Nations Decade for Women, 1975 to 1985, and they began, funded by Nongovernmental organizations such as the Agency for International Development, the World Bank, and the CEPAL, all seeking to find a means to combat poverty in the region. The programs dealt primarily with education, reproduction, and labor and sought to produce field studies that would help transform laws and public policy.

2. The programs needed to address the large indigenous populations in countries such as Guatemala, Peru, and Ecuador, populations that are often rural, isolated, and in many cases non-Spanish speaking.

3. They needed to address the challenges of internal migration to big cities or the seasonal migration of men out of the country, leaving women as temporary heads-of-household.

4. In some of the countries where programs emerged, such as Guatemala, Colombia, and Peru, this period was characterized by violence and conflicts that displaced significant numbers of the population. These conflicts have also affected the neighboring countries that have received these communities. Thus, the programs needed to address how the wars and violence affect women economically, psychologically, and socially as well as how they affect gender relations.

5. In the Southern Cone, the period of authoritarianism from the 1960s (in the case of Brazil), 1970s and 1980s (Argentina, Chile, Uruguay) also left its indelible mark, particular in each case, on the development of programs and women's activism. In some cases, women's activism in these countries was directly tied to exalting their feminine role as moral gatekeepers for the nation and their struggle as women took the backseat to the struggles against the dictatorships.

6. Programs faced oppositions as the result of ingrained cultural notions of the cult of virility and machismo, for men, and Marianismo, for women, tied to Catholicism, that were/are very much a part of the social fabric of the region (though the degree varies significantly from country to country) (Norma Fuller, Universidad Pontificia del Perú).

While in the United States, programs tended to place an emphasis on the humanities, on the development of theoretical models to understand the roots of gender inequity, in Latin America—due in large part to some of the reasons listed above—programs were much more focused on engaging in fieldwork and analysis of women's situations in order to affect changes in public policy. That said, as Fuller points out, it couldn't be ignored that the agendas for women's studies programs were often created according to national or funding agency priorities. This connection framed both the course of research for the centers and the possibility of moving toward a greater theoretical analysis of the information gathered. In other words, in many programs the injustices that women faced were documented. But moving to try to understand the roots of those injustices, for the lack of practical application to specific problems, was not as easy for funding agencies to swallow.

What is clear from looking at this list is that whatever obstacles might have presented themselves in the United States for the establishment and development of women's and gender studies programs, they were small in comparison to what Latin American women endured. The endless theoretical debates common in programs to the North were not practical given the situation of Latin American women, one that often required direct action to address immediate concerns. Their issues were practical, rooted in the urgent survival needs of the here and now. Endless theoretical debates would only lead to paralysis in terms of taking direct action.

Clear also is the fact that women's studies and later gender studies programs developed in each country in ways that were, in general, more scientifically oriented, based on fieldwork, and that they often included outreach programs designed to help women escape poverty.

Women's Studies and Gender Studies Programs and Networks

It is all too often overlooked in the United States, or simply unknown, that by the time the first institution for higher education, Harvard University, was founded in this country in 1636, there were already six universities in Latin America: University of Santo Domingo in what is today the Dominican Republic (1538), Universidad Mayor de San Marcos (1551) in Lima, what is today Peru, Universidad Nacional, Universidad Michoacana (both from 1551), and Universidad de Puebla (1578), all in Mexico, and Universidad de Córdoba in Argentina (1578) (Didriksson 7). History notwithstanding, the fact remains that internationally, the Latin American universities do not fare well when compared with their northern counterparts.[3]

Today the region's largest public universities are: Universidad de Buenos Aires in Argentina, La Universidad Autónoma de México, and Universidad Nacional de Córdoba (Argentina). These are followed by Universidad de Panamá, Universidad de San Carlos in Guatemala, Universidad de la República in Uruguay, and Universidad Central de Venezuela. All of these universities have gender studies or women's studies programs.

In 2002, in an effort to work together and share resources, following an initiative from UNAM and Universidad Central de Venezuela (UCV) and under the auspices of UNESCO's International Institute for Higher Education in Latin America and the Caribbean (IESALC-UNESCO), a network was formed called the *Red de Macrouniversidades de América Latina y el Caribe* [Network of Macrouniversities of Latin America and the Caribbean]. The idea was that the institutions would work together to find a solution to some of the greatest problems faced on the continent and improve the quality of higher education throughout the region (3).

The universities included in the network were chosen based on five factors: (1) size (generally between 40,000 to 60,000 students, in the case of UNAM and UBA (Universidad de Buenos Aires) much more, and in the case of a few less, 30,000 to 40,000); (2) for the variety of disciplines in each, covering a wide body of knowledge and a complex organizational structure, including not just science and technology but also social sciences and the humanities and the arts; (3) for their research profiles, particularly scientific, the weight and quality of the research done as well as the greatest number of graduate students and researchers; (4) for having the largest public financing in their respective countries and, finally, (5) for serving as the guardians of cultural patrimony (ibid. 10–12). In other words, these were the big cheeses.

The Macrouniversities of Latin America and the Caribbean comprised 10 percent of the 9,400,000 students in higher education in Latin America in 2000.[4] Twenty-four of these 27 principal institutions have women's studies or gender studies programs; the majority of programs are housed in the Social Sciences. This speaks to the level of legitimacy that the discipline has garnered in the region.

In examining programs at some of these institutions it becomes clear that in most cases they are training experts for roles in development, public health, and public policy, areas in which there remains a critical need in Latin America. Research involves diagnosing the situation that women experience with the ultimate goal of designing public policy that would help less favored sectors on the population with regard to education, health, reproductive planning, domestic violence and work as well as finding other survival strategies. Many studies have analyzed the penetration of these rural communities into the urban centers as well as the division of labor within families. In the case of Mexico and Central America, studies have also addressed the effect on women of the seasonal migrations of men to the United States for work. Women not only become heads of the family but also active in the local governments and work. Globalization has also had a profound effect on women in developing countries, a matter discussed in the journals examined in Chapter Three.

The earliest institutions to have women's studies programs in Latin America included the Universidad Nacional de Costa Rica, which founded the

Centro de Estudios de Mujer [Women's Studies Center] in 1976 in the Facultad
de Humanidades; the program at the Colegio de México, Programa Interdisciplinario de Estudios de la Mujer [Interdisciplinary Program of Women's
Studies] (now called Gender Studies) (PIEG), founded in 1983; and the Instituto Tecnológico de Santo Domingo in the Dominican Republic, which
founded the Centro de Estudios de Género [Center for Gender Studies] in 1987
as part of the Facultad de Ciencias Sociales. The Universidade de São Paulo
began its own program in 1985, the Núcleo de Estudos da Mulher e Relações
Sócias de Gênero [Center for Women's Studies and Social Relations of Gender].
Meanwhile, in Brazil, UNICAMP started PAGU, in 1993, Núcleo de Estudos de
Gênero (Center for Gender Studies) and, as we saw in Chapter Three, produces the journal *Cadernos Pagu*.

Attempts to build networks connected to women's studies began when
the Latin American Network of Women's Studies University Programs met in
November 1989 at the University of Puerto Rico, Cayey. The objective was to
strengthen the creation and development of women's studies programs in
universities of Latin America and the Caribbean, to contribute to a perma-
nent and scientific exchange among the existing programs, and to optimize
the academic level of the different women's studies programs in Latin America
through the exchange of scholars. Finally, the goal was also to support the
teaching and research initiatives that contribute to bringing a Latin American
perspective to women's studies programs in the region. In 1991, it was comprised the following programs: Universidad de Buenos Aires; Women's Studies Project at the Universidad de Puerto Rico, Cayey; Women and Gender
Studies Program at Universidad of Los Andes, in Colombia; Interdisciplinary
Women's Studies Program at the Colegio de Mexico; Women' Studies Institute
of the Technological Institute of Santo Domingo, in the Dominican Republic,
and the Interdisciplinary Program for Gender Studies at the Universidad of
Costa Rica (Taule 450–51). Unfortunately, this network was not maintained.

That said, other networks have emerged recently to establish links between
programs. In April 2006, seven programs in Central America banded together
to form the "Red Regional de Institutos y Centros de Investigación y Estudios
de las Mujeres, Género, y/o Feministas de las Universidades Publicas"
[Regional Network of Institutes and Centers of Investigation and Women's,
Gender and/or Feminist Studies in the Public Universities].[5] According
to Fidelina Martinez Castro, Director of Gender Studies at the Universidad de El
Salvador, the organization was formed because throughout Central America

there are problems that affect the physical, psychological, economic, and social well-being of women, as a result of patriarchal culture that has been learned through socialization. The organization agreed that public universities had the ethical and constitutional imperative to join forces to promote equality and environmental concerns. Members wrote a manifesto that demanded that public universities acknowledge their responsibility and their leadership role and meet the challenge to strengthen existing programs in women's studies and gender studies and help them address the issues of globalization, and the wide sectors of the population that continue to live in poverty and violence in the region.

One month later, in May 2006, another regional network was fortified by way of the Seminario Internacional "Equidad de Género en las Reformas Educativas de América Latina" [Gender Equity in Latin American Educational Reforms] meeting held in Santiago, on May 17 and 18. This was sponsored by universities in Argentina, Columbia, and Peru and had the financial backing of the Ford Foundation's Program for Educational Reform in Latin America and was cosponsored by UNESCO and CEPAL.

While there is an ever-growing list of graduate programs in Latin America for gender studies, doctoral programs are few, a fact that is due in large part because doctoral programs are not nearly as present in any field.[6] That said, there are programs and centers in every Latin American country, and in most capitals where both graduate and undergraduate coursework is possible. Lists of women's organizations, both formal state-funded and private research centers, may be found easily on the Internet on lists such as the "Federación Latinoamericana de Mujeres Rurales"[7] [Latin American Federation of Rural Women], and the site, "Mujeres y Estudios de Género" [Women and Gender Studies], from the Latin American Information Network Center run by the University of Texas.[8]

The decision of many programs to maintain their designation as "women's" studies was strategic. The Web page for Centro de Estudios de la Mujer [Center for Women's Studies] (CEM) at the Universidad Central de Venezuela explains why they elected to keep "mujer" [women] instead of making the change to "gender" or for that matter to "feminist" studies, stating that while some Spanish academics have opted to use the term "feminist" studies to avoid using what they felt was a diluted term, "gender" studies—one that also was used by many in an effort to appear more acceptable to their institutions and, especially, to the agencies on which they depend for funding. In Latin America women have to be very careful of misunderstandings that can arise from the use of the word "feminism," miscommunications that can affect any sort of program, academic or not. It is for this reason that the "women's" studies programs and centers proliferate in Latin America. "We avoid the misunderstanding from the 'subversive' term while specifying that we are working specifically with a problematic of women, which is to say the discrimination of one half of the population of the world and sexual discrimination" (my translation from CEM Web site at the Universidad Central de Venezuela).

Returning to Chile, the Chilean senate was suspicious of the word "gender," specifically of its origins in international feminism, causing ample political majorities to mistrust the cultural model from the north that, according to them, did nothing but confirm the "penetration into the social framework of lifestyles that clash with our culture and all that has been considered positively traditional" (Richard *Cultural Residues* 135).

Jean Franco was the inaugural speaker for the opening of the new gender studies program at the University of Chile. She gave a presentation on transvestite parody, one that showed how gender is the site of multiple entrances and exits, avoiding closure, avoiding the definitive identity (*Cultural Residues* 141). It is safe to assume that the politicians were not amused.

It must be understood that gender studies in Chile is a field that grew out of the struggles against the dictatorship. During the 1990s, government policies on higher education did not clearly express the need to establish women's or gender studies programs, and public officials were silent on the question of providing greater access for women to the university (Oyarzún 24). In spite of the lack of support during the 1990s when most programs were established, the majority of Chilean women were not in agreement with the government. At the time, one-fourth of the Chilean households were headed by women, one in three pregnancies ended in abortion, and botched abortions were responsible for a third of maternal deaths (ibid. 24). At the same time, studies showed that the majority of Chilean women believed in a woman's right to work, in the right to have sex before marriage, and in the use of contraception, inside or outside of marriage (ibid. 24). There was a great need for women's studies programs, and yet women were reluctant to be perceived as troublemakers for demanding such programs during a time in which there was an overzealous attempt in the country to reach a consensus on everything, ignoring the very real and legitimate differences among different sectors of the population.

In Santiago, the first women's studies center was established in 1984 as an independent, nonprofit organization called CEM or the "Centro de Estudios de la Mujer." It was focused on conducting research, training, and consulting programs, and it concentrated on the fields of labor and employment, citizenship and political participation and public policy planning.[9] Three areas were given priority at the center: work, political participation, and public policy. In terms of the founding of women's studies programs in public education in Chile, because the country was held up as the model of neoliberalism, this produced an odd contradiction. Neoliberalism,

> on the one hand, constitutes one of the principal forces that eliminate traditions on all sides, as a consequence of the driving market forces and of an aggressive individualism. On the other hand, its legitimacy and its links with conservatism base themselves on the persistence of tradition in the areas of the nation, religion, the sexes, and the family . . . It is no surprise that the doctrines of the new right mix the liberal freedoms with authoritarianism—even fundamentalism—in an unstable and uncomfortable way. (Anthony Giddens qtd. in Richard *Cultural Residues* 107)

In spite of the conservative groups within the country that sought to curtail anything that might be a threat to the status quo, programs were established in the early 1990s. The University of Chile currently has two gender studies centers, one in philosophy and the other in social sciences. As Oyarzún points out, similar to the United States, "Professors had to confront patriarchal suspicions and resistance from within academia itself" (25). The program on Gender and Culture in Latin America was founded in 1990. In 1999 it changed from a program (PGCAL) to a Center (CEGECAL) and in 1995 the graduate program was inaugurated.

According to Oyarzún, the most important factor to consider in terms of gender studies and women's studies programs in Chile was that they " . . . must rebuild the ties with civil society that were shredded during the dictatorship years. In particular, they need to coordinate their work with the networks of women's and gay rights organizations. Otherwise gender studies run the risk of becoming academic ghettos" (26). Gender studies cannot be isolated but instead must be integrated into the broader democratic changes in the university and the country.

Brazilian women's and gender studies programs, on the other hand, have a long and stable history and are most likely the largest such scholarly communities in Latin America today. They encompass not only the centers at universities, but also several research centers such as the Carlos Chagas Foundation, one that began to conduct research on women beginning in 1980.[10]

Albertina Costa has argued that there were many factors that had an impact on the development of women's studies in Brazil, including migration to the cities, urbanization, and the expansion of mass media, among others. In Brazil, as in other Latin American countries, the areas that have been historically privileged have been related to rural women, "Women's studies initially marked tendency toward social intervention meant that a clear separation emerged between concerns which emphasized public policy and development and those tending toward reflection and study" (Costa 39–40).

In the late 1980s, when many women who had been living in exile during the dictatorship returned to Brazil, they brought with them some of the theoretical concerns that were paramount at the time including sexuality and the body. As a result, Brazilian women's studies programs began to examine areas beyond development and economics, including literature, history and politics.

In Brazil, gender as an analytical category came to replace the category "woman." According to Ana Alicia Costa and Cecilia Sardenberg, the areas of research remained the same, which is to say, women, and as such, "studies continued to conceptualize woman as a preexisting essence, not taking into account how the category is constructed both socially and relationally. Gender studies was a way for some women to keep studying women without running the risk of the feminist label" (Costa and Sardenberg 747). Thus women's studies remained entrenched in the social sciences, such as sociology, anthropology, economics, without venturing into the humanities (Castro and Lavinas 1992).

NEIM-Núcleo de Estudos Interdisciplinares sobre a Mulher [Center for Interdisciplinary Studies on Women] at UFBA, the Universidade Federal da Bahia, is one of the oldest programs in Latin America, begun in 1983. It is part of that university's College of Philosophy and Human Sciences. The mission statement reaffirms NEIM's commitment to contributing to the process of overcoming the inequality of gender and creating a critical conscience about the importance of women in society. It offers both a masters and Ph.D. in gender studies. The objectives of the program include: (1) carrying out interdisciplinary research on women and gender relations; (2) developing teaching about the topic through the promotion of courses, putting on seminars and debates; (3) supporting public projects that foment equality of gender; (4) developing advising and consulting activities, contributing to finding practical solutions to questions regarding problems related to women; (5) participating in national and international events relative to the question of women and gender; (6) publishing and divulging the results of research about women and gender relations; and finally, maintaining a center of documentation with national and foreign publications on the topic, as well as unpublished works.

In Costa Rica, women's studies programs date from 1991 at the Universidad Nacional de Costa Rica (UNA) and from 1987 at the Universidad de Costa Rica (UCR). In 1993, these two programs joined forces to begin a jointly offered MA program. The joint MA program is interdisciplinary, activist in focus, committed to diversity and providing a regional vision about the state of women and gender relations in Costa Rica. There is the stated need for participants to develop policies, strategies, methods and alternative and appropriate techniques that contribute toward the elimination of oppression and subordination.[11]

According to Silvia Chavarria, former chairperson of women's studies at the Universidad of Costa Rica,

> It was a hard, long, time consuming, negotiated, emotionally-laden, heart-wrenching process to be able to start a Master's Program in women's studies. It required convincing the administrative and academic authorities of the two biggest universities of Costa Rica of its economic feasibility, that gender was an issue, that it had an academic space, that we could work with the regulations and the bureaucracy of both universities, that even though there could be power struggles, that both academic groups could share it to make the program work. And we made it! It is still the only inter-institutional program in the whole country! And it is still going and going . . . (Leitinger)

In the Dominican Republic, the Center for Gender Studies at the Instituto Tecnológico de Santo Domingo (CGS) was one of Latin America's first programs, founded in 1987. It was created because of the lack of places that allowed for the production, reflection, and theoretical diffusion of social problems from the perspective of gender. The program seeks to "contribute to the production, analysis and diffusion of knowledge about women and gender in order to work towards the necessary transformations of discriminatory practices that are obstacles to women's living out her full potential as human beings." The CGS publishes the journal *Género y Sociedad* three times a year, offers courses as electives and requirements, and provides students with the theoretical and methodological base necessary so that they may incorporate gender into their own work. The program sponsors debates, teaching, research and the elaboration and implementation of educational, social, and economic policies.[12]

In Colombia, at the Universidad Nacional de Colombia, Bogotá, the Escuela de Estudios de Género was founded in 1994 and actually lists, among its objectives, the need to promote policies that recognize difference of identity that may be feminine, masculine, homosexual or "otras opciones sexuales" [other sexual options]. There is graduate coursework available to work on public policy issues from the standpoint of gender and a series of projects that includes Socialization, Sexuality and Identity and Masculinity Studies.[13] Elsewhere in Colombia, at the Universidad del Valle in Cali, the Center for Gender, Women and Society was established in 1993. The center includes research, teaching, courses, seminars, workshops, extension classes, meetings, forums, conferences, and publications. The Universidad del Valle played an important role in encouraging debate about women's rights and gender inequity.[14] The start of the program was met with great opposition, something that ran counter to the ideas of equality and tolerance the women were trying to espouse. They were called crazy, or "Women with long hair and short intellects." The inauspicious beginning notwithstanding, women's studies at the Center has remain stable through the last 14 years, examining the status of women with regard to education, communication and culture, history, linguistics, health, family, jurisprudence, sexuality, violence, work, ethnicity, politics and democracy, local development, and citizenship.

Latin America's oldest Women's Studies program, from the Colegio de México from 1983, is the PIEM, the Programa Interdisciplinario de Estudios de la Mujer [The Interdisciplinary Program of Women's Studies]. PIEM offers a master's degree in Gender Studies that seeks to bridge the social sciences and the humanities. It also is focused on an analysis of national problems and public policy. What is most intriguing about the program is that the first two semesters are devoted to building a conceptual and theoretical understanding of the social construct of gender, especially in institutions such as the family. In the third semester specific themes are examined, and finally there is the elaboration and design of the thesis in the fourth semester. Some of the elective courses offered in the program include Gender and Human Rights, Gender and Power in International Contexts, and History of Women.[15] The program at the Colegio de México received a $467,525 grant from the Ford Foundation on August 24, 2006 ("Grants and Awards" 46) to fund a study exploring the barriers to including sexuality research and teaching in five countries.

The Emergence of Men's Studies in Latin America and the United States

Men's Studies emerged in the United States and Australia in the 1990s and has recently also become active in Latin America. A conference cosponsored by organizations in Brazil and Mexico was held November 14–16, 2007, entitled "Men Engage Mexico." They put their conference proceedings on a series of 12 videos available for viewing on YouTube. The majority of men related to men's studies are profeminist and agree that women have been faced with inequality at work, at home, and under law. While a fairly common complaint among some women is that every study is already a "men's" study, Men's Studies courses typically concern men's rights, feminist theory, and queer theory as well as cultural constructions of masculinity. They discuss male privilege and the fear of loss of the privilege that the women's movement has occasioned.

In North America, such programs emerged in the 1990s. There are currently more than 500 courses offered at schools across the United States. The first school to create a minor in men's studies was Hobart and William Smith Colleges in 1998. That same year, the Núcleo de Pesquisa em Gênero e Masculinidades [Center for Research in Gender and Masculinities] of the Universidade Federal de Pernambuco (GEMA-UFPE) in Brazil was founded. Among the objectives listed for the program were the need to promote multidisciplinary research on health, sexuality, and reproduction; to further studies on gender violence and conduct analyses of programs designed to work with male offenders; to break cultural barriers for men in public health issues and finally, to promote activism and research that is against homophobia.[16]

Also in Brazil, the Instituto Papai [Father Institute], a nongovernmental, feminist organization, was formed in 1997. Though not connected to a university, it is educational in scope and focus, informative and political, and focused on men in poverty and fomenting equal rights for men and women with regard to health, sexuality, and reproduction.

Papai connects its mission to the struggles of other groups, not only women and feminists but also those in favor of sexual rights, principally of gays and lesbians. It conducts educational forums, and research about gender and masculinity from a feminist standpoint that is based strongly on psychology, social sciences, and public health. Almost as if to prove that "real" men can, or should, care about such issues, on the portal to their Web site, they include a famous quote from the last letter that revolutionary Che Guevara wrote to his children, in which he tells them, "Grow up as good revolutionaries. Remember that each of us, alone, has no value. Above all, always be capable of feeling profoundly any injustice committed against anyone at all, anywhere in the world. This is the most beautiful quality of a revolutionary."

While programs that began in the United States and Europe initially inspired the establishment of women's studies and gender studies programs in Latin America, the programs themselves developed in very different ways and with distinctive priorities. In general, they are tied to addressing immediate needs with regard to women's lives, labor, and legal issues, particularly women in rural areas and women of color, and tend to be less focused on the humanities or in the development of theoretical models for understanding the roots of women's oppression.

There is a distinctly activist bent in many of the programs. In terms of sexuality, this takes the form of outreach programs designed to help women who have been the victims of rape, to provide information regarding the prevention of sexual harassment at work and in school, to offer information on what to do in the event someone is a victim of sexual discrimination or violence; to provide businesses with training for employees on the topics of sexual harassment and abuse. As we have seen above, there is also a growing interest in addressing the needs and the basic human rights of sexual minorities.

In spite of our humorous start to this side dish, the myriad areas that must be addressed both in Latin America (and in the United States) with regard to the place of gender studies and activism related to sex, gender, and sexuality within an institutional setting remains a serious topic of concern. As long as there is rampant gross intolerance of sexual minorities, sexual and domestic violence against mostly women but also men, and continuing inequities based on gender, race, class, and sexual orientation in virtually all realms of society, the challenge to promote social justice through education remains formidable.

And that's no laughing matter.

EPILOGUE
LEFTOVERS

There is a revolution brewing. It turns out that many restaurant patrons are now opting out of ordering entrees altogether.[1] Marketing executives have found that often they prefer to fill their plates with side dishes and appetizers and nothing more. They graze, until they have their fill. As Julie Hayes, marketing manager of Basic Vegetable Products in Suisin, California, has said:

> The popularity of side dishes is definitely increasing. As Americans become more health conscious, they are moving away from typical "meat" entrees toward a focus on vegetables and protein substitutes. Vegetables and side dishes are increasingly taking over the traditional role of meat as the focus of the meal, as evidenced by the growing presence of vegetarian entrees and lengthy side dish menus. Moreover, side dishes provide variety in tastes that many look for in their dining experience. With this in mind, consumers have become more experimental. (qtd. in Kuntz)[2]

I began this book with the humble assertion that under-examined side dishes should be allowed on the plate in courses on Latina American women's cultural production. I finish convinced that what I had thought was the entrée was really just a side dish all along. Sure, it was a heftier portion, but basically it was the result of a few possibilities thrown together, cooked into a stew and plopped onto the center of the plate. And this became our entire understanding of Latina American women's cultural production.

But what if other possibilities such as those contained on these pages are picked for our entire meal, and not merely as side dishes? After all, one person's side dish may be another's entrée. This is the case with pasta, and some rice combinations, and even the occasional "dressed up" baked potato.

No one is advocating tossing Sor Juana down the garbage disposal, but rather for seeing her oeuvre as just one dish among many.

The artifacts examined in this book have been a very small sampling of the tastes, textures and colors that await us if we make an attempt to broaden our notions of authorship and respectable topics of scholarly analysis to include the practice of everyday life. Other menu possibilities could include the work on Mexican feminist photographers of Magdalena Maiz Peña and on that of Brazilian and Argentine women photographers written by David William Foster, or the work on Latinas, performativity and popular culture done by Eliana Rivero or Roselyn Constantino. The book edited by Danny J. Anderson and Jill S. Kuhnheim, *Cultural Studies in the Curriculum: Teaching Latin America* (2003) would also be a fine point of departure. The menu could include the many cultural studies essays on Latin American women's cultural production found on the pages of *Studies in Latin American Popular Culture*, *Revista de crítica cultural*, or the *Journal of Latin American Cultural Studies*, all of which regularly offer enticing options.

The elements included in this book can be used as leftovers, mixed later with other ingredients to create an entirely new dish. But here is another thought, what if we customize the experience for our students by allowing them to pick and choose directly from the menu of available options and categories to fill their plates, just like the customers mentioned at the start of this epilogue? How could such a pedagogical decision transform or even electrify the classroom experience, both for the students and for the educators?

The tone of this book has been intentionally playful, but transforming the curriculum is serious business. I seek with *Side Dishes* to broaden the range of cultural expressions taught with regard to Latino America, specifically Latina American women, in order to move beyond literary studies and embrace a cultural studies approach that involves as much a transformation in what we teach as in the ways in which we teach it. Such an approach forces us to examine the power relations inherent in the legitimization of a particular discipline, as well as to acknowledge the market factors that affect production and consumption of cultural artifacts. It requires us to examine not only what has been done in the past in our institutions of higher education but to be in a continual process of self-interrogation concerning what we are doing in the present—what is missing from our courses, and why? What voices have been excluded? Beyond this, the method fosters a greater understanding of consumer society, mass culture, and the presence of marginal groups. By widening our notions of texts available for analysis, the world itself opens up to our students, allowing them to engage with the material as perhaps never before. It enables them to understand that culture is dynamic, or, to paraphrase Walter Mignolo, culture is not something one *has*, but rather something one *does* (Anderson and Kuhnheim 11).

Another dimension that *Side Dishes* seeks to underscore is how today, perhaps more than ever, there is a conversation, often literal, between those who produce and those who consume cultural expressions, as we saw most vividly in *Side Dishes* in the case of Marga Gomez or of Cecilia Rossetto, or even in the discussions on feminist pornography, and in the academic Web sites examined. The level of engagement of consumers has changed. What I have tried to demonstrate in this book, is that while typically what is studied in civilization or literature courses related to Latin America, even those "progressive" courses devoted to women, are examples of high culture, the best examples of a given country's essay, narrative, theater and poetry, art, or laudable historical achievements, there is a wealth of information that can be gleaned about a country or region by examining the everyday, a country's mass media, websites, television programs, comedy, journals or the topics prioritized in academic programs. The inclusion and analysis of such materials in our courses demonstrates for students that intellectual authority is not merely gleaned from studying the Great Books. When students ask me what topics they should write about for their research paper in my course on Latin American Popular Culture, I play the song "Dear Prudence" at full volume, so that they may have the refrain, "Look around, round round round round, round, round, round round round," echoing in their heads when they leave the classroom. I want them to see that the immediate world that surrounds them is ripe for their fresh intellectual insights; they just have to open their eyes.

While finding ways to reach students in ways that are relevant to them might seem like a fairly straightforward, even logical, aspiration, there are some who take exception to such an endeavor. Susan Jacoby, whose book *The Age of American Unreason* was published in early 2008, discusses the "consequences of a culture of serious reading being replaced by a rapid-fire, short-attention-span-provoking, over-stimulating, largely visual, information-spewing environment."[3] Jacoby would have failed my course. What she is unable to grasp is that 'serious reading' does not require a book, it requires understanding that all cultural expressions may be 'read' and approached intellectually, be it a video on YouTube, graffiti, magnets on a refrigerator, a newspaper, or, yes, a poem or novel.

Like Michelle Habell-Pallán's examination of Chicana and Latina popular culture, *Loca Motion: The Travels of Chicana and Latina Popular Culture* (2005), *Side Dishes* argues against any totalizing vision of Latina and Chicana women as defined strictly by their literary texts. Or to continue with the metaphor of the book, it argues against serving students what is essentially a Latina American TV dinner. Pre-packaged, pre-digested, and with cliff notes readily available in any bookstore.

The different sorts of cultural texts included within *Side Dishes* respond to the Modern Language Association's Ad Hoc Committee on Foreign Languages report, "Foreign Languages and Higher Education: New Structures for a Changed World," published in May 2007 on the crisis in language education and the need for a reorganization of our programs.[4] The questions that the committee addressed include: How can we provide a broad, intellectually driven approach to teaching language and culture in higher education today? How can we make our courses relevant? How can we prepare our American students to deal with people from other cultures both here and abroad with a more nuanced understanding of the range of cultural production available? How can we make students not just linguistically conversant, but culturally conversant? The committee argued that one possible model would be to shift the focus from canonical literature and define transcultural understanding as the ability to comprehend and analyze the cultural narratives that appear in every kind of expressive form—from essays, fiction, poetry, drama, journalism, humor, advertising, political rhetoric, and legal documents to performance, visual forms, and music (4). As Danny Anderson and Jill S. Kuhnheim and also argue in the book *Cultural Studies in the Curriculum: Teaching Latin America* (2003).

> The goal is to examine culture in ways that are meaningful to students, to allow for new ideas of what can be called a text, find new ways to motivate students, to articulate the centrality of cultural difference in our future, and provide new strategies for promoting critical thinking. (x)

But how can we connect this general discussion of cultural studies to an understanding of specifically women's cultural production? Teresa de Lauretis opens her book *Alice Doesn't* with an excerpt from *Alice in Wonderland* before clarifying "Far from proposing Alice (or any other) as yet another 'image' of woman or as the symbol of a struggle too real or too diversified to be even minimally 'represented' in a single text, character or person, I like to think of her tale as a parable suggesting—merely suggesting—the situation, the predicament, and the adventure of critical feminism" (2). Indeed, almost 25 years after De Lauretis wrote these words, the feminist critical journey remains an adventure. De Lauretis speaks of being forced to use the master's tools with regard to language, and asserts that there is the need to "formulate questions that will redefine the context, displace the terms of the metaphors, and make up new ones" (3). Her ideas may be extended to all forms of cultural expression because, if anything has been learned since she published her study, transformation involves more than simply allowing for a women's voice within the traditional schema of academic programs. It is not enough to alter the content of traditional courses in literature or civilization and simply add women's voice to the mix. Doing so demonstrates a subconscious acceptance of the institutional legitimization of knowledge as it has been configured until now.

In *Alice Doesn't*, De Lauretis makes another point relevant to *Side Dishes*: "The argument begun by feminism is not only an academic debate on logic and rhetoric—though it is that too, and necessarily, if we think of the length and influence that formal schooling has on a person's life from pre-school to secondary and/or higher education, and how it determines social place. That argument is also a confrontation, a struggle, a political intervention in institutions and in the practices of everyday life" (3). She argues that our task is to make visible the invisible by analyzing the semiotics of everyday life, or what she refers to as the "semiotics of experience." De Lauretis also reminds us that strategies of writing and reading are forms of cultural resistance. As she says, "the only way to position oneself outside that discourse is to position oneself within it—to refuse the question as formulated, or to answer deviously (through its own words), even to quote (but against the grain)" (7).

An analysis of the everyday is not restricted to contemporary intellectuals or philosophers. German writer Sigfried Kracauer (1889–1966) explored in *The Mass Ornament* (1927) myriad topics including shopping arcades, the cinema, bestsellers and their readers, photography, dance, hotel lobbies, Kafka, the Bible, and boredom. For him, it was not through a critical engagement exclusively with the master works but rather precisely through an examination of the ordinary, or the marginal, that great insights about given culture or society may be found. He argued that these cultural expressions of great importance, for what they revealed as part of a web of signification of a given society, one that many, according to Kracauer, take part in writing, but few ever actually read.

The examination of the everyday and revalorization of alternative forms of cultural expression in Latina America was not something that came about as an offshoot of European or U.S. schools of thought, as the *The Latin American Cultural Studies Reader* proves. Instead it developed as "specific sociohistorical continuities in the Latin American political and cultural milieus" (5). Many of the most important thinkers in the field have been discussed within the pages of *Side Dishes*, including Chilean Nelly Richard, Argentines Néstor Garcia Canclini, Beatriz Sarlo, Walter Mignolo, and Francine Masiello, and Mexican Carlos Monsiváis.

Teaching about alternative forms of cultural expression and the need for students to evaluate all cultural texts demonstrates my personal desire to transform the educational experience for our students, something akin to what bell hook describes in her *Teaching to Transgress*. I want my students to think globally, to be effective communicators and original thinkers. I seek to make them actively engaged with life, to foster in them the ability to look beyond our borders and become involved in critical discussions with those of other countries and here about issues of concern for all of us, such as the environment, racism, sexism, classicism, and homophobia, the "isms" that separate us from others, both within the United States and around the world. These are some of the issues I seek to examine both in my teaching and my research, as exemplified in *Side Dishes*, issues that also often become paramount in my effort to prepare my students for the to confront the challenges of life in the global community.

The concept of a meal is the governing metaphor that ties the themes of each chapter together. My simple goal with *Side Dishes* is to put an array of cultural artifacts related to women in Latina America on the table. My selection of side dishes does not pretend to be exhaustive. It has had to do exclusively with my own particular cravings and the dishes may not be seasoned to everyone's liking.

But it is getting late. Come join me at the table. There is no main course. The serving plates are filled only with side dishes. So enjoy. ¡Buen provecho!

APPENDIX

Latin American Women Film Festival Winners

Year	Film Festival	Name	Country	Film	Award
1980	Cannes	Tizuka Yamasaki	Brazil	Gaijin – Os Caminhos da Liberdade	FIPRESCI Prize – Special Mention
	Gramado	Tizuka Yamasaki	Brazil	Gaijin – Os Caminhos da Liberdade	Golden Kikito – Best Film, Best Screenplay
	Havana International	Tizuka Yamasaki	Brazil	Gaijin – Os Caminhos da Liberdade	Grand Coral – First Prize
1983	Gramado	Ana Carolina	Brazil	Das Tripas Coração	Golden Kikito – Best Director
1985	Cannes	Fina Torres	Venezuela	Oriana	Golden Camara
	Cartagena International	Fina Torres	Venezuela	Oriana	Golden India Catalina – Best Screenplay, Best Film
1986	Berlin International	Suzana Amaral	Brazil	A Hora da Estrela	C.I.C.A.E. Award, OCIC Award
	Havana International	Suzana Amaral	Brazil	A Hora da Estrela	Grand Coral – First Prize
	Sundance	Lourdes Portillo	Mexico	Las Madres de la Plaza de Mayo	Grand Jury Prize – Honorable Mention
1987	Havana International	Tetê Moraes	Brazil	Terra para Rose	Grand Coral First Prize – Best Documentary
1989	Havana International	María Novaro	Mexico	Lola	Coral – Best First Work

(Continued)

(Continued)

Year	Film Festival	Name	Country	Film	Award
1990	Berlin International	Jeanine Meerapfel	Argentina	La Amiga	Peace Film Award – Honorable Mention
	Bogatá	Paz Alicia Garciadiego	Mexico	Mentiras piadosas	Golden Pre-Columbian Circle
	Venice	María Luisa Bemberg	Argentina	Yo, la peor de todas	OCIC Award – Honorable Mention
1991	Berlin International	María Novaro	Mexico	Lola	OCIC Award
	Gramado	Tata Amaral	Brazil	Viver a Vida	Golden Kikita – Best Screenplay for Short Film
1992	Guadalajara	Dana Rotberg	Mexico	Ángel de fuego	DICINE Award, FIPRESCI Prize
1993	Havana International	Alice de Andrade	Brazil	Luna de miel	Grand Coral – Third Prize
		María Luisa Bemberg	Argentina	De eso no se habla	Special Jury Prize
1994	Gramado	Susana de Moraes	Brazil	Mil e Uma	Special Jury Award
	Havana International	María Novaro	Mexico	El jardín del Edén	Grand Coral – Second Prize
1995	Havana International	Helena Solberg	Brazil	Carmen Miranda: Bananas Is My Business	Grand Coral – First Prize
		Lucrecia Martel	Argentina	Rey muerto	Coral – Best Short Film
		Paz Alicia Garciadiego	Mexico	Profundo carmesí	Best Unpublished Screenplay
1996	Bogotá	Maryse Sistach	Mexico	La línea paterna	Golden Pre-Columbian Circle
	Guadalajara	Sabina Berman	Mexico	Entre Pancho Villa y una mujer desnuda	Audience Award
	Havana International	Eliane Caffé	Brazil	Caligrama	Coral – Best Experimental Work
	Venice	Paz Alicia Garciadiego	Mexico	Profundo carmesí	Golden Osella – Best Original Screenplay

Year	Film Festival	Name	Country	Film	Award
1997	Bogotá	Gabriela Rangel	Venezuela	Corazones negros	Silver Pre-Columbian Circle
	Gramado	Maryse Sistach	Mexico	La línea paterna	UNESCO Special Award – Special Mention
	Havana International	Tata Amaral	Brazil	Um Céu de Estrelas	Coral Award – Best First Work, FIPRESCI Prize – Special Mention
1999	Havana International	Marianne Eyde	Peru	La Carnada	FIPRESCI Prize – Special Mention
		Mercedes García Guevara	Argentina	Río escondido	OCIC Award – Special Mention
		Lourdes de los Santos	Cuba	Identidad	El Mégano Award
	Sundance	Lucrecia Martel	Argentina	La ciénaga	NHK Award
2000	Havana International	María Inés Roque	Argentina	Papá Iván	Grand Coral – First Prize
		Ana María Zanotti	Argentina	Seguir siendo	Imagen Comunitaria Award
		Tetê Moraes	Brazil	O Sonho de Rose – 10 Anos Depois	Memoria Documentary Award
	Rio de Janeiro International	Ângela Pires; Liliana Sulzbach	Brazil	O Branco	Première Brazil – Best Short Film
		Tetê Moraes	Brazil	O Sonho de Rose – 10 Anos Depois	Première Brazil – Best Documentary
	San Sebastián International	Paz Alicia Garciadiego	Mexico	Perdición de los hombres	Best Screenplay
	São Paulo International	Tetê Moraes	Brazil	O Sonho de Rose – 10 Anos Depois	Audience Award – Best Documentary
	Sundance	Dana Rotberg	Mexico	Otilia Rauda	NHK Award
2001	Berlin International	Lucrecia Martel	Argentina	La ciénaga	Alfred Bauer Award
	Guadalajara	Marisa Sistach	Mexico	Nadie te oye: Perfume de violetas	National Critics Award

(Continued)

(Continued)

Year	Film Festival	Name	Country	Film	Award
		Ângela Pires; Liliana Sulzbach	Brazil	O Branco	Glass Bear Special Mention – Best Feature Film
	Havana International	Lucrecia Martel	Argentina	La ciénaga	Grand Coral – First Prize, Best Director
		Marisa Sistach	Mexico	Nadie te oye: Perfume de violetas	Grand Coral – Second Prize, Martin Luther King Memorial Center Award
		Beatriz Flores Silva	Uruguay	En la puta vida	Radio Havana Award
		Mariem Pérez Riera	Puerto Rico	Cuando lo pequeño se hace grande	Memoria Documentary Award, Saúl Yelín Award
		Carmen Luz Parot	Chile	Estadio Nacional	Saúl Yelín Award
	Huelva Latin American	Beatriz Flores Silva	Uruguay	En la puta vida	Golden Colon
		Verónica Chen	Argentina	Vagón fumador	Best New Director
	Sundance	Sandra Werneck	Brazil	Amores Possíveis	Latin American Cinema Award
		María Novaro	Mexico	Sin dejar huella	Latin American Cinema Award
2002	Bogatá	Beatriz Flores Silva	Uruguay	En la puta vida	Golden Pre-Columbian Circle – Best Director
	Gramado	Anna Muylaert	Brazil	Durval Discos	Audience Award, Golden Kikito for Best Film and Kikito Critics Prize for Best Director
	Havana International	Lourdes Portillo	Mexico	Señorita extraviada	Grand Coral – First Prize, Memoria Documentary Award

Year	Film Festival	Name	Country	Film	Award
	Huelva Latin American	Suzana Amaral	Brazil	Uma Vida em Segredo	Silver Colon – Best Director, Special Jury Award
	Sundance	Lourdes Portillo	Mexico	Señorita extraviada	Special Jury Prize
2003	Berlin International	Lucía Cedrón	Argentina	En ausencia	Silver Berlin Bear – Best Short Film
	Cartagena International	Suzana Amaral	Brazil	Uma Vida em Segredo	OCLACC Award – Honorable Mention
	Rio de Janeiro International	Eliane Caffé	Brazil	Narradores de Javé	Audience Award – Best Film, Première Brazil – Best Film
		Celina Murga	Argentina	Ana y los otros	FIPRESCI Prize – Best Latin American Film
	Venice	Celina Murga	Argentina	Ana y los otros	Cult Network Italia' Prize – Special Mention
2004	Bogotá	Elia Schneider	Venezuela	Punto y raya	Golden Pre-Columbian Circle – Best Director
	Gramado	Helena Solberg	Brazil	Vida de Menina	Audience Award, Golden Kikito for Best Film and Best Screenplay
	Havana International	María Victoria Menis	Argentina	El cielito	FIPRESCI Prize
	Rio de Janeiro International	Lúcia Murat	Brazil	Quase Dois Irmãos	FIPRESCI Prize – Best Latin American Film, Première Brazil – Best Director
		Helena Solberg	Brazil	Vida de Menina	Audience Award – Best Film

(Continued)

(Continued)

Year	Film Festival	Name	Country	Film	Award
	San Sebastián International	María Victoria Menis	Argentina	El cielito	Arte, CICAE, SIGNIS Future Talent, and Solidarity Awards
	São Paulo International	Lucrecia Martel	Argentina	La niña santa	Critics Award Honorable Mention
2005	Berlin International	Anahí Berneri	Argentina	Un año sin amor	Best Feature Film
	Gramado	Tizuka Yamasaki	Brazil	Gaijin – Ama-me Como Sou	Golden Kikito – Best Film, Best Director,
		Mara Mourão	Brazil	Doutores da Alegria	Audience Award, Special Jury Award
		Elia Schneider	Venezuela	Punto y raya	Kikito Critics Prize
	Huelva Latin American	Lúcia Murat	Brazil	Quase Dois Irmãos	Radio Exterior de España Award, Special Jury Award
	Mar del Plata	Lúcia Murat	Brazil	Quase Dois Irmãos	Audience Award – Best Film
		Anahí Berneri	Argentina	Un año sin amor	FIPRESCI Prize
2006	Cannes	Paz Encina	Paraguay	Hamaca paraguaya	FIPRESCI Prize
	Gramado	Andrea Tonacci	Brazil	Serras da desordem	Golden Kikito – Best Film, Best Cinematography
	Guadalajara	Maryse Sistach	Mexico	La niña en la piedra	Mayahuel Award – Best Film
	Mar del Plata	Claudia Llosa	Peru	Madeinusa	Roberto Tato Miller Award – Best Latin American Feature Film
	São Paulo International	Tata Amaral	Brazil	Antônia – O Filme	Special Jury Award
		Paz Encina	Paraguay	Hamaca paraguaya	Critics Award International

Year	Film Festival	Name	Country	Film	Award
	Sundance	Elena Soarez	Brazil	Casa de Areia	Alfred P. Sloan Feature Film Prize
2007	Berlin International				
	Cannes	Elisa Miller (II)	Mexico	Ver llover	Norman McLaren Award
		Lucía Puenzo	Argentina	XYZ	Grand Golden Rail
	Cartagena International	Claudia Llosa	Peru	Madeinusa	Special Mention
	Havana International	Camila Guzmán Urzúa	Cuba	El Telón de azúcar	Grand Coral – First Prize
	Rio de Janeiro International	Sandra Kogut	Brazil	Mutum	Première Brazil – Best Film
	Sundance	Lucía Cedrón	Argentina	Agnus Dei	NHK Award
	Toronto International	Anahí Berneri	Argentina	Encarnación	Innovation Award

NOTES

Chapter 1: Lust

1 www.goodforher.com/.

2 *La nación* Chile 9/9/2005 www.lanacion.cl.

Chapter 2: Pop

1 Critical theorist Susan Bennett expands this notion of the interactive state of flux in the relationship between culture and performance when she writes, "Both the audience's reaction to a text (or performance) and the text (performance) itself are bound within cultural limits. Yet, as a diachronic analysis makes apparent, those limits are continually tested and invariably broken. Culture cannot be held as a fixed entity, a set of constant rules, but instead it must be seen as in a position of inevitable flux" (101).

2 In a study conducted by the Fundación de las Cajas de Ahorro (Funcas), only one out of every four Spaniards feels that foreigners are greeted with friendliness, while 46 percent view them with suspicion, and 12 percent say there is outright disdain and even aggression against them. This same study shows that almost one-half of the Spanish population, 46 percent, now thinks there are "too many" immigrants and they blame the immigrants for growing urban unrest ("Ola de inmigrantes" *La nación*, 22 enero, 2004, 4). On the bright side, at least for Argentines, a study conducted by the Centro de Investigaciones Sociológicas in Spain did a ranking of all of the foreigners to determine which countries the Spaniards preferred. Argentines won the popularity contest, while U.S. Americans ranked in the penultimate position, just above the much despised Moroccans ("Los españoles y argentinos: El país más amigo"*endoscontinentes* No. 1 Marzo, 2004, 26).

3 According to Richard, the culture-spectacle is a show "filled with visibility and mathematical calculation to the point that the complacent symbols of majority culture erase any nuance of critical-reflective layering and dissipate the ambiguities of everything that does not contribute directly to the performances show worthiness. There is no confrontation, no discord, merely presentation. While it shows tolerance for the maximum diversity of opinions, that same tolerance is "insufficient for that diversity to articulate competing readings that design alternative meanings" (*Insubordination* 73).

4 Later that year Rossetto would be named Argentina's cultural attaché in Spain by Argentine president Néstor Kirchner.

5 Juan Villegas explains this self tropicalizing inherent in representing one's country in Spain in terms of the annual Festival Internacional de Cadíz, in which groups from Latin America come to perform each year: "Al buscar la satisfacción o aceptación de la auto-representación dirigida a los practicantes de las culturas del 'otro' un festival puede conducir a una preferencia por teatralidades esterotipadoras de sistemas culturales o identidades nacionales. Aún puede darse el caso que rasgos aparentemente esterotipadores que en los contextos nacionales adquieren una dimensión subversiva, en el contexto políticamente neutralizado del festival, son leídos como definitivamente esterotipadores. En varias versiones del Festival de Cádiz han recurrido modalidades aparentemente definitorias de identidades nacionales. Es el caso de Cuba, por ejemplo, que tiende a definirse con baile afrocubanos y teatralización de leyendas africanas, como indicio de la redefinición de los popular en la Cuba revolucionaria. La teatralidad brasilenña, por otra parte, tiende a reinterar espectáculos con bailes, música, gran actividad física o corporal y desnudos. En los grupos argentinos, con frecuencia se habla del tango o se le baila en el escenario. [. . .]Estos sistemas de teatralidad confirman las imágenes de lo nacional desde la mirada del otro, descontextualizado su potencial subversión o su búsqueda de aceptación por parte del 'otro' europeo que espera al final del puente de la entrada a Europa" (214–15).

6 Interesting to note that books most often stolen from bookstores include cookbooks, books on sex ("because people are too embarrassed to buy them"), and science fiction ("because the majority of the readers are thirteen and have no money). *New York Times Book Review*, "Sticky Fingers," 19 November 2006.

7 A few sites include: *Ciencia y Ficción*, http://orbita.starmedia.com/cienciayficcion/; *Com Ciência*, www.comciencia.br/reportagens/2004/10/11.shtml; Jorge Forte, *Guía de Recursos de la Ciencia Ficción en español*, www.geocities.com/Athens/7037/guia.html; *Sitio de Ciencia-Ficción*, www.ciencia-ficcion.com/bienvenida.html; *Portal de Ciencia Ficción*, www.portal-cifi.com/; *Scarium—Ficção Científica, Fantasia, Horror, e Mistério*, Scarium Magazine, www.scarium.com.br/; *Silente—Ciencia ficción y fantasia*, www.silente.net/; *Simetria,* Associação Portuguesa de Ficção Científica e Fantástico, www.simetria.org/.

8 She argues, "authors in Brazil use icons of humanity to confront the fear of technology and the new type of colonization that threatens to destroy Brazilian culture. In the case of Brazil, science fiction technology generally stands for a neocolonialist power that threatens national identity. Brazilian stories involving humanoid aliens tend to be rewritings of Brazilian myths of identity and tend also to emphasize harmony of the three races. Nonhumanoid aliens tend to reproduce the Brazilian experience with foreigners, colonizers on traders, who have often exploited the country's resources while maintaining distance between themselves and the Brazilians (469).

Chapter 3: Issues

1 To give a brief overview of feminist journals in the United States, *Signs* is probably the most well known feminist journal, as are *differences* and *Feminist Studies*. Many of the same scholars publish in these journals and/or serve on the editorial boards (Judith Butler is an example). *Differences* is focused on feminist cultural theory. *Feminist Studies* was the first feminist journal in the United States, dating from 1972. *Genders* includes studies on masculinity and men and gender and sexuality in general. The *NWSA Journal,* meanwhile, is the publication of the

National Women's Studies Association and was founded in 1988. The purpose of the journal is to link theory with activism and underscore the interdisciplinarity of women's studies. There are also many feminist journals that have emerged that are focused on feminist approaches to particular disciplines. Some of these include: *Hypatia*, devoted to philosophy, *Gender & History*, and *camera obscura*, about feminist film theory, and the *Journal of Women's History*.

2 Examples include "Amor y democracia" [Love and Democracy] (1.1.1990); "Fronteras, límites, negociaciones" [Borders, Limits and Negotiations] (4.8. 1993); "Crítica y censura" [Criticism and Censorship] (5.9. 1994); "Identidades" [Identities] (7.14.1996); "Ciudad, espacio y vidas" [City, Space and Lives] (9.17.1998); "Público privado, sexualidad" [Private Public, Sexuality] (9.18.1998); "Sexo y violencia" [Sex and Violence] (13.26.2002).

3 Clear examples of this bias can be seen in numerous articles such as "Stonewall 25, Marcha ante las naciones unidas y algo más" [Stonewall 25, March in front of the United Nations and More] (5.10.1994); "Maricrónica de un viaje al arcoiris" [Fag-chronicle of a Trip to the Rainbow] (5.10.1994); "Stonewall, el mensaje" [Stonewall: The Message] (5.10.1994); "El cine gay, a 25 años de Stonewall" [Gay Film 25 years after Stonewall] (5.10.1994); "Hombres chicanos, una cartografía de la identidad y del comportamiento homosexual" [Chicano Men: A Cartography of Identity and Homosexual Behavior] (6.11.1995); "Valores sexuales en la era de Sida" [Sexual Values in the Age of AIDS] (6.11.1995); "La actuación de la identidad a través del performance chicano gay" [Enacting Identity through Gay Chicano Performance] (7.13.1996); "Volviendo todo perfectamente queer" [Making Things Perfectly Queer] (8.16.1997) and "Aspectos del comercio sexual masculino en la ciudad de México" [Aspects of Masculine Sexual Commerce in Mexico City] (9.18.1998).

4 The Chiapas conflict began on January 1, 1994, when Zapatista rebels—primarily indigenous (called the EZLN or Zapatista Army of National Liberation)—revolted against the federal government because of Mexico's decision to be part of the North American Free Trade Agreement. The indigenous people of the impoverished region had long felt that the federal government had done little to help them by not following through on promises for land reform and they believed that NAFTA would only worsen their situation.

5 Sexuality later appeared as the central theme in volume 18, "público/privado sexualidad"; in volume 22, "intimidad y servicios"; in volume 26, "sexo y violencia"; in addition to the previously mentioned volume 29, "las raras."

6 E-mail to author January 28, 2002.

7 http://feminaria.com.ar/default.asp.

8 Among the awards Fletcher has won are the Premio Fundación Alícia Moreau de Justo in 1992 for her "destacada tarea como investigadora, editora y feminista" [noteworthy work as researcher, editor, and feminist] and the Premio Julio Cortázar in 1999, as director of *Feminaria*, "an alternative journal that foments intellectual creation inside and outside of the country." She also received the Marzo Margarita de Ponce Award in 2000 for contributions to gender theory, as well as other awards that have recognized the role of the journal in the diffusion and promotion of women's rights and feminism.

9 Iberoamerican Cultural Foundation: www.iberoamerican.org/honorary.htm.

10 E-mail to author January 21, 2002.

11 This observation was made by my research assistant on this project, Jennifer Phillips.

12 Among the theorists translated or interviewed for the journal are Linda Alcoff (U.S.) 4 [1989]; Hélène Cixous (France) 4 [1989]; Marilyn Strathern (England) 6 [1990]; Lucia Guerra Cunningham (Chile) 8 [1992]; Emma Kaplan (U.S.) 8 [1992]; Fiorella Di Carlantonio (Italy) 8 [1992]; Miriam Lang (Germany) 9 [1992]; Rossana Rossanda (Italy) 8 [1992], Teresa de Lauretis (U.S.) 10 [1993] Jane Tompkins (U.S.) 12 [1994]; Gayatri Spivak (India/U.S) 12 [1994]; Donna Guy (U.S.) 14 [1995]; Seyla Benhabib (U.S.) 12 [1994]; Ian Forbes (England) 14 [1995]; Judith Butler (U.S.) 20 [1997], 22/23 [1999]; Diane Elam (U.S.) 20 [1997]; Nancy Chodorow (U.S.) 24/25 [2000]; Sara Mills (Sheffield Hallam University) 24/25 [2000]; Gemma Corradi Fiumara (Italy) 24/25 [2000]; Toril Moi (U.S.) 26/27 [2001], as well as the ongoing presence of many nationally known feminists such as July Cháneton, Tununa Mercado, Nora Domínguez, Jutta Marx, Eva Giberti, and Fletcher herself.

13 Found in *Feminaria Literaria* 10.16. 2000.

14 E-mail to author January 21, 2002.

15 www.unicamp.br/pagu/.

16 Issue 14.2 from 2006 had a similar dossier on "Conjugalities and Parenthoods of Gays, Lesbians and Transgenders in Brazil" that included an article by Richard Miskolci on the film *Brokeback Mountain*.

17 www.laneta.apc.org/debate/.

18 http://socialsciences.scielo.org/.

19 www.artemisanoticias.com.ar.

20 www.creatividadfeminista.org/index.htm.

21 www.cimacnoticias.com/site/.

22 Centro Feminista de Estudos e Assessoria, www.cfemea.org.br/.

Chapter 4: Flicks

1 www.Antoniaofilme.globo.com/English/html/picture/index.

Chapter 5: Class

1 PBS chief operating officer Wayne Godwin and spokesperson Lea Sloan gave a variety of reasons for PBS's decision to censor the show, saying it conflicted with PBS's purpose: "The presence of a couple headed by two mothers would not be appropriate curricular purpose that PBS should provide." And yet, public television's mandate as set forth in the 1967 Carnegie Commission Report is to "provide a voice for groups in the community that may otherwise be unheard," to serve as "a forum for controversy and debate," and to broadcast programs that "help us see America whole, in all its diversity."

2 An example of the rural-urban divide is found in the story told by Brazilian scholar Claudia de Lima Costa, who gives an illuminating account of her initial field experience when she went to study the women in the Sem Teto [Without Roof] movement. She had just returned to Brazil, after many years living in the United States very involved in feminist theoretical debates. She went to help women clear dirt and garbage at a squatter settlement in Florianópolis. After shoveling dirt for 15 minutes, the women were laughing at her. She had worn all white.

3 According to the Educational Supplement of the *London Times*, of the 200 best universities in the world, only one, at 195, is in Latin America, UNAM. This is from the educational supplement of the *London Times* based on certain criteria, among them: (1) interviews with academics in 88 countries; (2) number of citations in academic publications; and (3) number of students to professor. Latin Americans argued that most academic publications are in English, thus publishing in Spanish works against scholars in the region. That said, 300 of the 1300 academic professionals interviewed in the survey were from Latin America.

4 The institutions include the following: Universidad Nacional de Córdoba (Argentina); Universidad Nacional de la Plata (Argentina); Universidad Mayor de San Andrés (Bolivia); Universidad de Río de Janeiro (Brasil); Universidad de São Paulo (Brasil); Universidad Nacional de Colombia (Colombia); Universidad Nacional de Costa Rica (Costa Rica); Universidad de Costa Rica (Costa Rica); Universidad de la Habana (Cuba); Universidad Central de Ecuador (Ecuador); Universidad de El Salvador (El Salvador); Universidad de San Carlos de Guatemala (Guatemala); Universidad Autónoma de Honduras (Honduras); Benemérita Universidad Autónoma de Puebla (México); Universidad Autónoma de Sinaloa (México); Universidad de Guadalajara (México); Universidad Nacional Autónoma de México (México); Universidad Nacional Autónoma de Nicaragua (Nicaragua); Universidad de Panamá (Panamá); Universidad Nacional de Asunción (Paraguay); Universidad Nacional Mayor de San Marcos (Perú); Universidad de Puerto Rico (Puerto Rico); Universidad Autónoma de Santo Domingo (Dominican Republic); Universidad de la República (Uruguay); Universidad Central de Venezuela (Venezuela); Universidad de los Andes (Venezuela); Universidad del Zulia (Venezuela).

5 El Instituto de Estudios de la Mujer–IEM [Institute for Women's Studies] of the Universidad Nacional de Costa Rica; El Centro de Investigaciones y Estudios de la Mujer–CIEM [Center for Investigations and Women's Studies] of the Universidad de Costa Rica; El Instituto Universitario de la Mujer [The University Women's Institute] from the Universidad de San Carlos de Guatemala–IUMUSAC; La Universidad Nacional Autónoma de Honduras, UNAH; El Programa de Genero [Gender Program] at Universidad Autónoma de Nicaragua; El Instituto de la Mujer [Women's Institute] of the Universidad de Panamá–IMUP; and El Centro de Estudios de Genero [Center of Gender Studies] of the Universidad de El Salvador–CEG-UES.

6 Lauritz B. Holm-Nielsen and Kristian Thorn, "Higher Education in Latin America—A Regional Overview." Today, an average of 27 percent of people aged 18–24 in Latin America are enrolled in postsecondary schools. This constitutes an annual growth rate of 4.4 percent since 1985. Argentina, Chile, and Uruguay are the national leaders. There is very low production of doctoral graduates, one per 70, in Brazil, one per 140,000 in Chile, and 1 in 700,000 in Colombia (in OECD countries this average is 1 per 5000) (Holm-Nielsen and Thorn). In Chile, Colombia, and Brazil, public higher education is restricted and private institutions have accounted for most of the growth. Chile and Colombia allocate very little public funding to higher education relative to GDP. Beyond them public institutions are tax-financed (2–9). Argentina and Brazil have zero-tuition policies for undergraduate programs in public universities, although graduate programs do cost. Attempts to insure academic standards and quality have led to national accreditation agencies, such as CONEAU (Comisión Nacional de Evaluación y

Accreditación Universitaria [National Commission of Evaluation and University Accreditation]), created in 1995 (9).

7 www.proyectorural.org/Enlacesom.htm.

8 http://lanic.utexas.edu/la/region/women/indexesp.html.

9 www.cem.cl.eque.htm.

10 Other major programs include NEMGE (Núcleo de Estudo da Mulher e Relações Sociais de Gênero [Center for the Study of Women and Gender at the University of São Paulo]); CFEMEA (Centro Feminista de Estudos e Assessoria [Feminist Center for Studies and Advice]) in Brasilia; CIM (Centro Informação Mulher) in São Paulo; Instituto Universitário de Pesquisas de Rio de Janeiro; Women's Studies Center at the Pontifical Catholic University in Rio de Janeiro and GEISH–Grupo de Estudo Interdisciplinar em Sexualidade Humana at UNICAMP-Universidade de Campinas; NEIM (Núcleo de Estudos Interdisciplinares sobre a Mulhe) at UFBA, the Universidade Federal da Bahia; NEMGE/USP (Núcleo de Estudos da Mulher e do Gênero da Universidade de São Paulo); NIEM/UFRGS (Núcleo Interdisciplinar de Estudos sobre a Mulher da Universidade Federal do Rio Grande do Sul) in Porto Alegre.

11 *The Costa Rican Women's Movement: A Reader.*

12 www.intec.edu.do/estudio-genero/home.html.

13 www.humanas.unl.edu.co/genero/.

14 www.univalle.edu.co/~cgenero/.

15 www.colmex.mx/centros/ces/piem/maestria/htm.

16 www.ufpe.br/papai/.

Epilogue

1 Richard Martin, "Sidestepping into the Spotlight—Restaurant Side Dishes," *Nation's Restaurant News*, 17 Apr. 1989, http://findarticles.com/p/articles/mi _m3190/is_n16_v23/ai_7535627.

2 Lynn A. Kuntz, "Side Dishes: Not Just a Side Issue," *Food Product Design*, 1 May 1996. Copyright 2007 Virgo Publishing. www.foodproductdesign.com/. Posted 1 May 1996. Accessed 30 Dec. 2007.

3 Pantheon, 2008, 15.

4 The complete report may be found at www.mla.org/flreport.

BIBLIOGRAPHY

Acosta, Magdalena. "Mujeres torturadas." *Fem* 2 (1977).

Aftab, Tahera. "Lobbying for Transnational Feminism: Feminist Conversations Make Connections." *NWSA* 14.2 (2002): 153–56.

Aitken, Leo E., and Stuart C. Zonn, eds. *Place, Power, Situation and Spectacle: A Geography of Film*. Lanham: Rowman and Littlefield, 1994.

Alcoff, Linda. Introduction. *Identities: Race, Class, Gender and Nationality*. Ed. Linda Alcoff and Eduardo Mendieta. Malden, MA: Blackwell, 2003.

——. "The Problem of Speaking for Others." *Who Can Speak: Authority in Critical Identity*. Ed. Judith Roof and Robyn Wiegman. Urbana: U of Illinois P, 1995. 97–119.

Alexander, M. Jacqui, and Chandra Talpade Mohanty, eds. *Feminist Genealogies, Colonial Legacies, Democratic Futures*. New York: Routledge, 1997.

Almeida, Miguel Vale de. "Corpos marginais: notas etnográficas sobre páginas 'de policia' epáginas 'de sociedad.'" *Cadernos Pagu* 14 (2000): 130–45.

Altamiranda, Daniel. "Alejandra Pizarnik." *Latin American Writers on Gay and Lesbian Themes*. Ed. David William Foster. Westport, CT: Greenwood, 1994. 326–34.

——. *Teorías literarias II. Enfoques desde la cultura*. Buenos Aires: Editorial Docencia, 2001.

Altbach, Philip. *The Knowledge Context: Comparative Perspectives on the Distribution of Knowledge*. Albany: State U of New York P, 1987.

Alvarez, Sonia E. "Articulación y transnacionalización de los feminismos latinoamericanos." *debate feminista* 8.15 (1997). www.laneta.apc.org/debate/artsquince.html. 1 Jan. 2002.

——. "Feminismos Latinoamericanos" *Revista de Estudos Feministas* 6.2 (1998). www.laneta.apc.org/debate/artsquince.html. 5 May 2003.

——. "The (Trans)formation of Feminism(s) and Gender Politics in Democratizing Brazil." *The Women's Movement in Latin America: Participation and Democracy*, 2nd ed. Ed. Jane Jaquette. Boulder: Westview, 1994. 13–64.

Amado, Ana. "Velocidades, generaciones, y utopias: a propósito de *La Ciénega* de Lucrecia Martel." *ALCEU* 6.12 (2006): 48–56.

Anderson, Danny, and Jill S. Kuhnheim. *Cultural Studies in the Curriculum: Teaching Latin America*. New York: Modern Language Association of America, 2003.

Anderson Lola. "Mexican Women Journalists." *PanAmerican Bulletin* 68 (1934): 315–20.

Andre, Maria Claudia. *Chicanas and Latin American Women Writers Exploring the Realm of the Kitchen as a Self-Empowering Site*. Lewiston, NY: Edwin Mellen Press, 2001.

Antônia-O filme. Dir. Tata Amaral. Perfs. Negra Li, Cindy Mendes. Film. Coração da Selva, Globo Filmes, O2 Filmes,Tangerina Entretenimento, 2006.

Antônia-O filme. http://antoniaofilme.globo.com/.

Anzaldúa, Glória, ed. *Making Face, Making Soul/Haciendo Caras: Creative and Critical Perspectives by Women of Color*. San Francisco: Aunt Lute Books, 1990.

Anzaldúa, Glória, and Cherríe Moraga, eds. *This Bridge Called My Back: Writings by Radical Women of Color*. New York: Kitchen Table, 1983.

Aparicio, Frances R., and Susana Chávez-Silverman. Introduction. *Tropicalizations: Transcultural Representations of "Latinidad."* Ed. Frances R. Aparicio and Susana Chávez-Silverman. Hanover: UP of New England, 1997. 1–17.

Araújo, Helena. "El tema de la violación en Armonía Somers y Griselda Gambaro." *Plural* 15.11 (1986): 21–23.

Arenson, Karen W. "Furor Over a Sex Conference Stirs SUNY's Quiet New Paltz Campus." *New York Times* 8 Nov. 1997. www.newyorktimes.com

"Argentina." *CIA Fact book Online*. 30 Mar. 2005. www.cia.gov/cia/publications/factbook/geos/ar.html#Econ.

Arrom, Silvia Marina. *The Women of Mexico City, 1790–1857*. Stanford, CA: Stanford UP, 1985.

"Assessing Films Directed by Women." *Issues in Feminist Film Criticism*. Ed. Patricia Erens. Bloomington: Indiana UP, 1990. 330–37.

Avellaneda, Andrés. "The Process of Censorship and the Censorship of the Proceso: Argentina 1976–1983." *The Redemocratization of Argentine Culture, 1983 and Beyond*. Ed. David W. Foster. Tempe: Arizona State University Center for Latin American Studies, 1989. 23–47.

Aydemir, Murat. *Images of Bliss: Ejaculation, Masculinity, Meaning*. Minneapolis: U of Minnesota P, 2007.

Azeredo, Sandra Maria da Mata. "Era uma vez . . . uma análise." *Cadernos Pagu* 20 (2003): 205–16.

Bacchetta, Paola, Tina Campi, Inderpal Grewal, Caren Kaplan, Minoo Moallem, and Jennifer Terry. "Por uma prática feminista transnacional contra a Guerra." *Revista de Estudos Feministas* 9.2 (2001): 353–59.

Baccoloni, Raffaella. "Gender and Genre in the Feminist Critical Dystopias of Catherine Urdekin, Margaret Atwood and Octavia Butler." *Future Females, The Next Generation: New Voices and Velocities in Feminist Science Fiction Criticism*. Ed. Marlene S. Barr. Lanham: Rowman and Littlefield, 2000. 13–34

Bakhtin, Mikhail. "Discourse in the Novel." *The Dialogic Imagination: Four Essays*. Ed. Michael Holquist. Trans. Caryl Emerson and Michael Holquist. Austin: U of Texas P, 1983.

———. *Problems of Dostoevsky's Poetics*. Minneapolis: U of Minnesota P, 1984.

Balderston, Daniel, David William Foster, Tulio Halperin Donghi. *Ficción y política: la narrativa argentina durante el proceso militar*. Buenos Aires: Alianza Editorial, 1987.

Barone, Roxana. "Provincia 25: La Argentina en España." *Endoscontinentes* I (2004): 1–2.

Barr, Marlene S. *Feminist Fabulation. Space/Postmodern Fiction*. Iowa City: U of Iowa P, 1992.

———. *Lost in Space. Probing Feminist Science Fiction and Beyond*. Chapel Hill: U of North Carolina P, 1993.

Bassani, Lorena. "Mujeres adictas a la pornografía: todo lo que entra, entra por los ojos." Clarin.com conexiones www.clarin.com/diario/2005/06/06/conexiones/t-990034.htm. 6 Jun. 2005. 18 Nov. 2007.

Bassnett, Susan. "Speaking with Many Voices: The Poems of Alejandra Pizarnik." *Knives and Angels: Women Writers in Latin America*. Ed. Susan Bassnett. London: Zed Books, 1990. 36–51

Baudrillard, Jean. *Simulations*. Trans. Nicola Dufresne. New York: Semiotext(e), 1983.

Bell, Andrea. "Science Fiction in Latin America: Reawakening." *Science Fiction Studies* 26 (1999): 441–46.

Bell, Andrea, and Yolanda Molina-Gavilán, eds. *Cosmos Latinos: An Anthology of Science Fiction from Latin America and Spain*. Middletown, CT: Wesleyan UP, 2003.

Bellessi, Diana, Magui Bellotti, Hayde Birgin, Lea Fletcher, Patricia Kolensnicol, Diana Mafia, and Monica Tarducci. "VII Encuentro Feminista Latinoamericano y del Caribe." *Feminaria* 10.19 (1997): 28–36.

——. "Todas ibamos a ser ancianas indecentes." www.fempress.cl/base/fem/bellesi. html. 1 Jan. 2002

Bellucci, Mabel. "Volviendo del silencio." *Feminaria* 14.26/27 (2001): 37–38.

Bennett, Susan. *Theater Audiences: A Theory of Production and Reception*. London: Routledge, 1990.

Bergmann, Emilie, Janet Greenberg, Gwen Kirkpatrick, Francine Masiello, Francesca Miller, Marta Morello-Frosch, Kathleen Newman, Mary Louise Pratt. *Women, Culture and Politics in Latin America. Seminar on Feminism and Culture in Latin America*. Berkeley: U of California P, 1992.

Beserra, Bernadete. "Sob a sombra de Carmen Miranda e do carnaval: brasileiras em Los Angeles." *Cadernos Pagu* 28 (2007): 313–44.

Bessa, Karla. "Os festivais GLBT de cinema e as mudanças estético-políticas na constituição da subjetividade." *Cadernos Pagu* 28 (2007): 257–83.

Besse, Susan Kent. "Freedom and Bondage: The Impact of Capitalism on Women in São Paulo, Brazil 1917–1937." Diss. Yale University, 1983.

Bhabha, Homi K. *The Location of Culture*. London: Routledge, 1994.

Birkerts, Sven. "Present at the Re-Creation: Margaret Atwood's Naïve Protagonist Works for the Brilliant, Monomaniacal Scientist." *New York Times Book Review*. 18 May 2003: 12.

Biron, Rebecca. "Feminist Periodicals and Political Crisis in Mexico: *Fem, debate feminista* and *La Correa Feminista* in the 1990s." *Feminist Studies* 22.1 (1996): 151–69.

Blackwood, Evelyn and Saskia Wieringa, eds. *Female Desires: Same-Sex Relations and Transgender Practices across Cultures*. New York: Columbia UP, 1999.

Blanco, Jorge Ayala. *La condición del cine mexicano*. México: Editorial Posada, 1986.

Boggs, Joseph M. *The Art of Watching Films*. 3rd ed. Mountain View, CA: Mayfield Publishing, 1991.

Bonini, Celina. "Entrevista con Gina Vargas" *Feminaria* 13 24/25 (2000): 47–52.

Bordo, Susan. "A Feminista Como O Outro." *Revista de Estudos Feministas* 8.1 (2000): 10–29.

Bornstein, Kate. Preface. *PoMoSexuals: Challenging Assumptions About Gender and Sexuality*. Ed. Carol Queen and Lawrence Schimel. San Francisco: Cleis Press, 1997.

"Brazil a Leader in Gay Hate Crimes." *United Press International* 23 April 2002. 15 Jul. 2005. http://www.upi.com/view.cfm?StoryID=23042002–052102–4811r.

Bueno Fischer, Rosa Maria. "Mídia e educação da mulher: uma discussão teórica sobre os modos de enunciar o femenino na TV." *Revista de Estudos Feministas* 9.2 (2001): 586–600.

Buikema, Rosemarie, and Anneke Smelik, eds. *Women's Studies and Culture. A Feminist Introduction.* London: Zed Books, 1995.

Bulbeck, Chilla. *Re-Orienting Western Feminisms. Women's Diversity in a Postcolonial World.* Cambridge: Cambridge UP, 1998.

Burundarena, Maitena. *Mujeres alteradas.* No. 1. 4ta. ed. Buenos Aires: Editorial Atlántida, 2000, c1994.

——. *Mujeres alteradas.* No. 2. 4ta. ed. Buenos Aires: Editorial Atlántida, 1999, c1995.

——. *Mujeres alteradas.* No. 2. Ed. rev. Buenos Aires: Editorial Atlántida, 2000, c1995.

——. *Mujeres alteradas.* No. 3. Buenos Aires: Editorial Atlántida, 2000, c1997.

——. *Mujeres alteradas* No. 4. Buenos Aires: Editorial Atlántida,1999, c1998.

——. *Mujeres alteradas.* No. 5. Buenos Aires: Editorial Sudamericana, 2001.

——. *Superadas.* La Nación online.

——. www://maitena.com.ar.

Butler, Judith. "Performative Acts and Gender Constitution: An Essay on Phenomenology and Feminist Theory." *Writing on the Body.* Ed. Kate Conboy, Nadia Medina, and Sarah Stanbury. New York: Columbia UP, 1997. 400–417.

Cabral, Mauro, and Gabriel Benzur. "Cuando digo intersex: un diálogo introductorio a la intersexualidad." *Cadernos Pagu* 24 (2005): 283–304.

Cadena, Agustín. La literatura erótica escrita por mujeres en México." *Ínsula: Revista de Letras y Ciencias Humanas* (Ínsula) (2004): 685–86.

Cadernos Pagu 14 (2000). Organizadoras: Adrianna Piscitelli and Filomena Gregori. Universidade Estadual de Campinas, UNICAMP.

Cadernos Pagu 29 (2007). Repensando relações familiares. Comitê Editorial. Universidade Estadual de Campinas, UNICAMP.

Cadernos Pagu 26 (2006). "Dossiê Diferenças em jogo." Universidade Estadual de Campinas, UNICAMP.

Cadernos Pagu 28 (2007). "Dossiê: Sexualidades disparatadas." Universidade Estadual de Campinas, UNICAMP.

Cadernos Pagu 20 (2003). "Dossiê: Erotismo: prazer, perigo." Universidade Estadual de Campinas, UNICAMP.

Caldwell, Kia Lilly. *Negras in Brazil: Re-Envisioning Black Women, Citizenship, and the Politics of Identity.* New Brunswick, N.J.: Rutgers UP, 2007.

Califia, Pat. *Public Sex: The Culture of Radical Sex.* San Francisco: Cleis Press, 2000.

——. *Sex Changes: The Politics of Transgenderism.* 2nd ed. San Francisco: Cleis Press, 2003.

"Camp." *Random House Dictionary of the English Language Second Edition.* New York: Random House, 1987. 301.

Cano, Gabriela. "Ni tanto ni tan poco: las reformas penales relatives a la violencia sexual." *debate feminista* 1.2 (1990).

Carlson, Marifran. *¡Feminismo! The Woman's Movement in Argentina from Its Beginnings to Eva Perón.* Chicago: Academy Chicago Publishers, 1988.

Carson, Diane, Linda Dittmar, and Janice R. Welsch, eds. *Multiple Voices in Feminist Film Criticism.* Minneapolis: U of Minnesota P, 1994.

Castillo, Debra. *Talking Back: Toward a Latin American Feminist Literary Criticism.* Ithaca: Cornell UP, 1992.

———. *Easy Women: Sex and Gender in Modern Mexican Fiction.* Minneapolis: U of Minnesota P, 1998.

Castillo Zapata, Rafael. "Bolero." *Encyclopedia of Contemporary Latin American and Caribbean Cultures Vol 1 A–D.* Ed. Daniel Balderston, Mike Gonzalez, and Ana M. López. London and New York: Routledge, 2000.

———. *Fenomenología del Bolero.* Caracas: Monte Avila, 1990.

Castro, Mary Garcia, and Lena Lavinas. "Do feminismo ao gênero: A construção de um objeto." *Uma Questão de Genêro.* Ed.Albertina de Oliier Costa and Cristina Bruschini. Rio de Janeiro: Editora Rosa dos Tempos/Fundação Carlos Chagas, 1992. 216–51.

Castro-Klarén, Sarah, Sylvia Molloy, and Beatriz Sarlo, eds. *Womens' Writing in Latin American: An Anthology.* Boulder: Western, 1991.

Cátedra Libre en Salud Reproductiva, Sexualidad y Género. Universidad de la República. 31 Jan. 2008. www.psico.edu.uy/academic/sexrep.htm.

Causo, Roberto de Sousa. *Ficção científica, fantasia e horror no Brasil 1875–1950.* Belo Horizonte: Editora UFMG, 2003.

"Cecilia Rossetto en Madrid." March 5–May 8, 2004. New Alcalá Theater. Dir. and Text Cecilia Rossetto. Poems Oscar Balducci. Lighting Ariel de Maestro.

Centro de Estudios de Género. Benemérita Universidad Autónoma de la Puebla. 31 Jan. 2008. www.estudiosmasculinidades.buap.mx/paginas/reporteelvarivera.htm.

Centro de Estudios de Género. Universidad de El Salvador. 31 Jan. 2008, www.ues.edu.sv/investigacion/institutos_y_centros.htm.

Centro de Estudios de Género. Universidad de Guadalajara. 31 Jan. 2008, www.cucsh.udg.mx/mxdivdep/phpdees/indexceg.php.

Centro de Estudios de la Mujer. Universidad Central de Venezuela. 31 Jan. 2008, http://cem.ve.tripod.com/.

Centro de Investigación en Estudios de la Mujer. Universidad de Costa Rica. 31 Jan. 2008. www.ciem.ucr.ac.cr/index.htm.

Centro de Investigaciones Socio-Educativas. Universidad Nacional Autónoma de Nicaragua. 31 Jan. 2008. www.unan.edu.ni/Cise/cise.htm.

CFEMEA. Dec. 2003. Centro Feminista de Estudos e Assessoria. 1 Jan. 2008. www.cfemea.org.br/.

Chaher, Sandra, and Sonia Santoro. *Artemisa Noticias—Periodismo de género para mujeres y varones.* 6 July 2005. Artemisa Comunicación. 1 Jan. 2008.

Chanan, Michael. *Cuban Cinema.* Vol. 14 of Cultural Studies of the Americas. Minneapolis: U of Minnesota P, 2004.

Chancer, Lynn S. *Reconcilable Differences. Confronting Beauty, Pornography, and the Future of Feminism.* Berkeley, CA, London: U of California P, 1998.

Chauncey, George. "The Ridicule of Gay and Lesbian Studies Threatens All Academic Inquiry." *Chronicle of Higher Education* 3 Jul. 1998: A40.

Chávez-Silverman, Susana. "Tropicolada: Inside the U.S. Latino/a Gender B(l)ender." *Tropicalizations: Transcultural Representations of "Latinidad."* Ed. Frances R. Aparicio and Susana Chávez-Silverman. Hanover: UP of New England, 1997. 101–18.

———. "Trac(k)ing Gender and Sexuality in the Writing of Alejandra Pizarnik." *Chasqui* (2006): 89–108.

Chaviano, Daína. *Fábula de una abuela extraterreste*. Havana: Letras Cubanas, 1988; Mexico City: Oceano, 2003.

———. "The Annunciation." *Cosmos Latinos: An Anthology of Science Fiction from Latin America and Spain*. Ed. Andrea Bell and Yolanda Molina-Gavilán. Middletown, CT: Wesleyan UP, 201–207.

"Chile: International Conference on Women's Literature in Latin America, August 17–21, 1987." *Resources for Feminist Research* 16.4 (1987): 62–63.

Chinchilla, Norma. "Marxism, Feminism and the Struggle or Democracy in Latin America." *Materialist Feminism: A Reader in Class, Difference, and Women's Lives*. Ed. and intro Rosemary Hennessy and Chrys Inraham. New York: Routledge, 1997. 214–26.

Christian, Barbara. "A disputa pela teoria." *Revista de Estudos Feministas* 10.1 (2002): 85–98.

Ciencia y Ficción. 18 Dec. 2007. http://orbita.starmedia.com/cienciayficcion/.

Cimac Noticias—Periodismo con perspectiva de género. Organización de Comunicación e Información de la Mujer. 1 Jan. 2008. http://www.cimacnoticias.com/site/.

Citeli, María Teresa. "Mulheres nas ciências: mapeando campos de estudo." *Cadernos Pagu* 15 (2000). www.unicamp.br/pagu/cadernos15.html. 10 May 2003.

Cleto, Fabio. Introduction. *Camp: Queer Aesthetics and the Performing Subject: A Reader*. Ed. Fabio Cleto. Ann Arbor: U of Michigan P, 1999. 1–42.

Clifford, James. *The Predicament of Culture: Twentieth-Century Ethnography, Literature and Art*. Cambridge: Harvard UP, 1988.

"Colegio de México Received a $467,525.00 Grant from the Ford Foundation." *Diverse: Issues in Higher Education* (24 Aug. 2006): 46.

Constantino, Roselyn. "Postmodernism and Feminism in Contemporary Mexican Theatre. *Aura y las once mil virgenes*. By Carmen Boullosa." *Latin American Theatre Review* 28 (1995): 55–71.

———. "Visibility as a Strategy: Jesusa Rodriguez's Body in Play." *Corpus Delecti: Performance Art of the Americas*. Ed. Coco Fusco. London and New York: Routledge, 2000. 63–77.

———, and Diana Taylor. Introduction. *Holy Terrors: Latin American Women Perform*. Durham: Duke UP, 2003. 1–24.

Cornell, Drucilla, and Janet Allured. *Feminism and Pornography*. Oxford, UK; New York: Oxford UP, 2000.

Corrêa, Mariza. "Do feminismo aos estudos de gênero no Brasil, um exemplo pessoal." *Cadernos Pagu* 16 (2001). www.unicamp.br/pagu/cadernos15.html. 10 May 2003.

Correa, Mariza. "Apresentação." *Cadernos Pagu* 23 (2004): 7–9.

Cortez, Beatriz. "Negociando la construcción de la identidad: La producción de tres directoras de cine latinoamericano." *Romance Languages Annual* X (1999): 512–18.

Costa, Albertina da, and Cristina Bruschini, eds. *Uma Questão de Gênero*. Rio de Janeiro: Editora Rosa dos Tempos/Fundação Carlos Chagas, 1992.

———. "Women's Studies in Brazil: Tightrope Walking Strategy." *Brazilian Issues on Education, Gender and Race*. Ed. Elba Siquiera de Sá Barretto and Dagmar M. L. Zibas. Trans. Johnathan Hannay. São Paulo: Fundação Carlos Chagas, 1996. 37–47.

Costa, Ana Alicia Alcântara, and Cecilia Sardenberg. "Teoria e praxis feminista na academia: Os núcleos de estudos sobre a mulher nas universidades brasileiras." *Revista de Estudos Feministas* 2, special number 2nd semester (1994): 387–400.

Costa, Claúdia de Lima. "As teorias feministas nas Américas e na política transnacional da tradução." *Revista de Estudos Feministas* 8.2 (2000): 43–48.

———. "Being Here and Writing There: Gender and the Politics of Translation in a Brazilian Landscape" *Signs* 25.3 (2000): 727–60.

———, and Sónia Weidner Maluf. "Feminismo fora do centro: Entrevista com Ella Shohat." *Revista de Estudos Feministas* 9.1 (2001): 147–63.

Costa, Maria Dolores. *Latina Lesbian Writers and Artists*. Binghamton, NY: Harrington Park P, 2004.

Couture, Mark. "The Importance of Being Agustín Lara: Cursilería, Machismo and Modernity." *Studies in Latin American Popular Culture* 21 (2002): 69–80.

Crang, Mike. *Cultural Geography*. London: Routledge, 1998.

Creatividad *Feminista—un espacio donde ser mujer no es un dato indiferente*. 3 Sept. 2007. 1 Jan. 2008. www.creatividadfeminista.org/index.htm.

Crumpacker, Bunny. *The Sex Life of Food: When Body and Soul Meet to Eat*. New York: Thomas Dunne, 2006.

Damasceno, Leslie. "The Gestural Art of Reclaiming Utopia: Denise Stoklos at Play with the Hysterical-Historical." *Holy Terrors: Latin American Women Perform*. Ed. Diana Taylor and Roselyn Costantino. Durham: Duke UP, 2003. 152–78.

Dauphin, Cécile. "Mujeres solas." *El siglo XIX/Actividades y reivindicaciones/Cuerpo, trabajo y modernidad*. Comp. Geneviève Fraisse and Michelle Perrot. Dir. George Duby and Michelle Perrot. Vol. 8 of *Historia de las mujeres*. Madrid: Taurus, 1993. 131–47.

De Barbieri, Teresita, and Gabriela Cano, "Ni tanto ni tan poco: las reformas penales relativas a la violencia sexual." *debate feminista* 1.2 (1990): 348–57.

"Debate de los directores del cine porno argentino." *Boletín Argentino: El portal del Boletín Argentino y de su Suplemento Cultural*. Ed. Osvaldo Parrondo. www .boletinargentino.com/index.php?p=1183.

debate feminista. Vols. 1–24 (1990–2005). Issues 5.9 (1994); 5.10 (1994); 6.11 (1995); 6.12 (1995); 7.13 (1996); 8.16 (1997); 9.17 (1998); 9.18 (1998); 10. 19 (1999); 10.20 (1999); 11.21 (2000); 11.22 (2000); 12.23 (2001); 12.24 (2001); 13.25 (2002); 13.26 (2002); 14.27 (2003): 14.28 (2003); 15.29 (2004); 15.30 (2004); 16.31 (2005); 16.32 (2005). Ed. Marta Lamas. Mexico City.

———. 8 Jan. 2008. www.laneta.apc.org/debate/.

———. Editorial. 11 Dec. 2001. www.laneta.apc.org/debate/editorial23.htm.

———. "Las raras." Editorial. *debate feminista* 15.29 (2004): ix–xii.

Decker, Alicia C. "Rethinking the North-South Intellectual Divide: The Future of Global Women's Studies." Proceeding of the 8th International Interdisciplinary Congress on Women's Studies and Gender Studies, Makerere University, Kampala-Uganda, July 18–26, 2002.

De la Hera, Alberto. "Hacerse con el público tiene su mérito." *Guía del Ocio*. "Críticas" Mar. 2004. 116.

De Lauretis, Teresa. *Alice Doesn't: Feminism, Semiotics, Cinema*. Bloomington: Indiana UP, 1984.

———. "Sexual Indifference and Lesbian Representation" *Theater Journal* 40.2 (1988): 155–77.

——. *Technologies of Gender: Essays on Theory, Film and Fiction*. Bloomington: Indiana UP, 1987.

Dellepiane, A. B. "Mester de fantasía o la narrativa de Angélica Gorodischer." *Revista Iberomericana* 51.132–133 (1985): 627–40.

Del Río, Ana María. *Los siete días de la Señora K*. Santiago: Planeta, 1993.

Del Sarlo, Ana, Alicia Rios, and Abril Trigo, eds. *The Latin American Cultural Studies Reader*. Durham: Duke UP, 2004.

De Moraes, Lisa. "Who Framed Buster Rabbit? The Fallout Continues." *Washington Post* 18 Feb. 2005: C07.

Denser, Márcia, comp. *Muito prazer: contos*. Rio de Janeiro: Editora Record, 1982.

——. *O prazer é todo meu*: Contos eróticos femeninos. 2nd ed. Rio de Janeiro: Editora Record, 1985.

De Russy, Candace. "Revolting Behavior: The Irresponsible Exercise of Academic Freedom." *Chronicle of Higher Education* 6 Mar. 1998: 26.

De Santis, Pablo. *Historieta y política en los '80*. Buenos Aires: Letra Buena, 1992.

——. "Sobre la condición femenina" reseña sobre. *Mujeres Alteradas* 5. Suplemento Cultural. La nación. www.lanacion.com.ar/suples/cultura/0203/B08.htm.

Desmond, Jane. "Embodying Difference: Issues in Dance and Cultural Studies." *Everynight Life: Culture and Dance in Latino/a America*. Ed. Celeste Fraser Delgado and José Esteben Muñoz. Durham: Duke UP, 1997. 33–64.

des-ubicadas.com. Gender Studies program at the Universidad Nacional Mayor de San Marcos in Lima, Peru.

Díaz Rönner, Lucila, and Teresa Azcárate. "Current Drawbacks of Feminisms in Argentina: A View from Paradoxes." 4th European Feminist Research Conference, July 2000. www.women.it/4thfemconf/workshops/politics6/luciladiazazcarate .htm. 12 Nov 2001.

Didriksson T, Axel. "Las macrouniversidades de América Latina y el Caribe." *Reunion de Macrouniversidades de America Latina y el Caribe*. Universidad Central de Venezuela (Estudio auspiciado por el IESACC-UNESCO), Caracas, June 13–14, 2002. 1–17.

Di Leonardo, Micaela. *Exotics at Home: Anthropolgies, Others, American Modernity*. Chicago and London: U of Chicago P, 1998.

——. *The Varieties of Ethnic Experience: Kinship, Class and Gender among California Italian-Americans*. Ithaca: Cornell P, 1984.

Doane, Mary Ann. *Femmes Fatales. Feminism, Film Theory, Psychoanalysis*. New York: Routledge, 1991.

——. *The Desire to Desire: The Woman's Film of the 1940s*. Bloomington: Indiana UP, 1987.

Dolan, Jill. *Presence and Desire: Essays on Gender, Sexuality, Performance* Critical Perspectives on Women and Gender. Ann Arbor: U of Michigan P, 1994.

Domínguez, Nora. "Entrevista con Reina Roffé." *Primer plano. Suplemento cultural de página 12* (26 Jun. 1994): 5–6.

——. "Diálogos del género o cómo no caerse del mapa." *Revista de Estudos Feministas* 8.2 (2000): 113–26.

Dominus, Susan. "What Women Want to Watch: In Porn, the Acting is Hideous; the Decor, Worse. Can Playgirl TV Do Better?" *New York Times*. Arts and Leisure. 29 Aug. 2004.

Donaldson, Laura E. *Decolonizing Feminisms*. Chapel Hill: U of North Carolina P, 1992.

Donaworth, Jane L., and Carol A. Kolmerten, eds. *Utopian and Science Fiction by Women: Worlds of Difference*. Syracuse, NY: Syracuse UP, 1994.

Dorsey, Xochitl. "Women Making Movies, Latin Style." www.wmm.com/news/Articles/wmmlatinstyle_ctarticle.pdf.

Doty, Alexander. *Making Things Perfectly Queer: Interpreting Mass Culture*. Minneapolis: U of Minnesota P, 1993.

Duncan, Cynthia. "Griselda Gambaro." *Latin American Writers on Gay and Lesbian Themes*. Ed. David William Foster. Westport, CT: Greenwood, 1994.

Duque, Félix. *Postmodernidad y apocalipsis: Entre la promiscuidad y la transgresión*. Buenos Aires: Serie Humanitas, 1999.

Eaglen Audrey. "Spreading the Word on Women: Contemporary Women's and Feminist Journals." *Women Library Workers Journal* 15.1 (1992): 4–8

Eagleton, Mary, ed. *A Concise Companion to Feminist Theory*. Oxford: Blackwell, 2003.

Ebert, Teresa L. *Ludic Feminism and After. Postmodernism, Desire, and Labor in Late Capitalism*. Critical Perspectives on Women and Gender Series. Ann Arbor: U of Michigan P, 1996.

Edelman, Lee. *No Future. Queer Theory and the Death Drive*. Durham: Duke UP, 2004.

Edwards, Julie, and Linda McKie. "Los sanitários públicos para mujeres: un asunto grave para la política del cuerpo." *debate feminista* 9.17 (1998): III–30.

Ejército Zapatista de Liberación Nacional. "Chiapas: el alzamiento de las mujeres indígenas. Ley revolucionaria sobre las mujeres." *debate feminista* 5.9 (1994): 16.

Elam, Diane. "Speak for Yourself." *Who Can Speak? Authority and Critical Identity*. Ed. Judith Roof and Robyn Wiegman. Chicago: U of Illinois P, 1995. 231–37.

"El canal Venus cumple 10 anos en la Argentina" diciembre 2004. Sitios Argentina-Notas y Noticias Destacadas e interesantes. 18 Nov. 2007. Source: www.pagina12web.com.ar.

Elena, Alberto, and Marina Díaz López, eds. *The Cinema of Latin America*. London and New York: Wallflower Press, 2003.

El placer de la palabra: literatura erótica femenina de América Latina: Antología crítica. México: Planeta, 1991.

El Sentido de la Vida. www.elsentidodelavida.net.

EME Masculinidades y Equidad de Género. Men Engage Mexico. Consulta Regional para Latinoamérica y el Caribe de la Iniciativa MenEngage (Involucramiento de los Hombres en la Equidad de Género). Ciudad de México, 14 al 16 de noviembre 2007. Convocada por: MenEngage, Instituto Promundo (Brasil), FAI (Save the Children, México) y Salud y Género, AC (México) Conference, November 14–16, 2007. http://eme.cl/.

Enloe, Cynthia. *Bananas, Beaches and Bases: Making Feminist Sense of International Politics*. 2nd ed. Berkeley: U of California P, 2000.

Eren, Patricia. "Assessing Films Directed by Women." *Issues in Feminist Film Criticism*. Ed. Patricia Erens. Bloomington: Indiana UP, 1990. 330–42.

Escuela de Estudios de Género. Universidad Nacional de Colombia. 31 Jan. 2008. www.estudiosgenero.unal.edu.co/.

"Estadística del movimiento migratorio de la Comunidad de Madrid 2003." *Instituto de Estadística, Comunidad de Madrid*. 7 Aug. 2005. www8.madrid.org/iestadis/fijas/efemerides/migrao3nt.htm.

Esteben, Rafael. "Entrevista con Cecilia Rossetto 'Durante el espectáculo canto, baile, lloro y hago chistes.'" 3 May 2004. *Elmundo.es*. 13 Nov. 2004. www.elmundo.es/metrópoli/2004/03/04/teatro/1078391149.html.

Eu, Tu, Eles. Dir. Andrucha Waddington. Writer Elena Soarez. Perfs. Regina Casé. DVD. Colombia Pictures Corporation, Colombia Tristar Filmes do Brasil, Conspiracção Filmes, 2001.

Ewen, Stuart. *All Consuming Images: The Politics of Style in Contemporary Culture*. New York: Basic Books (Perseus) 1988. Rev. ed. 1999.

Faderman, Lillian. *Odd Girls and Twilight Lovers*. New York: Penguin, 1991.

———. *Surpassing the Love of Men*. New York: William Morrow, 1981.

Fares, Gustavo, and Eliana Hermann. "Exilios internos: el viaje en cinco escritoras argentinas." *Hispanic Journal* 15.1 (1994): 21–29.

Fausto-Sterling, Anne. *Sexing the Body: Gender Politics and the Construction of Sexuality*. New York: Basic Books, 2000.

Felipe, Jane. "Afinal, quem é mesmo pedófilo?" *Cadernos Pagu* (2006): 201–223.

Felski, Rita. *Beyond Feminist Aesthetics. Feminist Literature and Social Change*. Cambridge: Harvard UP, 1989.

Feminaria. 2.4 (1989); 3.6 (1990); 5.8 (1992); 5.9 (1992); 6.10 (1993); 6.11 (1993); 7.12 (1994); 7.13 (1994); 8.14 (1995); 9 17/18 (1996); 10.19 (1997); 10.20 (1997); 11.21 (1998); 10.22/23 (1999); 13. 24/25 (2000); 14.26/27 (2001); 28/29 (2002). Ed. Lea Fletcher. Buenos Aires.

Feminaria Editora. 8 Jan. 2008. http://feminaria.com.ar/default.asp.

"Feminismo vs pornografia?" des-ubicadas: genero y feminismo en la red. 16 febrero. www.Des-ubicadas-peg.blogspot.com/2007/02/feminismo-vs-pornografia.html. 18 Nov. 2007.

"Feminist Science Fiction" www.litencyc.com/php/stopics.php?rec=true&UID=382.

feministasanónimas.com "Queremos una pornografia para mujeres." 7 Nov. 2006. http://feministasanonimas.blogspot.com/2006/11/queremos-una-pornografa-para-mujeres.html. 18 Nov. 2007.

"Ficção *Científica*." 10 Oct. 2004. Com Ciência. Accessed 18 Dec. 2007. www.comciencia.br/reportagens/2004/10/11.shtml.

Field Listing—Internet Users. 13 Dec. 2007. Central Intelligence Agency. 8 Jan. 2008. www.cia.gov/library/publications/the-world-factbook/fields/2153.html.

Figueroa Perea, Juan Guillermo. "Derechos Reproductivos y Feminismo en la experiencia de los varones." *Revista de Estudos Feministas* 8.1 (2000): 131–44.

Fiol-Matta, Licia. "'Raras' por mandato: la maestra, lo queer, y el estado en Gabriela Mistral." *debate feminista* 15.29 (2004): 118–37.

Fitz, Earl E. *Brazilian Narrative Traditions in a Comparative Context*. World Literatures Reimagined Series. New York: The Modern Language Association of America, 2005.

Fletcher, Lea. "Re: Mensaje para Lea Fletcher." E-mail to Melissa A. Fitch. 20 Jan. 2002.

———. "Un silencio a gritos: tortura, violación y literatura de la Argentina." *Feminaria* 9.17/18 (1996): 49–53.

Flinn, Caryl. "The Deaths of Camp." *Camp: Queer Aesthetics and the Performing Subject: A Reader*. Ed. Fabio Cleto. Ann Arbor: U of Michigan P, 1999. 433–57.

Forcinto, Ana. "Mirada Cinematográfica y Genero Sexual: Mímica, Erotismo y Ambigüedad en Lucrecia Martel." *Chasqui: Revista de Literatura Latinoamericana* 35.2 (2006): 109–30.

"Foreign Languages and Higher Education: New Structures for a Changed World." MLA Ad Hoc Committee on Foreign Languages. May 2007 *Profession* 2007. 1–11.

Forte, Jorge. *Guía de Recursos de la Ciencia Ficción en español.* 18 Dec. 2007. www .geocities.com/Athens/7037/guia.html.

Foster, David William. *Sexual Textualities: Essays on Queer/ing Latin American Writing.* Austin: U of Texas P, 1997.

———, and Roberto Reis, eds. *Bodies and Biases: Sexualities in Hispanic Cultures and Literatures.* Minneapolis: U of Minnesota P, 1996.

———. "The Case for Feminine Pornography in Latin America." *Bodies and Biases*: 246–73.

———. *From Mafalda to los Supermachos: Latin American Graphic Humor as Popular Culture.* London: Lynne Rienner, 1989.

———. *Gay and Lesbian Themes in Latin American Literature.* Austin: U of Texas P, 1991.

———. "*Mulher no espelho.*" *Chasqui* 19.1 (1990): 123.

———. "Of Power and Virgins: Alejandra Pizarnik's *La condesa sangrienta.*" *Violence in Argentine Literature: Cultural Responses to Tyranny.* Columbia: U of Missouri P, 1995. 98–114.

———. *Gender and Society in Contemporary Brazilian Cinema.* Austin: U of Texas P, 1999.

Foster, Gwendolyn Audrey. *Women Film Directors : An International Bio-critical Dictionary.* Westport, CT: Greenwood, 1995.

Foucault, Michel. *The Archeology of Knowledge: The Discourse on Language.* Trans. A. M. Sheridan Smith. New York: Harper and Row, 1972.

———. *Discipline and Punishment: The Birth of the Prison.* Trans. A. M. Sheridan Smith. New York: Random, 1977.

———. *The History of Sexuality: An Introduction.* Trans. Robert Hurley. Vol. I, New York: Vantage Books, 1980.

Foxley, Ana María. "Acoplamiento incestuoso." *Hoy* 12.18 (Aug. 1985): 41.

———. " Me interesa todo aquello que esté a contrapelo del poder." *La época* 20 (Nov. 1988): 4–5.

———. "¿Una palabra sospechosa?" [Santiago de Chile] *La época* (15 May 1988): 5.

Franco, Jean. "Beyond Ethnocentrism: Gender, Power, and the Third World Intelligencia." *Marxism and the Interpretation of Culture.* Ed. and intro. Carl Nelson and Lawrence Grossberg. Urbana: U of Illinois P, 1988. 503–15.

———. "Afterword. From Romance to Refractory Aesthetic." *Latin American Women's Writing: Feminist Readings in Theory and Crisis.* Ed. Anny Brooksbank Jones and Catherine Davies. New York: Oxford UP, 1996. 226–37.

Frank, Thomas, and Matt Weiland, eds. *Commodify Your Dissent.* New York: W.W. Norton, 1997.

Frederick, Bonnie. *Wily Modesty: Argentine Women Writers, 1860–1910.* Tempe: Arizona State University, Center for Latin American Studies, 1998.

Fuller, Norma. "Los estudios de genero en el ámbito sudamericano." *Global Education Digest 2005.* Montreal: UNESCO Institute for Statistics, 2005. http://inicia.es/ de/cgarciam/Fuller.html.

Gall, Olivia. Editorial. *debate feminista* 12.24 (2001). www.laneta.apc.org/debate/ editorial24.htm

Gambaro, Griselda. *Dios no nos quiere contentos.* Barcelona: Lumen, 1979.

———. *Ganarse la muerte: novela.* Buenos Aires: Ediciones de la Flor, 1976.

———. *Lo impenetrable*. Buenos Aires: Torres Agüero, 1984.

———. *The Impenetrable Madam X*. Trans. Evelyn Picon Garfield. Detroit: Wayne State UP, 1991.

Garber, Marjorie B. *Vice Versa: Bisexuality and the Eroticism of Everyday Life*. New York: Simon & Schuster, 1995.

Garciá, Irene. "Mimi Derba and Azteca Fjilms: The Rise of Nationalism and the First Mexican Woman Director." Natividad Gutiérrez-Chong. *Women, Ethnicity and Nationalism in Latin America*. Aldershot, England; Burlington, VT: Ashgate, 2007.

García Canclini, Néstor. "¿Ciudades multiculturales o ciudades segregadas?" *debate feminista* 9.17 (1998): 3–19.

———. *Consumers and Citizens: Globalization and Multicultural Conflicts*. Trans. and intro. George Yúdice. Minneapolis/London: U of Minnesota P, 2001.

———. *Culturas híbridas: estrategias para entrar y salir de la modernidad*. México: Editorial Grijalbo, 1990.

———. *Imaginarios urbanos*. 2nd ed. Buenos Aires: Editorial Universidad de Buenos Aires. 1999.

García-Corales, Guillermo. "Crítica cultural: Relaciones del poder y carnavalización en la novela chilena contemporanea." Diss. University of Colorado, 1993.

———, and Sandra Garabano. "Entrevista." *Hispamérica* 21.62 (1992): 65–75.

Geertz, Clifford. *Works and Lives: The Anthropologist's Author*. Stanford, CA: Stanford UP, 1988.

Género, investigación y formación. Mujeres en red. 31 Jan. 2008. www.nodo50.org/mujeresred/investigacion.htm.

Gever, Martha, John Greyson, and Pratibha Parmar. *Queer Looks. Perspectives on Lesbian and Gay Film and Video*. New York: Routledge, 1993.

Gilbert, Sandra M. "Literary Paternity." *Critical Theory Since 1965*. Ed. Hazard Adams and Leroy Searle. Tallahassee, Florida: Florida UP, 1986. 485–96.

Gimbernat González, Ester. "*La rompiente* o la integración de la escritura." *Aventuras del desacuerdo: novelistas argentinas de los 80*. Buenos Aires: Danilo Albero Vergara, 1992. 186–90.

Ginway, M. Elizabeth. *Brazilian Science Fiction. Cultural Myths and Nationhood in the Land of the Future*. Lewisberg, PA: Bucknell UP, 2004.

———. "A Working Model for Analyzing Third World Science Fiction: The Case of Brazil." *Science Fiction Studies* 32 (2005): 467–95.

———. "Vampires, Werewolves and Strong Women: Alternate Histories or the Re-writing of Race and Gender in Brazilian History." *Extrapolation* 44.3 (2003): 283–97.

Global Education Digest 2005. Montreal: UNESCO Institute for Statistics, 2005.

Glória, Maria da. "Mutilating the Written Word." *Index on Censorship* 8.4 (1979): 27–30.

Gomes, Helena. *O arqueiro e a feiticeira* [The Archer and the Enchantress]. São Paulo: Editora Devir, 2003.

Gómez, Leila. "El cine de Lucrecia Martel: La Medusa en lo recóndito." *Lehman Collage*. 10 Dec. 2007. www.lehman.cuny.edu/ciberletras/v13/gomez.htm.

Gomez, Marga. *Hung Like a Fly*. Prod. David Drozen and Irene Pinn. Recorded at Jessie's Cabaret, San Francisco. Uproar Entertainment. Westlake Village, CA, 1997.

———. www.myspace.com/margagomezcomedy.

——. www.margagomez.com.

——. www.youtube.com/user/GomezMarga.

——. Vlog YouTube. 10 Aug. 2007. www.youtube.com/view_play_list?p=03B47D9FIA6464F0.

——. Anna Nichole Smith. 26 Feb. 2007.

——. Dinah, Lesbians, Golf and Cookies. 2 Apr. 2007.

——. Intimate Details.www.margagomez.com.

——. The L Word.Berkeley, CA. Apr. 2007.

——. Mojitos and Labels. 22 Feb. 2007.

Gómez, Mercedes. "Crímenes de odio en Estados Unidos. La distinción analítica entre excluir y discrimar." *debate feminista* 15.29 (2004): 158–86.

Good Girl. Dir. Erica Lust, 2004.

Good For Her. Feminist Porn Awards. 2007.

Gorodischer, Angélica. "Narrativa fantástica y narrativa de ciencia-ficción." *Plural: revista cultural de excelsior* 188 (1987): 48–50.

——. *Casta luna eletrónica*. Buenos Aires: Andrómeda, 1977.

——. *Kalpa Imperial. Libro I: La casa del poder*. Buenos Aires: Minotauro, 1983. Barcelona: Martínez Roca, 1990.

——. *Kalpa Imperial. Libro II: El imperio más vasto*. Buenos Aires: Minotauro, 1984.

——. *Mala noche y parir hembra*. Buenos Aires: La Campana, 1983.

——. *Opus Dos*. Buenos Aires: Minotauro, 1967. Barcelona: Ultramar, 1990.

——. *Las repúblicas*. Buenos Aires: La Campana, 1991.

——. *Trafalgar*. Buenos Aires: El Cid, 1979. Rosario: Ediciones El Peregrino, 1984. Barcelona: Orbis, 1986.

Gramugli, María Teresa. "Aproximaciones a *La rompiente*." Roffé, *La rompiente*. Buenos Aires: Puntosur, 1987. 127–35.

"Grants and Awards." *Diverse: Issues in Higher Education* 23.14 (2006): 46.

Greenberg, Janet. "Toward a History of Women's Periodicals in Latin America: A Working Bibliography." Bergmann et al. *Women, Culture and Politics*. 172–231.

Greenblatt, Stephan. "Me Myself and I." *New York Review of Books* 51.6 (2004).

Greene, Gayle, and Coppelia Kahn, eds. *Changing Subjects: The Making of Feminist Literary Criticism*. London: Routledge, 1993.

Grewal Inderpal, and Caren Kaplan, eds. *Scattered Hegemonies: Postmodernity and Transnational Feminist Practices*. Minneapolis: U of Minnesota P, 2002.

Grossi, Miriam Pillar. "Gênero e parentesco: famílias gays e lésbicas no Brasil. *Cadernos Pagu* 21 (2003): 261–80.

Groves, Sharon. "News and Views." *Feminist Studies* 29.3 (2003): 673–75.

Gruppelli Loponte, Luciana. "Sexualidade, artes visuais e poder pedagogias visuais de femenino." *Revista de Estudos Feministas* 10.2 (2002): 283–300.

Grussing Abdel Moneim, Sarah. "Virtual Voices: Electronic Bodies: Women and Resistance in Cyber-Chiapas." *Feministas Unidas* 19.2. (1999): 34–42.

Habell-Pallán, Michelle. *Loca Motion: The Travels of Chicana and Latina Popular Culture*. New York and London: New York UP, 2005.

Habell-Pallán, Michelle, and Mary Romero, eds. *Latino/a Popular Culture*. New York: New York UP, 2002.

Hahner, June Edith. "Recent Research on Women in Brazil." *Latin American Research Review* 20.3 (1985): 163–79.

Haraway, Donna J. "A Cyborg Manifesto: Science, Technology, and Socialist-Feminism in the Late Twentieth Century." *Simians, Cyborgs, and Women: The Reinvention of Nature.* New York: Routledge, 1991. 149–81.

Harrington C. Lee, and Denise D. Bielby. *Popular Culture: Production and Consumption.* Oxford: Blackwell, 2001.

Hartsock, Nancy. "Foucault on Power: A Theory for Women?" *Feminism/Postmodernism.* Ed. Linda J. Nicholson. New York: Routledge, 1990. 157–75.

Harvey, David. "Urbanization of Consciousness." *The Urban Experience.* Baltimore: Johns Hopkins UP, 1989. 229–55.

——. *The Condition of Postmodernity.* Cambridge: Cambridge UP, 1989.

——. *The Urban Experience.* Padstow, UK: TJ Press, 1989.

Haskell, Molly. *From Reverence to Rape. The Treatment of Women in the Movies.* New York: Penguin Books, 1974.

Hausman, Bernice L. *Changing Sex: Transsexualism, Technology, and the Idea of Gender.* Durham: Duke UP, 1995.

Hautzinger, Sarah J. *Violence in the City of Women: Police and Batterers in Bahia, Brazil.* Berkeley: U of California P, 2007.

Hawley, John C., ed. *Post-colonial Queer: Theoretical Intersections.* Albany: State U of New York P, 2001.

Hershfield, Joanne. *Mexican Cinema, Mexican Woman: 1940–1950.* Tucson: U of Arizona P, 1996.

Hershfield, Joanne, and David Maciel. "Women and Gender Representations in the Contemporary Cinema of Mexico." *Mexico's Cinema: A Century of Film and Film-makers.* Ed. Joanne Hershfield and David Maciel. Wilmington DE: Scholarly Resources, 1999.

Hiriart, Berta, and Adriana O. Ortega, "Notas sobre feminismo y sexualidad" *Fem* 41 (1985).

Hodgdon, Tim. " '*Fem*:' A Window onto the Cultural Coalescence of a Mexican Feminist Politics of Sexuality." *Mexican Studies/Estudios Mexicanos* 16.1 (2000): 79–104.

Hoeg, Jerry Van. "Angélica Gorodicher." *Latin American Science Fiction Writers: An A to Z Guide.* Ed. Darrell B. Lockhart. Westport, CT: Greenwood, 2004. 95–99.

Hollanda, Heloisa Buarque de. "Os estudos de mulher e literature no Brasil: Uma primeira avaliação." *Costa and Bruschini* (1992): 54–92.

Holm-Nielsen, Lauritz B., and Kristian Thorn. "Higher Education in Latin America: A Regional Overview." The World Bank, 2005. www.worldbank.org.

hooks, bell. *Teaching to Transgress: Education as a Practice of Freedom.* New York: Routledge, 1994.

Hoover, Eric. "The New Sex Scribes: Female Columnists Spark Interest and Controversy at Student Newspapers" *Chronicle of Higher Education* 14 Jun. 2002. http://chronicle.com Sec.: Students. A33.

Hopkins, J. "Mapping of Cinematic Places: Icons, Ideology and the Power of (mis) representation." *Place, Power, Situation and Spectacle: A Geography of Film.* Ed. Leo Aitken and Stuart Zonn. Lantham: Rowan and Littlefield, 1994. 47–65.

Hutcheon, Linda. *The Politics of Postmodernism.* New York: Routledge, 1989.

————. *Narcissistic Narrative: The Metafictional Paradox.* Waterloo, Ontario: Wilfrid Laurier UP, 1980.

Iglesias, Francisco José Súñer. *Sitio de Ciencia-Ficción.* 17 Dec. 2007. www.ciencia -ficcion.com/bienvenida.html.

"International Press." *Maitena.com.* www.clubcultura.com/clubhumor/maitena/notas 04_eng.htm.

Instituto de Derechos Humanos. Universidad Nacional de la Plata. 31 Jan. 2008. www.derechoshumanos.unlp.edu.ar/ddhh/areas.php?categ=36.

Instituto de Estudios de la Mujer. Universidad Nacional de Costa Rica. 31 Jan. 2008. www.una.ac.cr/iem/principal.htm.

Instituto Papai. www.ufpe.br/papai/.

Internet Filter Review. "Pornography."

Internet Movie Datebase (IMDB). 21 Jan. 2008. www.imdb.com.

Iron Chef America: The Series The Food Network. Presented by Alton Brown, Kevin Brauch. Starring Mario Batali, Cat Cora, Bobby Flay, Masaharu Morimoto Michael Symon, Mark Dacascos.

Jackson, Rosemary. *Fantasy: The Literature of Subversion.* London: Methuen, 1981.

Jacoby, Susan. *The Age of Unreason.* New York: Pantheon, 2008.

Jagose, Annamarie. *Queer Theory: An Introduction.* New York: New York UP, 1996.

Jameson, Fredric. "Posmodernismo y sociedad de consumo." *La posmodernidad.* Ed. and prologue Hal Foster. Trans. Jordi Filba. Original title: *The Anti-aesthetic: Essays on Postmodern Culture* (Bay Press: 1st ed. 1984; 2nd. 1986). Barcelona: Editorial Kairós, 1985.

————. "The Cultural Logic of Late Capitalism." *Postmodernism, or, The Cultural Logic of Late Capitalism.* Durham: Duke UP, 1991.

Johnson, Randal, and Robert Stam, eds. *Brazilian Cinema.* Austin: U of Texas P, 1988.

————, eds. *Brazilian Cinema.* Expanded ed. New York: Columbia UP, 1995.

Johnson, Reed. "A Self-baring Strip: Her Comic's Candor Wins Argentina's Maitena a Far Flung Following." *Los Angeles Times.* 11 Apr. 2006.

Juliano, Dolores. "El trabajo sexual en la mira: polémicas y estereotipos." *Cadernos Pagu* 25 (2005): 79–106.

Kadir, Djelal. *The Other Writing: Postcolonial Essays in Latin America's Writing Culture.* West Lafayette, IN: Purdue UP, 1993.

Kaminsky, Amy. "Issues for an International Feminist Literary Criticism." *Signs* 19 (1993): 213–27.

————. *Reading the Body Politic: Feminist Criticism and Latin American Women Writers.* Minneapolis: U of Minnesota P, 1993.

Kantaris, Geoffrey. "Lola/Lolo: género y violencia en películas de la Ciudad de México." *Guaraguo* 8.18 (2004): 57–78.

Kaplan, Ann. *Women and Film: Both Sides of the Camera.* New York: Routledge, 1983.

Kaplan, Carla. *The Erotics of Talk: Women's Writing and Feminist Paradigms.* New York: Oxford UP, 1996.

Karp, Marcelle, and Debbie Stoller, eds. *The Bust Guide to the New Girl Order.* New York: Penguin, 1999.

Katz, Johnathon Ned. *The Invention of Heterosexuality.* New York: Plume, 1996.

Kempadoo, Kamala. "Mudando o debate sobre o tráfico de mulheres." *Cadernos Pagu* 25 (2005): 55–78.

Kerr, Sharon Hybki, and George D. Oberle III. "Women's Resources." *College and Research Libraries News* (May 2005): 366–70.

Khamsi, Roxanne. "Women Become Sexually Aroused as Quickly as Men." www .newscientist.com. 2 Oct. 2006. 19 Nov. 2007.

King, John. *Magical Reels: A History of Cinema in Latin America.* London; New York: Verso, 1990.

Kirkwood, Julieta. *Ser política en Chile: Las feministas y los partidos.* Santiago, Chile: FLASCO, 1986.

Klautau, Michelle. *O crepúsculo da fé.* São Paulo: Devir, 2001.

——. *A legendária Hy Brasil.* São Paulo: Devir, 2005.

Knaster, Meri. "Women in Latin America: State of Research, 1975." *Latin American Research Review* 11.1 (1976): 3–74.

——. "Women in Spanish America: *An Annotated Bibliography from Pre-Conquest to Contemporary Times.* Boston: G. K. Hall, 1977.

Kracauer, Siegfried. *The Mass Ornament: Weimar Essays.* Ed., Trans., and intro Thomas Y. Levin. Cambridge, MA: Harvard UP, 2005.

Kuhn, Annette. *Women's Pictures: Feminism and Cinema.* London: Verso, 1994.

Kulick, Don. *Travesti: Sex, Gender, and Culture among Brazilian Transgendered Prostitutes.* Chicago: U of Chicago P, 1998.

Kuntz, Lynn A. "Side Dishes: Not Just a Side Issue." *Food Product Design.* 1 May 1996. Copyright 2007, Virgo Publishing. www.foodproductdesign.com/. Posted: 1 May 1996. Accessed 30 Dec. 2007.

Kupstas, Marcia. "Gepetto." *Como era gostosa a minha alienígena.* Ed. Gerson Lodi-Ribeiro. São Caetano do sul: Ano Luz, 2002.

Lacombe, Andrea. "De entendidas e sapatonas: socializações lésbicas e masculinidades em um bar do Rio de Janeiro." *Cadernos Pagu* 28 (2007): 207–25.

La Fountain-Stokes. "De sexilio(s) y diáspora(s) homosexual(es) latina(s): cultura puertorriqueña y lo nuyorica queer." *debate feminista* 15.29 (2004) : 138–57.

Lamas, Marta. "Re: *debate feminista.*" E-mail to Melissa A. Fitch. 28 Jan. 2002.

——. "*debate feminista* y el debate feminista." Unpublished essay sent to author. 28 Jan. 2002.

——. "De la autoexclusión al radicalismo participativo. Escenas de un proceso feminista." Unpublished essay sent to author. 28 Jan. 2002.

——. "Opresión y frigidez." *Fem* 4 (1977): 6.

Landini, Tatiana Savoia. "Violência sexual contra crianças na mídia impressa: gênero e geração." *Cadernos Pagu* 26 (2006): 225–52.

Landow, George P. *Hyper/text/theory.* Baltimore: Johns Hopkins UP, 1994.

——. *Hypertext 2.0.* Baltimore, MD; London: Johns Hopkins UP, 1997.

La perspectiva de género en las ciencias sociales y humanas. Universidad Nacional de Córdoba. 30 Jan. 2008. www.ffyh.unc.edu.ar/index2.php.

Laqueur, Thomas W. *Solitary Sex: A Cultural History of Masturbation.* New York: Zone Books, 2003.

"Las pelis porno." *El Sentido de la Vida.* 10 Apr. 2004. www.elsentidodelavida.net/ las-pelis-porno. 18 Nov. 2007.

Latina Feminist Group. *Telling to Live: Latina Feminist Testimonios.* Durham: Duke UP, 2001.

Laudano, Claudia "De mujeres y discursos: veinte anos es mucho." *Feminaria* 9:17/18 (1996). 23–26.

"La violación en México: una lucha por los derechos humanos e las mujeres." *Fem* 28 (1983): 49.

Lavrín, Asunción. "Recent Studies on Women in Latin America (Review Article)." *Latin American Research Review* 19.1 (1984): 181–89.

———. "Sources for the Study of Women in Latin America." *Latin American Masses and Minorities: The Images and Realities.* Ed. Dan Hazen. Madison, WI: SALALM, 1987.

Lefanu, Sarah. *Feminism and Science Fiction.* Bloomington: Indiana UP, 1988.

Lefebvre, Henri. *The Production of Space.* Oxford: Blackwell, 1991.

Leitinger, Ilse Abshagen. *The Costa Rican Women's Movement: A Reader.* Pittsburgh, PA: U of Pittsburgh P, 1997.

Lerner, Gerda. *The Creation of Patriarchy.* New York: Oxford P, 1986.

Lockhart, Darrell B. Introduction. "Latin American Science Fiction A-Z." *Latin American Science Fiction Writers, an A-to-Z-Guide.* Ed. Darrell Lockhart Westport, CT: Greenwood, 2004.

———. "Ana María Shua." *Latin American Science Fiction Writers, an A-to-Z-Guide.* Ed. Darrell Lockhart. Westport, CT: Greenwood, 2004. 190–93.

Lopes Louro, Guacira. "Teoria Queer-uma política pos identificatória para a educação." *Revista de Estudos Feministas* 9.2 (2001): 541–53.

Lorde, Audré. *The Uses of the Erotic: The Erotic as Power.* Trumansburg, NY: Out and Out Books, 1978.

Lovink, Geert. *Dark Fiber: Tracking Critical Internet Culture.* Cambridge, MA; London: MIT Press, 2002.

Lugones, Maria, and Elizabeth Spelman. "Have We Got a Theory for You! Feminist Theory, Cultural Imperialism and the Demand for 'The Woman's Voice.'" *Women's Studies International Forum* 6.6 (1983): 573–81.

Lyotard, Jean-François. *The Postmodern Condition: A Report on Knowledge.* Trans. Geoffrey Bennington and Brian Massumi. Minneapolis: U of Minnesota P, 1984.

Lyra, Jorge, and Benedito Medrado. "Gênero e paternidade nas pesquisas demográficas: o viés científico." *Revista de Estudos Feministas* 8.1 (2000): 145–58.

Maciel, David R., and María Herrera-Sobek, eds. *Culture Across Borders: Mexican Immigration and Popular Culture.* Tucson: U of Arizona P, 1998.

Maffia, Diana. "Informe del seminario Feminismos Latinoamericanos: Retos y Perspectivas, realizado por P.U.E.G. México, Abril 2002." *Feminaria* 28/29 (2002): 40–42.

Magalhaes Junior, R. (Raimundo). *O conto feminino.* Rio de Janeiro: Editora Civilização Brasileira, 1959.

Maines, Rachel. *The Technology of Orgasm: 'Hysteria' the Vibrator and Women's Sexual Satisfaction.* Baltimore, MD: Johns Hopkins UP, 1998.

Maranghello, César. *Breve Historia del Cine Argentino.* Barcelona: Artes, 2004.

Marchant, Elizabeth A. *Critical Acts: Latin American Women and Cultural Criticism.* Gainesville: UP of Florida, 1999.

Martin, Richard. "Sidestepping into the Spotlight—Restaurant Side Dishes." *Nation's Restaurant News.* 17 Apr. 1989. http://findarticles.com/p/articles/mi_m3190/is_n16_v23/ai_7535627.

Martínez de Richter, Marily. "Textualizaciones de la violencia: *Informe bajo llave* de Marta Lynch y *La rompiente* de Reina Roffé." *Siglo XX/20th Century* II.I–2 (1993): 89–II7.

Martinez, Elena M. *Lesbian Voices From Latin America: Breaking Ground.* New York: Garland, 1996.

Martinez, Marilyn. MySpace. www.myspace.com/latindivamarilynmartinez.

Masiello, Francine. *The Art of the Transition: Latin American Culture and Neoliberal Crisis.* Durham: Duke UP, 2001.

——. "La Argentina durante el proceso: las múltiples resistencias de la cultura." Balderston et al. *Ficción y política: la narrativa argentina durante el proceso militar.* Buenos Aires: Alianza; Minneapolis: Institute for the Study of Ideologies and Literature, U of Minnesota P, 1987. II–29.

——. "Conhecimiento suplementar: Queering o eixo norte/sul." *Revista de Estudos Feministas* 8.2 (2000): 49–62.

——. "Contemporary Argentine Fiction: Liberal (Pre)-texts in the Reign of Terror." *Latin American Research Review* 16.2 (1981): 218–24.

——. "Cuerpo/presencia: mujer y estado social en la narrativa argentina durante el proceso militar." *Nuevo texto crítico* 2.4 (1989): 155–72.

——. "Discurso de mujeres: lenguaje de poder." *Hispamérica* 45 (1986): 53–60.

Mattelart, Armand. *Transnationals and the Third World: The Struggle for Culture.* Trans. David Buxton. South Hadley, MA: Bergin and Garvey, 1983.

Maxwell, Richard, ed. *Culture Works: The Political Economy of Culture.* Vol. 18 of Culture Politics. Minneapolis, and London: U of Minnesota P, 2001.Tucson: U of Arizona P, 2000.

Mayne, Judith. *The Woman at the Keyhole: Feminism and Women' Cinema.* Bloomington: Indiana P, 1990.

McCann, Carole R., and Kim Seung-Kyung, eds. *Feminist Theory Reader: Local and Global Perspectives.* New York and London: Routledge, 2003.

McClintock, Anne. "Couro imperial: raça, travestismo e o culto da domesticidade." *Cadernos Pagu* 20 (2003): 7–85.

McDermott, Patrice. *Politics and Scholarship: Feminist Academic Journals and the Production of Knowledge.* Urbana: U of Illinois P, 1994.

——. "The Risk and Responsibilities of Feminist Academic Journals." *National Women's Studies Association Journal* 6.3 (1994): 373–83.

McLaren, Angus. *Impotence: A Cultural History.* Chicago: U of Chicago P, 2007.

Mercer, Marilyn. "Feminism in Argentina." www.cddc.vt.edu/feminism/arg.html. Copyright 1998, Marilyn Mercer. 1 Jan. 2002.

Meyer, Bente. "Women's Time, Women's Space: Reflections on the International Network of Women's Studies Journals Workshop." *National Women's Studies Association Journal.* 14.2 (2002): 148–52.

Miguel, María Esther de, ed. *Mujeres argentinas: el lado femenino de nuestra historia.* Buenos Aires: Alfaguara, 1998.

Millán, Márgara. "Género y representación: El cine hecho por mujeres y la representacion de los géneros." *Actas Sociologicas* 16 (1996): 175–94.

Miller, Francesca. "The International Relations of Women in the Americas." *The Americas: A Quarterly Review of Inter-American Cultural History* 43.2 (1986): 171–82.

Miller, Nancy K. *Getting Personal: Feminist Occasions and Other Autobiographical Acts.* London and New York: Routledge, 1991.

Miller, Nancy K., ed. *The Poetics of Gender.* Gender and Culture Series. New York: Columbia UP, 1986.

Minh-ha, Trinh T. *Framer Framed.* New York and London: Routledge, 1992.

Miskolci, Richard, and Júlio Assis Simoes. Apresentação. *Cadernos Pagu* 28 (2007): 9–18.

——. "Pânicos morais e controle social: reflexões sobre o casamento gay." *Cadernos Pagu* 28 (2007): 101–28.

Modleski, Tania. "Questioning Scholars' Torrid Romance with Popular Culture." *Chronicle of Higher Education* 5.12 13 Nov. 1998. Opinion and Arts: B8.

Mohanty, Chandra Talpade. "Cartographies of Struggle: Third World Women and the Politics of Feminism." *Race Critical Theories: Text and Context.* Ed. Philomena Essed and David Theo Goldberg. Malden, MA: Blackwell Publishers, 2002. 195–219.

——. "Feminist Encounters: Locating the Politics of Experience." *Social Postmodernism: Beyond Identity Politics.* Ed. Linda J. Nicholson and Steven Seidman. Cambridge, England: Cambridge UP, 1987. 30–44.

Molina-Gavilán, Yolanda. "Alternative Realities from Argentina: Angélica Gorodischer's "Los embriones del violeta." *Science Fiction Studies* 26 (1999): 401–411.

——, and Miguel Ángel Fernández Delgado, Andrea Bell, Luis Pestarini, Juan Carlos Toledana. "Cronología de CF latinoamericana 1775–1999." *Chasqui* 29.2 (2000): 43–72.

Molloy, Sylvia and Robert McKee Irwin, eds. *Hispanisms and Homosexualities.* Durham: Duke UP 1998.

Monoghan, Peter. "Knowing Thyself: A Historian Explains How the Stigma of 'Solitary Sex' Rose . . . and Fell." *Chronicle of Higher Education* 7 Mar. 2003: A14.

Monsiváis, Carlos. "Bolero: A History." *Mexican Postcards.* Ed. Trans. Intro. John Kraniauskas. London and New York: Cerso, 1997. 166–95.

——. "Los espacios marginales." *debate feminista* 9.17 (1998): 20–38.

——. "La emergencia de la Diversidad: las comunidades marginales y sus batallas por la visibilidad." *debate feminista* 15.29 (2004): 187–208.

Montecino, Sonia. "De la mujer al género: Implicancias académicas y teóricas." *Mujer y género: Nuevos saberes en las universidades chilenas.* Ed. Sonia Montecino and Loreto Rebolleo. Santiago: University of Chile, 1995.

Moore, Lisa Jean. *Sperm Counts: Overcome by Man's Most Precious Fluid.* New York: New York UP, 2007.

Moraga, Cherríe. *Loving in the War Years: Lo que nunca pasó por sus labios.* Boston: South End, 1983.

——. *Heroes and Saints & Other Plays.* Albuquerque: West End, 1994.

Mosier, Patricia. "Women in Power in G's Kalpa Imperial." *Spectrum of the Fantastic: Selected Essays from the Sixth International Conference in the Fantastic in the Arts.* Ed. David Palubo. Westport, CT: Greenwood, 1998. 145–61.

Mott, Maria Lucia. "Bibliografia comentada sobre assistência ao parto no Brasil (1972–2002)." *Revista de Estudos Feministas* 10.2 (2002): 493–509.

Moura, Clovis. "Climate of Terror." *Index on Censorship* 8.4 (1979) 8–10.

Moutinho, Laura. " 'Raça,' sexualidade e gênero na construção da identidade nacional: uma comparação entre Brasil e África do Sul." *Cadernos Pagu* 23 (2004): 55–88.

"Mujeres infieles en España." www.chile.com/tpl/articulo/detalle/print.tpl?cod _articulo=78066.

Mujeres infieles [Unfaithful Women]. Film. Dir. Rodrigo Ortuzar Lynch. 2004.

Mukerji, Chandra, and Michael Schudson, eds. *"Rethinking Popular Culture." Contemporary Perspectives in Cultural Studies*. Berkeley: U of California P, 1991.

Mulvey, Laura. "Visual Pleasure and Narrative Cinema." *Screen* 16:3 (1975): 6–18.

Munck, Ronaldo. "Postmodernism, Politics and Paradigms in Latin America." *Latin American Perspectives* 27.4 (2000): 11–26.

Munerato, Elice, and Maria Helena Darcy de Oliveira. "When Women Film." *Brazilian Cinema*. Ed. Randal Johnson and Robert Stam. New York: Columbia UP, 1995.

Muñoz, José Esteben. *Disidentifications: Queers of Color and the Performance of Politics*. Vol. 2 of Cultural Studies in the Americas. Minneapolis and London: U of Minnesota P, 1999.

Naber, Nadine. "Interseccionalidade em uma era de globalização: as implicações da Conferência Mundial contra o Racismo para as practicas feministas transnacionais." *Revista de Estudos Feministas* 10.1 (2002): 189–98.

Narayan, Uma, and Sandra Harding. *Decentering the Center: Philosophy for a Multicultural, Postcolonial and Feminist World*. Bloomington: Indiana UP, 2000.

Nari, Marcela. "Abrir los ojos, abrir la cabeza": el feminismo en la Argentina de los anos 70." *Feminaria* 9:17/18 (1996) 15–21.

Negrón-Muntaner, Frances. "Cherríe Moraga." *Latin American Writers on Gay and Lesbian Themes*. Ed. David William Foster. Westport, CT: Greenwood, 1994.

Nicholson, Linda. "Interpretando o gênero." *Revista de Estudos Feministas* 8.2 (2000): 9–42.

Niebylski, Dianna C. *Humoring Resistance: Laughter and the Excessive Body in Contemporary Latin American Women's Fiction*. Albany: State U of New York P, 2004.

Nieto, Linda. "Entrevista con Cecilia Rossetto." *Teatros* 5.34 (Mar. 2004): 21.

Niña Santa, La. Dir. Lucrecia Martel. Perfs. Mercedes Morán, Maria Alche. Film. Senso, La Pasionaria, R & C, Teodora, 2004.

Noble, Andrea. *Mexican National Cinema*. London and New York: Routledge, 2005.

Novães Coelho, Nelly. *A literatura feminina no Brasil contemporâneo*. São Paulo: Siciliano, 1993.

Novarro, Chico. "Cuenta conmigo" (Song). Music by Raúl Parentella, 1979. *Tango Lyrics homepage* 10 Nov. 2004. http://argentina.informatik.uni-muenchen.de/tangos/msg06915.html.

Núcleo de Estudos da Mulher e Relações Sociais de Gênero. Universidade de São Paulo. 31 Jan. 2008. www.usp.br/nemge/.

Nussbaum, Emily. "Does the Exotic Become Erotic? A Cornell Psychologist's Bold New Theory on Who is Gay and Why." *Lingua Franca* 8.4 (1998): 38–44.

Nussbaum, Martha. "Feminists and Philosophy." *New York Times Review of Books* 41.17 (1994): 59–63.

———. "The Professor of Parody." *The New Republic Online*. 28 Nov. 2000. www.tny.com/index.mhtml.

———. *Sex and Social Justice*. Oxford: Oxford UP, 2000.

Oppenheimer, Andres. "Las universidades latinoamericanas reciben mala nota." *Miami Herald* 13 Mar. 2005.

Original Latin Divas of Comedy. Sandra Valls, Marilyn Martinez Monique Marvez, Sara Contreras. November 25–26, 2007. San Bernardino Theater of Performing Arts. Payaso Entertainment, Kosmic Films Entertainment. Prod. Neal Marshall. Dir. Scott Montoya.

Oyarzún, Kemy. "Engendering Democracy in the Chilean University." *NACLA Report on the Americas* 33.4 (2000): 24–29.

Parente Cunha, Helena. *Mulher no espelho*. São Paulo: Arte Editora, 1985.

———. *Woman Between Mirrors*. Trans. Fred P. Ellison and Naomi Lindstrom. Austin: U of Texas P, 1989.

Pelucio. Larissa. "Na noite nem todos os gatos são pardos: notas sobre a prostituição travesti." *Cadernos Pagu* 25 (2005): 217–48.

Penley, Constance, ed. *Feminism and Film Theory*. New York: Routledge, 1988.

Peters, Mike. "Argentina's Female-centric Funnies Making their Way to the US." *Dallas Morning News*, 2 Jan. 2005.

Petro Patrice. *Aftershocks of the New. Feminism and Film History*. New Brunswick, N.J. and London: Rutgers UP, 2002.

Pino, Nádia Perez. "A teoria queer e os intersex: experiências invisíveis de corpos des-feitos." *Cadernos Pagu* 28 (2007): 149–74.

Pisani, Silvia. "Beneficiará a los argentinos un blanqueo de ilegales en España." *La nación*. 23 Aug. 2004. www.lanacion.com.ar/629851.

———. "Nuestro país fue el que más indocumentados exportó a la península en 2002; en dos años sumó 235.000." *La nación* 11 Jul. 2003. 15 Nov. 2004. www.lanacion.com.ar/03/07/11/dx_510465.asp.

———. "Ola de inmigrantes en España: en 2015 serán el 27% de la población." *La nación* 22 Jan. 2004. 10 Nov. 2004. www.lanacion.com.ar/04/01/22/dx_566036.asp.

Piscitelli, Adriana. "Apresentação: gênero no mercado do sexo." *Cadernos Pagu* 25 (2005): 7–23.

———. "Viagens e sexo on-line: a internet na geografia do turismo sexual." *Cadernos Pagu* 25 (2005): 281–326.

———. "Exotismo e autenticidade: relatos de viajantes à procura de sexo." *Cadernos Pagu* 19 (2002):195–231.

Pizarnik, Alejandra. *El infierno musical*. Buenos Aires: Siglo XXI, 1971.

———. *La condesa sangrienta*. Buenos Aires: López Crespo, 1971.

———. *Textos de sombra y últimos poemas*. Ed. Olga Orozco and Ana Becciú. Buenos Aires: Sudamericana, 1982.

———. *Obras completas. Poesía y prosa*. Buenos Aires: Corregidor, 1990.

"Pornografía argentina: Todo lo que siempre quiso saber y nunca se animó a preguntar" *No pretendo agradarles*. 14 Jan. 2005. www.nopretendoagradarles.blogspot.com/2005/01/pornografia-argentina.html.

"Pornografia para mujeres: videos, enlaces, películas, libros." *Inner, El Pendejo*. 8 Aug. 2007. www.blog.innerpendejo.net/2007/08/pornografia-para-mujeres-videos.html.

Portal de Ciencia Ficción. 18 Dec. 2007. www.portal-cifi.com/.

Pratt, Mary Louise. "Arts of the Contact Zone." *Mass Culture and Everyday Life*. Ed. Peter Gibian. New York and London: Routledge, 1997. 61–72.

———. *Imperial Eyes: Travel Writing and Transculturation*. London and New York: Routledge, 1992.

Pribram, E. Deidre, ed. *Female Spectators. Looking at Film and Television*. London: Verso, 1988.

Prins, Bukje, and Irene Costera Meijer. "Como os corpos se tornam matéria: Entrevista com Judith Butler." *Revista de Estudos Feministas* 10.1 (2002): 155–68.

Programa Universitario de Estudios de Género. Universidad Nacional Autónoma de México. 31 Jan. 2008. www.pueg.unam.mx/investigacion/est.php.

Proyecto de Estudios de la Mujeres. Universidad de Puerto Rico. 31 Jan. 2008. http://promujeres.cayey.upr.edu/index.htm.

Quart, Barbara Koenig. *Women Directors. The Emergence of a New Cinema*. New York: Praeger, 1988.

Queen, Carol, and Lawrence Schimel. *PoMoSexuals: Challenging Assumptions about Gender and Sexuality*. San Francisco: Cleis, 1997.

Quiñones, Juan Gómez. *Chicano Politics: Reality and Promise 1940–1990*. Alburquerque: U of New Mexico P, 1990.

Rama, Ángel. "La facinación del horror." *Marcha* 1188 (Montevideo) (27 Dec. 1963).

———. *La generación crítica 1939–1969*. Montevideo: Arca, 1972.

Ramos, José Mario Ortiz. "O Cinema Brasileiro Contemporâneo (1970–1987)." *História do Cinema Brasileiro*. 2nd ed. Org. Ramos Fernao. São Paulo: Arte Editora, 1990. 399–454.

Rangil, Viviana. "Changing the Face of Argentinean Cinema: The Vibrant Voices of Four Women." *Afterimage* 28.6 (2001).

———. *Otro punto de vista: Mujer y cine en Argentina*. Rosario: Beatriz Viterbo Editora, 2005.

Raphael, Chad. "The Web." *Culture Works: The Political Economy of Culture*. Vol. 18 of Culture Politics. Ed. Richard Maxwell. Minneapolis, MN and London: U of Minnesota P, 2001. 197–224.

Rashkin, Elissa. *Women Filmmakers in Mexico: The Country of Which We Dream*. Austin: U of Texas P, 2001.

Raymond, Janice G. *The Transsexual Empire: The Making of the She-male*. Boston: Beacon, 1979.

Redding, Judith M., and Victoria A. Brownsworth. *Film Fatales. Independent Women Directors*. Seattle: Seal Press, 1997.

Reddock, Rhoda, Eudine Barriteau, Jeanette Morris, Joan Cuffie. "Studying Men and Masculinities in the Caribbean Gender/Women's Studies Programs." Proceedings of the 8th International Interdisciplinary Congress on Women's Studies and Gender Studies. Makerere University, Kampala-Uganda, July 18–26, 2002.

Rêgo, Cacilda M. "Brazilian Cinema: Its Fall, Rise, and Renewal (1990–2003)." *New Cinemas: Journal of Contemporary Film* 3.2 (2005): 85–100.

Revista de Estudos Feministas. 27 Nov. 2007. 8 Jan. 2008. www.scielo.br/scielo.php?pid=0104–026X&script=sci_serial.

Revista de Estudos Feministas. 7 and 7.2 (1999); 8.1 (2000); 8.2 (2000); 9.1 (2001); 9.2 (2001); 10.1 (2002); 10.2 (2002). Instituto de Filosofia e Ciências Sociais, Universidade Federal Rio de Janeiro (1999); Universidade Federal do Santa Catarina (2000–2002).

——. Volumes 0–6.2. www.cfh.ufsc.br/~ref/como.html. 8 May 2003.

Rich, Adrienne. "Compulsory Heterosexuality and Lesbian Existence." *Signs* 5.4 (1980): 631–60.

Rich, Ruby. "Making Argentina Matter Again." *New York Times* 30 Sep. 2001, late ed.: 15.

Richard, Nelly. "Cultural Peripheries: Latin America and Postmodern Decentering." *The Postmodern Debate in Latin America*. Ed. John Beverly, Jose Oveido, and Michael Aronna. Durham: Duke UP, 1995. 217–22.

——. "*Feminismo*, Experiencia y Representación." *Revista Iberoamericana* 62.176–77 (1996): 733–44.

——. *The Insubordination of Signs: Political Change, Cultural Transformation, and Poetics of the Crisis*. Trans. Alice A. Nelson and Silvia R. Tandeciarz. Durham: Duke UP, 2004.

——. *La estratificación de los márgenes*. Santiago, Chile: Francisco Zegers, 1989.

——. *Masculine/Feminine: Practices of Difference(s)*. Trans. Alice A. Nelson and Silvia R. Tandeciarz. Durham: Duke UP, 2004.

——. *Cultural Residues: Chile in Transition*. Trans. Theodore Quester and Alan West-Durán. Minneapolis: U of Minnesota P, 2004.

Ríos, Alicia, Abel Trigo, and Ana Del Sarto, eds. *The Latin American Cultural Studies Reader*. Durham: Duke UP, 2004.

Rivero, Eliana. "I Can Fly: Of Dreams and Other Nonfictions," *Telling to Live: Latina Feminist Testimonios*. The Latina Feminist Collective. Durham: Duke UP, 2001. 156–66.

——. "Precisiones de lo femenino y lo feminista en la practica literaria hispanoamericana." *Inti: Revista de Literatura Hispanica* 40.41 (1994): 21–46.

Robertson, Pamela. *Guilty Pleasures: Feminist Camp from Mae West to Madonna*. Durham: Duke UP, 1996.

Robin, Diana, and Ira Jaffe, eds. *Redirecting the Gaze. Gender, Theory and Cinema in the Third World*. SUNY Ser. Cultural Studies in Cinema/Video. New York: SUNY Press, 1999.

Robles, Oscar. *Identidades maternacionales en el cine de María Novaro*. New York: Peter Lang, 2005.

Rodriguez, Juana María. *Queer Latinidad: Identity Practices, Discursive Spaces*. New York: New York UP, 2003.

Rodríguez, Mariana. "Maryse Sistach: filma desgracias." *Contenido* (Dec. 2001): 89–91.

Roen, Paul. *High Camp. A Gay Guide to Camp and Cult Films*. Vol.I. San Francisco: Leyland Publications, 1994.

Roffé, Reina. "Omnipresencia de la censura en la escritura argentina." *Revista iberoamericana* 51.131–33 (1985): 909–15.

——. "Qué escribimos las mujeres en la Argentina de hoy." *Literatura Argentina hoy: de la dictadura a la democracia*. Ed. Karl Kohut and Andrea Pagni. Frankfurt: Vervuert Verlag, 1989. 205–13.

——. *Llamado al puf*. Buenos Aires: Pleamar, 1972.

——. *La rompiente*. Buenos Aires: Puntosur, 1987.

——. *Monte de Venus*. Buenos Aires: Corregidor, 1976.

Rohter, Larry. "A Sassy Appraisal of the Sexes." *New York Times* 23 Mar. 2004. www.clubcultura.com/clubhumor/maitena/notas03_eng.htm.

Rojas, Mario A. "La experiencia teatral como evento sociocultural: *El Galpão* y la búsqueda de una estética sertaneja." *Propuestas escénicas de fin de siglo: FIT 1998.* Ed. Juan Villegas. Irvine: Colección Historia del Teatro 3, 1999. 173–92.

Román, David, and Alberto Sandoval. "Caught in the Web: Latinidad, AIDS, and Allegory in Kiss of the Spiderwoman, the Musical." *Everynight Life: Culture and Dance in Latino/o America.* Ed. Celeste Fraser Delgado and José Esteben Munñoz. Durham: Duke UP, 1997. 255–87.

Rönner, Lucila Díaz, and Teresa Azcárate. "Current Challenges and Drawbacks of Feminisms in Argentina: A View from Paradoxes." Presented on September 30 at the IV Conferenza Europea di Ricerca feminista. Bologna, Italy, September 28-October 1, 2000. www.women.it/4thfemconf/workshops/politics6/luciladiazazcarate.htm. 12 Nov. 2001.

Ropelato, Jerry. "Internet Pornography Statistics" *Internet Filter Review.* http://internet-filter-review.toptenreviews.com/internet-pornography-statistics.html#anchor7.

Rufino, Alzira. "Vocês não podem mais adiar nossos sonhos . . ." *Revista de Estudos Feministas* 10.1 (2002): 215–18.

Ruiz García, Samuel. "Documental pastoral sobre el aborto." *debate feminista* 5.9 (1994): 435–56.

Russ, Joanna. "The Image of Women in Science Fiction." *Images of Women in Fiction.* Ed. Susan Koppelman Cornillon. Bowling Green: Bowling Green University Popular Press, 1972. 79–94.

Sadlier, Darlene J. "Introduction." *One Hundred Years After Tomorrow: Brazilian Women's Fiction in the 20th Century.* Bloomington/Indianapolis: Indiana UP, 1992. 1–12.

Sánchez, Jorge A. "Nota post-liminar." Angélica Gorodischer. *Trafalgar.* Buenos Aires: El Cid, 1979. 221–35.

Sandoval, Joshua. "Last Laughs in Honor of Marilyn Martinez: Comedians Gather at the Comedy Store to Eulogize Funny Woman Marilyn Martinez." *Los Angeles Times* 16 Nov. 2007.

Sarlo, Beatriz. "Política, ideología y figuración literaria." *Ficción y política: la narrativa Argentina durante el proceso militar.* Ed. René Jara and Hernán Vidal. Buenos Aires; Minneapolis: Institute for the Study of Ideologies and Literature; Alianza Editorial, 1987. 30–59.

———. "Strategies of the Literary Imagination." *Fear at the Edge: State Terror and Resistence in Latin America.* Ed. Juan E. Corradi, Patricia Weiss Fagen, and Manuel Antonio Garretón. Berkeley; Los Angeles; Oxford: U of California P, 1992. 236–49.

Saueressig, Simone. "O ano da lua." *Como era gostosa a minha alienígena.* Ed. Gerson Lodi-Ribeiro. São Caetano do Sul: Ano Luz, 2002. 155–74.

Savary, Olga. *Carne Viva.* Rio de Janiero: Anima, 1984.

Scarium—Ficção Científica, Fantasia, Horror, e Mistério. *Scarium* Megazine. 18 Dec. 2007. www.scarium.com.br/.

Schaefer, Claudia. *Bored to Distraction. Cinema of Excess in End-of-the-Century Mexico and Spain.* New York: SUNY Press, 2003.

Schmink, Marianne. "Women in Brazilian *Abertura* Politics." *Signs* 7.1 (1981): 115–34.

Schneider, Rebecca. *The Explicit Body in Performance.* London: Routledge, 1997.

Schumater, Maria Aparecida, and ElizabethVargas. "A Place in Government: Alibi or Conquest." Spec. Issue of *Revista de Estudos Feministas* (1999): 141–52.

Schwartz, Marcy E. *Writing Paris: Urban Topographies of Desire in Contemporary Latin American Fiction*. New York: SUNY Press, 1999.

SciELO (Social Science English Edition). http://socialsciences.scielo.org/.

Scott, A. O. "The Stirrings of Sensuality for a Pilgrim on the Road." *New York Times* 9 Oct. 2004, late ed.: 11.

Sedgwick, Eve Kosofsky. *Epistemology of the Closet*. Berkeley: Los Angeles: U of California P, 1990.

Seger, Linda. *When Women Call the Shots. The Developing Power and Influence of Women in Television and Film*. New York: Henry Holt, 1996.

——. "Women and Gender Representations in the Contemporary Cinema of Mexico." *Mexico's Cinema*. Ed. Joanne Hershfield and David Maciel. 249–65.

Selden, Raman. *A Reader's Guide to Contemporary Literary Theory*. Lexington: UP of Kentucky, 1985.

SEMIac Cuba—Una Mirada diferente a la información. Agencia Servicio de Noticias de la Mujer de Latinoamérica y el Caribe. 1 Jan. 2008. www.redsemlac-cuba.net/.

Shaw, Deborah. *Contemporary Cinema of Latin America: Ten Key Films*. New York: Continuum, 2003.

Shohat, Ella. "A vinda para a América: reflexões sobre perda de cabelos e de memória." *Revista de Estudos Feministas* 10.1 (2002): 99–118.

Shohat, Ella, ed. *Talking Visions. Multicultural Feminism in a Transnational Age*. New York: MIT Press, 1995.

Showalter, Elaine. *Hystories: Hysterical Epidemics and Modern Media*. New York; Chichester, England: Columbia UP, 1997.

Shteir, Rachel. *Striptease: The Untold History of the Girlie Show*. Oxford: Oxford UP, 2005.

——. "Striptease, Porn, and Gender Politics: An Academic's Dilemma." *Chronicle of Higher Education*. Sec.: *The Chronicle Review* 52. 2 2 Sept. 2005.

Shua, Ana María. *Viajando se conoce gente*. Buenos Aires: Editorial Sudamericana. 1988. 123–42.

Silente—Ciencia ficción y fantasia. 18 Dec. 2007. www.silente.net/.

Silva, Ana Paula da, and Thaddeus Blanchette. "'Nossa Senhora da Help': sexo, turismo e deslocamento transnacional em Copacabana." *Cadernos Pagu* (2005): 249–80.

Silva, Ana Paula da, Thaddeus Blanchette, Anna Marina Madureira de Pinho et al. "Prostitutas, "traficadas" e pânicos morais: uma análise da produção de fatos em pesquisas sobre o "tráfico de seres humanos." *Cadernos Pagu* 25 (2005): 153–184.

Simetria. Associação Portuguesa de Ficção Científica e Fantástico. 18 Dec. 2007. www.simetria.org/.

Simon, Adriana. "Dainara." *Como era gostosa a minha alienígena*. Ed. Gerson Lodi-Ribeiro. São Caetano do Sul: Ano Luz, 2002. 225–36

Sin dejar huella. Dir. Maria Novaro. Perfs. Aitana Sánchez-Gijón, Tiaré Scanda. Film. Tabasco Films, Altavista Films, Tornasol Films, 2000.

Singh, Amritjit, and Peter Schmidt, eds. *Postcolonial Theory and the United States. Race, Ethnicity and Literature*. Jackson: UP of Mississippi, 2000.

Sinha, Mrinalini, Dona Guy, and Angelea Woollacott. *Feminisms and Internationalisms.* Oxford, UK, and Malden MA: Blackwell, 1999.

Sjogren, Britta. *Into the Vortex. Female Vortex and Paradox in Film.* Urbana: U of Illinois P, 2006.

Slater, David. "Exploring Other Zones of the Postmodern: Problems of Ethnocentrism and Difference Along the North South Divide." *Racism, Modernity and Identity.* Ed. Ali Rattansi. Cambridge, MA: Polity Press, 1994. 87–125.

Steimberg, Alicia. *Amatista.* 2nd ed. Barcelona: Tusquets, 1989. 1990.

———. *Músicos y relojeros.* Buenos Aires: Centro Editorial de América Latina, 1971.

Stephan, Lynn. *Women and Social Movements in Latin America: Power from Below.* Austin: U of Texas P, 1997.

Strinati, Dominic. "Postmodernism and Popular Culture." *Cultural Theory and Popular Culture—A Reader.* By John Storey. London: Harvester Wheatsheaf, 1994. 428–38.

Subercaseaux, Bernardo. "Nueva sensibilidad y horizonte 'post' en Chile: (Aproximaciones a un registro)." *Nuevo Texto Crítico* 6 (1990): 135–45.

Sutherland, Romy. "Journeys and Destinations: The Films of María Novaro." *Senses of Cinema.* Nov. 2002. www.sensesofcinema.com/contents/directors/02/novaro .html.

Suvin, Darko. *Metamorphoses of Science Fiction: On the Poetics and History of a Literary Genre.* New Haven: Yale UP, 1979.

Szurmuk, Mónica. "La textualización de la represión en *La rompiente* de Reina Roffé." *Nuevo texto crítico* 3.5 (1990): 123–29.

Taule, Ginny "Latin American Women's Studies Programs." *NSWSA Journal* 3.3 (1991): 450–51.

Taylor, Diana, and Roselyn Costantino, eds. *Holy Terrors: Latin American Women Perform.* Durham: Duke UP, 2003.

Taylor, Mark C., and Esa Saarinen. *Imagologies: Media Philosophy.* London; New York: Routledge, 1994.

Taylor, Sally. "Publishing in Latin America: South of the Border, They're Hanging in There by Pulling Together." *Publishers Weekly* 13 Sept. 1999. 45–52.

Toledano, Juan C. "Daína Chaviano." *Latin American Science Fiction Writers: An A-Z Guide.* Ed. Darrell B. Lockhart. Westport, CT: Greenwood, 2004. 54–56.

Tomlinson, John. *Globalization and Culture.* Chicago: U of Chicago P, 1999.

Tompkins, Cynthia. "Las *Mujeres alteradas* y *Superadas* de Maitena Burundarena: Feminismo Made in Argentina." *Studies in Latin American Popular Culture* 22 (2003): 35–60.

———. *Latin American Postmodernisms: Women Writers and Experimentation.* Gainesville: UP of Florida, 2006.

Trelles Plazaola, Luis. *Cine y mujer en América Latina: Directoras de largometrajes de ficción.* Río Piedras: Editorial de la Universidad de Puerto Rico, 1991.

Trujillo, Carla, ed. *Living Chicana Theory.* Berkeley: Third Woman Press, 1998.

Turner, William B. *A Genealogy of Queer Theory.* Philadelphia: Temple UP, 2000.

Tuñon, Julia. *Mujeres de luz y sombra en el cine mexicano: la construcción de una imagen (1939–1952).* Mexico, D.F.: Colegio de México: Instituto Mexicano de Cinematografía, 1998.

Tyson, Lois. *Critical Theory Today: A User-Friendly Guide.* New York: Routledge, 1999.

Ubersfeld, Anne. *Diccionario de términos claves del análises teatral.* Colección teatrología. Dir. Osvaldo Pelletieri. Buenos Aires: Galerna, 2002.

Unterburger Amy L., ed. *The St. James Women Filmmakers Encyclopedia. Women on the Other Side of the Camera.* Detroit: Visible Ink Press, 1999.

Urraca, Beatriz. "Angélica Gorodischer's Voyages of Discovery: Sexuality and Historical Allegory in Science Fiction's Cross-Cultural Encounter." *Latin American Literary Review* 45 (1995): 85–102.

Valls, Sandra. MySpace. www.myspace.com/sandravalls.

———. "Coming out Mexican, Calling in Gay." The Outlaugh Festival on Wisecrack. May 7, 2007. www.youtube.com/watch?v=AovF_7VrsRQ&feature=related.

Vásquez, Maria Esther. "Angélica Gorodischer: una escritora lationamericana de ciencia ficción." *Revista Iberoamericana* 49 (1983): 123–24.

Velada da Silva, Susana. "Os estudos de gênero no Brasil: Algumas considerações." Biblio 3W. *Revista Bibliográfica de Geografía y Ciencias Sociales* 262 (15 Nov. 2000). Universidad de Barcelona [ISSN 1138–9796].

Villegas, Juan. "Palabras finales: los festivales y las instituciones culturales." *Propuestas escénicas de fin de siglo: FIT 1998.* Ed. Juan Villegas. Irvine: Colección Historia del teatro 3, 1999. 209–15.

Wainerman, Catalina. "El mundo de las revistas femeninas." *Del deber ser y el hacer de las mujeres: Dos estudios de caso en Argentina.* Mexico: El Colegio de Mexico/PISPAL, 1984. 113–19.

Walsh, Andrea S. *Women's Film and Female Experience, 1940–1950.* New York: Praeger, 1984.

Weidner Maluf, Sônia. "Corporalidade e desejo: *Tudo sobre minha mãe* e o gênero na margem." *Revista de Estudos Feministas* 10.1 (2002):143–54.

Wendland, Albert. *Science, Myth and the Fictional Creation of the Alien World.* Ann Arbor: UMI Research Press, 1985.

West-Duran, Alan. "Devo(ra)ciones: sabores y saberes de la memoria en el bolero." *Studies in Latin American Popular Culture* 22 (2004): 61–73.

Wilchins, Riki. *Queer Theory, Gender Theory: An Instant Primer.* Los Angeles: Alyson, 2004.

Williams, Linda. *Hard Core: Power, Pleasure and the "Frenzy" of the Visible.* Berkeley: U of California P, 1999.

———, ed. *Porn Studies.* Durham: Duke UP, 2004.

Williamson, Judith. *Consuming Passions. The Dynamics of Popular Culture.* London: Marion Boyars, 1986.

Wiscon, The World's Leading Feminist Science Fiction Convention. www.wiscon.info/.

Women, Culture, and Politics in Latin America/Seminar on Feminism and Culture in Latin America. Introduction. Berkeley and Los Angeles: U of California P, 1990. 1–9.

"Writing Women In: Developing Knowledge Tools for the New Millennium." International *Network* of Women's Studies Journals Workshop held at Hotel Equatorial and Makerere University, Kampala-Uganda, July 18–26, 2002. *Australian Feminist Studies* 18.40 (2003): 99–102.

Xavier, Elódia. Introduction. *Todo no feminino.* Ed. Elódia Xavier. Rio de Janeiro: Francisco Alves, 1991. 9–16.

———. "Reflexões sobre a narrativa de autoria feminina." *Todo no feminino.* Ed. Elódia Xavier. Rio de Janeiro: Francisco Alves, 1991. 17–42.

Yáñez, Cecilia. "Strippers son la puerta de entrada a la pornografia para mujeres." *La nacion* (Chile) 9 Sept. 2005. www.lanacion.cl/.

Yarbrough, Stephen R. *Deliberate Criticism Toward a Postmodern Humanism.* Athens, GA: U of Georgia P, 1992.

Zarrilli, Phillip B. "For Whom Is a King a King? Issues in Intercultural Production, Perception, and Reception in a Kathakali King Lear." *Critical Theory and Performance.* Ed. Janelle G. Reinelt and Joseph R. Roach. Ann Arbor: U of Michigan P, 1992. 16–40.

Zavala, Iris. *El bolero: historia de un amor.* Madrid: Celeste, 1989.

Zavarzadeh, Mas'ud. *Seeing Films Politically.* Albany: State U of New York P, 1991.

Zavarzadeh, Mas'ud, and Donald Morton. *Theory as Resistance. Politics and Culture After (Post)Structuralism.* Critical Perspectives Series. New York: Guilford, 1994.

Zavella, Patricia. "Comentários sobre teorias feministas nas América(s) Latinas, a política transnacional da tradução." *Revista de Estudos Feministas* 8.2 (2000): 109–12.

Zayas, Josefina, and Isabel Larguía. "La Mujer: Realidad e Imagen." *La Mujer en los Medios Audiovisuales: Memorias del VIII Festival Internacional del Nuevo Cine Latinoamericano.* México D.F.: Coordinacion de Difusión Cultural, Universidad Nacional Autónoma de Mexico, 1987.

INDEX

ABOUT THE AUTHOR

Melissa A. Fitch was born in Los Angeles and raised in San Francisco. Her research interests lie in the representation of gender and sexuality in popular culture, theater, film, television, and narrative in Argentina, Brazil, and the U.S. borderlands. The theoretical underpinnings of her work are found in postmodernism, queer theory, cultural studies theory, postcolonial and gender studies. From 2002 to 2008 she was editor-in-chief of the academic journal *Studies in Latin American Popular Culture*. Her essays have been published in *Latin American Theater Review; Gestos: Teoría y práctica del teatro hispánico; Chasqui: Revista de literatura latinoamericana; ADFL Bulletin; Luso-Brazilian Review; Romance Languages Annual; ADE Bulletin;* and in the books *¡Dale Nomas! ¡Dale que va!* (2006); *Latino/a Popular Culture* (2002); and *Interventions: Feminist Dialogues on Third World Women's Literature and Film (1997).* She is coauthor of the book *Culture and Customs of Argentina* (1998). Professor Fitch is past president of the Arizona Languages Association and the statewide Languages Articulation Task Force. She directed the UA Study Abroad programs in Fortaleza, Brazil (2001), Alcalá de Henares, Spain (2004), and Segovia, Spain (2007). In 2008, she received the University of Arizona's Five Star Teaching Award, the university's highest teaching honor. She doesn't cook.

Printed in the United States
219142BV00002B/1/P